Case Studies in Business, Society, and Ethics

Tom L. Beauchamp
Georgetown University

Prentice-Hall, Inc.   Englewood Cliffs, New Jersey 07632

78409

Library of Congress Cataloging in Publication Data

BEAUCHAMP, TOM L.
 Case studies in business, society, and ethics.

  Includes bibliographical references.
  1. Industry—Social aspects—United States—Case
studies. 2. Industry and state—United States—Case
studies. 3. Trade regulation—United States—Case
studies. I. Title.
HD60.5.U5B38 1983   658.4'08'0973   82-20453
ISBN 0-13-119263-9

Editorial/production supervision
  and interior design: Chrys Chrzanowski
Cover design: Miriam Recio
Manufacturing buyer: Harry P. Baisley

Printed in the United States of America

10 9 8 7 6 5 4 3 2 1

ISBN 0-13-119263-9

PRENTICE-HALL INTERNATIONAL, INC., *London*
PRENTICE-HALL OF AUSTRALIA PTY. LIMITED, *Sydney*
EDITORA PRENTICE-HALL DO BRASIL, LTDA., *Rio de Janeiro*
PRENTICE-HALL CANADA INC., *Toronto*
PRENTICE-HALL OF INDIA PRIVATE LIMITED, *New Delhi*
PRENTICE-HALL OF JAPAN, INC., *Tokyo*
PRENTICE-HALL OF SOUTHEAST ASIA PTE. LTD., *Singapore*
WHITEHALL BOOKS LIMITED, *Wellington, New Zealand*

Contents

Expanded Contents

This alternative listing of cases is an expansion of the basic Contents. It is offered as a guide for teachers and students. It should be especially useful for teachers who plan a large segment of a course around a restricted range of topics. Thus, for example, a teacher who devotes a major part of a course to the topic of business and government can easily locate below the large number of cases relevant to this subject. (The headings in the basic Contents are unchanged, but a much larger set of cases is included under most headings.)

chapter **2**   The Consumer

chapter **3**   The Environment

chapter **6**   The Multinational

Preface

This book presents thirty-three case studies concerning social and ethical issues of contemporary concern to corporate officers, academics, government officials, and the broader public. The aim is to create an appreciation for the complexity of the circumstances and motives involved, as well as to make students aware of professional situations that require evaluative reflection and decision. The book was not produced to create a platform for moralistic criticism of the behavior of individual persons, corporations, or governmental agencies that play leading roles in the cases.

Of course, some cases do contain dramatic instances of professional irresponsibility, where it is reasonably clear that something went wrong or that some conduct is distinctly immoral, illegal, or unprofessional. It should not be inferred from these cases that conduct in the relevant profession generally follows this pattern. Irresponsible actions are occasionally featured because more can sometimes be learned from wrongful behavior than from rightful. However, learning through the study of wrongful or negligent behavior is *not* the orientation of this volume. The focus is on the complexities of circumstances in which hard choices must be made. More is to be learned, in my judgment, from reasoning under circumstances of controversy, personal quandary, and incompleteness of information than from paradigmatic cases of irresponsibility.

Some explanation of the length and structure of the cases is needed. Many cases that now circulate in the general literature of business, society, and ethics are either too short to contain enough detail for discussion or contain so much detail that discussion is retarded by the particulars and their connections. Living as we do in a society saturated by journalistic writing and rapid information dissemination, most of us encounter severe limitation regarding the amount of information we can study and remember about any sequence of events. We thus prefer tidy cases that come quickly to the essence of the matter. Most cases in this book conform to this model. However, any experienced executive will rightly insist that the situations under which decisions are made in business are almost infinitely complex, and usually call for more information than can be obtained. Executives thus see cases as inherently complex, and are disappointed with quick summaries. This point of view certainly has its merits. It is important for every student to appreciate that cases almost always contain complexities far beyond the factors presented. This is so even when described at book length—as, for example, the Love Canal and Reserve Mining cases reported in this volume have been studied. Moreover, judgments about the cases become progressively more difficult as the description of the case is enriched by detail.

On the other hand, discussion of cases is facilitated by a reasonably tidy display of the pertinent materials. I have therefore tried to write and otherwise collect cases that contain sufficient detail to facilitate discussion in the classroom without becoming bogged down in detail. Cases of this length also make it possible to produce a book with a variety of issues at an affordable cost to students. At the same time, the problem of having far too many cases for use in a single course is avoided.

Many teachers of the subject matter found in this book prefer cases that take an "inside" view of a corporation or institution under investigation in the case. The reasons behind this preference for an inside-view are set forth in the Introduction to this volume. I endorse the importance of this form of pedagogy, and several cases in this book are so oriented. However, this approach incorporates only one profitable style of case study. An outside look at corporate activities is sometimes the only look that one can obtain, and moreover, it is usually the best approach to writing cases that require public-policy decisions. A spread of approaches to case writing is therefore used in this book, some taking the inside look, some the outside perspective, and some using a mixture of perspectives.

I also note a lack of enthusiasm for questions at the end of each case that focus students on particular features of the cases. I believe this is an editorial disservice rather than a service. A teacher may, of course, choose to provide questions to a class, but the problem with this approach in a text is twofold: (a) teachers teach the cases with very different approaches and purposes; (b) students can easily be impeded from novel approaches by being funneled in a particular direction. Thus, no questions or aids other than general introductions to chapters accompany the cases. (I discuss these problems of pedagogy further in the Introduction.)

A talented research staff assisted in the collecting and writing of these cases, and we were in turn generously supported by a grant from the Exxon Foundation and the Landegger Program in International Business Diplomacy at Georgetown University. The Kennedy Institute of Ethics also supported this work. Special research was undertaken by R. Jay Wallace, Martha Elliott, Barry Smith, Nancy Blanpied, William Pitt, Barbara Humes, Sarah Westrick, Louisa W. Peat O'Neil, Andrew Rowan, Linda Kern, Cathleen Kaveny, and Sara Finnerty Kelly. Ted Moran and John Kline of the Landegger Program steered me in a number of important directions, as did Ruth Faden, Norman Bowie, Theodore Purcell, Carl Kaufman, Lisa Newton, Robert Cooke, William H. Hay, Thomas L. Carson, Archie B. Carroll, George Lodge, Henry W. Tulloch, Vivian Weil, Michael Hooker, Deborah G. Johnson, David P. Boyd, Richard E. Wokutch, Burton Leiser, Homer B. Sewell, and John H. Bubar. Some useful and substantive suggestions for improving the final draft of the Introduction were made by Terry Pinkard, Ruth Faden, Judith Areen, and Alex Capron. In the final stages Mary Ellen Timbol helped put the whole together, assisted by Tim Hodges, Fred Hoffman, Margaret Pumper, and Kyle Ward.

A number of corporations discussed in the cases in this volume also provided important materials and criticisms. A couple threatened law suits, but most were extraordinarily kind and patient in providing criticism, otherwise unavailable information, and data by telephone. Only Polaroid was fully convinced of the slant taken in the case as written in this book. This clearly evidences that most of these companies would not see the situation quite as the case-writer has depicted it. Nonetheless, almost every case in this book was aided by the contributions of representatives of the corporations, and I am pleased to be able to name the following constructive critics: Carol A. Boyd of Procter & Gamble, James M. Green of Hooker Chemical, Fred Shippee of the American Apparel Manufacturers Association, Leo J. Feuer of the William Carter Co., Robert Jeffrey of A.T. & T., Kathryn Ribbey of Ruder Finn & Rotman, Thomas J. Moore of Tampax, Robert M. Palmer of Polaroid, E. N. Brandt of Dow Chemical, Aracelia Garcia-Vila of Warner Lambert, John T. Sant of McDonnell Douglas, Frank Tomlinson of McDonnell Douglas, Craig Shulstad of General Mills, Susan K. Hartt of Kellogg Cereals, Carl Kaufman of Du Pont, Martha Beauchamp of the American Petroleum Institute, Barry F. Scher of Giant Food Inc., Don Price of the Lakewood Bank & Trust, Tom McCollough of Abbott/Ross Laboratories, C. L. Scarlott of Exxon, A. A. Gioia of Gulf Oil, J. Lee Bailey of the Cleveland Electric Illuminating Co., and Roger Shelley of Revlon.

I was also aided by a great many persons in organizations other than corporations. They too were exceedingly generous with their time and printed information. I thus also express gratitude to Alan Shakin of the Consumer Product Safety Commission, Peggy Charron of Action for Children's Television (ACT), Robert B. Choate of the Council on Children, Media and Merchandising (CCMM), and unknown sources of The Coalition for Environmental-Energy Balance. (Persons who supplied information I was not able to use because of cases deleted from the volume include Craven Crowell of the Tennessee Valley Authority, J. Kenneth Clark of the Duke Power Co., Greg LaBrache of Mobil Oil, and Marc Covington of B. F. Goodrich.)

I am grateful for all of these sources of encouragement, support, and criticism.

T.L.B.

Introduction: The Uses of Cases

The cases collected in this volume emerge from the intersection of professional practice in business, economics, law, and government. The cases can be profitably read from all of these perspectives. There are, however, better ways to analyze the cases if the reader is to obtain a due appreciation of the questions and possible answers they present. The purpose of this first chapter is to explore: (1) how different perspectives can structure the problems located in the case; (2) the history of "case methods"; (3) whether there exists more than one case method; (4) pitfalls in case analysis; and (5) reservations about "facts" presented in cases.

DIFFERENT PERSPECTIVES ON CASE STUDY

Most students and teachers who profit from the study of cases agree that cases help focus and dramatize problems and, at the same time, locate problems in real-life situations. Beyond this initial point of agreement, diverse orientations and styles of case analysis are plentiful. For example, orientations provided by the disciplines of economics, management, and philosophy direct a reader to pick out different elements in the cases as problematic and deserving of careful reflection. This pluralism of approaches dominantly occurs in the general area of business, society, and ethics as a result of two fundamentally distinct, though not incompatible, orientations: (1) the perspective of *ethics*, and (2) the perspective of the professional in *business*.

The ethics orientation tends to categorize its endeavor as "business ethics," and then proceeds to analyze cases in such ethical categories as justice, utility, and rights. Cases about reverse discrimination in hiring, for example, are studied in light of theories of justice and what these theories demand or permit. Moral decisions and quandaries found in cases are emphasized as fundamental to the case and to a proper understanding of it—although one's ethical presuppositions and evalua-

1

tions in examining cases might be taken to be as important as the presuppositions and evaluations of the central figures. Ethical theories may not be studied in detail and may not be called on for the analysis of each case, but such theories are generally regarded as heuristically useful. A common presumption is that without some understanding of ethical theory one is ill-equipped for the critical examination of the cases.

The business orientation tends to categorize its endeavor as "business and society," and then proceeds to analyze cases in terms of various relationships between business and industry, on the one hand, and government and society, on the other hand. Cases about environmental pollution, for example, are studied by detailing empirical facts about pollution and disease and by examining social processes that have tended to diminish the scope of decisionmaking in business and have created new responsibilities through government requirements. The economic aspects of pollution control are central to any such discussion. The responses of corporations to changing legal and regulatory situations as well as the importance of skillful management are often heavily emphasized, as are the considerations of what has been and may become public policy. Tax policies and the economic consequences of proposed public policies may be studied in detail, and almost certainly will be taken as central to the analysis of cases. The difference between political interests and business interests too are taken as fundamental for a proper understanding of cases. This orientation somewhat deemphasizes the importance of both one's ethical presuppositions and the ethical presuppositions of persons featured in the cases. Ethical principles may not be mentioned at all—just as those who examine the cases with an ethical interest may wholly ignore questions of good and bad management.[1]

There is no reason to suppose that these different orientations are mutually exclusive or that one orientation is preferable to another. A more constructive approach is to admit that cases invite multiple forms of analysis. This judgment reflects a general truth about good cases: They can be analyzed from many points of view, and increased complexity increases the possibilities for different forms of analysis.

THE CASE METHOD IN LAW

Just as different *perspectives* on cases lead to different conceptions, so different *strategies* in analyzing cases yield different outcomes. This fact of life is not to be deplored. Something can be learned from cases only

[1]An instructive example of this approach is found in the Introductions and cases in *Business and Society*, eds., Robert D. Hay, Edmund R. Gray, and James E. Gates (Cincinnati: South-Western Publishing Co., 1976).

if a framework of questions is brought to the cases; otherwise a case merely offers a sequence of events and thoughts. The oldest and most extensive body of thought on strategies for analyzing cases (apart from religious traditions) is found in law, where the case method has long been a staple of legal training and where "case law" establishes precedents of evidence and justification. It is instructive to look first to the history of and problems in legal case analysis.

The single most important development in the history of the case method in law occurred shortly after 1870, when Christopher Columbus Langdell became Dean of the Law School at Harvard. Upon his ascending he immediately proceeded to revolutionize previous academic standards and teaching techniques by introducing "the case method." He intended this method to replace the prevailing textbooks and lecture methods, which he condemned as promoting rote learning and worthless acumen for passing examinations. Langdell's idea was to use casebooks, rather than textbooks, for the entire law school curriculum. The casebooks were composed of cases selected, edited, and arranged to reveal to the student the pervasive meanings of legal terms, as well as the "rules" and "principles" of law. This approach used a dialectical or Socratic manner of teaching to reveal how concepts, rules, and principles are found in the legal reasoning of judges, as exhibited in the cases. The skillful teacher presumably could extract these fundamental principles, in the way a skillful biographer extracts the true principles of a person's reasoning by studying his or her considered judgments over a lifetime.

Langdell was no mere disenchanted teacher who disliked conventional methods of lecturing. He had theoretical reasons for his reforms. In his view the law was no perfunctory profession that any clerk could learn by boning up on textbook wisdom. Langdell believed that the law was a science, resting on an inductive method modeled on the "scientific method" of the natural sciences. Teachers and students developed hypotheses in their dissection of cases, and landed on principles just as any scientist did. In law, he argued, one extracts from cases a select body of principles that frame the English common law.[2] Even though the many particulars in cases vary and their judicial conclusions are sometimes at odds, the principles of judicial reasoning need not vary. Also, one could study by this method exactly how far a principle extends, including where its employment is invalid. In the process the student presumably acquired a facility and sophistication to move from particular circumstances to generalizations and back.

[2]Langdell's first casebook, *Contracts*, is treated in Lawrence M. Friedman, *A History of American Law* (New York: Simon and Schuster, 1973), pp. 531f. The general account of the case method in this section is indebted to this source, and also to G. Edward White, *Tort Law in America: An Intellectual History* (New York: Oxford University Press, 1980).

At Harvard students were horrified at Langdell's innovation, and they cut his classes in massive numbers. They disliked recitation, criticism by questioning, and the preparation required for every class. There was also a faculty revolt, and the school's enrollment slipped noticeably. But in the end Langdell was victorious: The method was adopted and spread quickly to other echelons of American legal education, and eventually every American law school of renown succumbed to the new method of pedagogy. Yet this outcome was in some ways unfortunate, for there were many problems and pretentious claims in the Langdell vision, not the least of which was the odd notion of making the law a science and making its essence a few abstract principles. This vision tended to suppress such matters as legislation, the politics of such legislation, particular historical circumstances, jurisdictional variations, and legal practice. These were easily dismissed as trivial and irrelevant, because historical development and political context were less important than abstract principle.

There were, however, important reasons why this method, with appropriate modifications, ultimately prevailed in American law schools and still persists as the basic model. By making analysis of case law a basic source of legal education, teachers had a powerful and attractive tool for generalizing from cases. Spanning the tangled web of details in particular cases were "the principles of law." Legal theory and its fundamental doctrines could thus be both *found in and applied to cases*. Moreover, and very importantly, training in the case method was believed to sharpen skills of legal reasoning—both legal analysis and legal synthesis. One could tear a case apart and then construct a better way of treating similar cases. In the thrust-and-parry classroom setting, teacher and student had to *think through* a case and its rights and wrongs; they could no longer simply memorize a section of a textbook that transmitted general wisdom about the right answer. The method prepared the student for the practice of the law, not merely for theoretical wisdom about it.

The case method was the soul of American legal education from roughly 1880–1910, and leading legal texts and practices today give testimony that its legacy endures. However, since 1910 the case method has been less grandiosely conceived than it was in the Langdell era, having been buttressed by other forms of study. Its minor decline, in retrospect, was inevitable.[3] For one thing, the principles did not prove to be as uniform across courts or time as had first been thought, for incompatible and even rival theories were found in the precedent cases. The method was also isolationist in the context of the modern university, making law a specialty without connections to other professions and undercutting interdisciplinary investigation.

[3]See White, *Tort Law in America*, esp. pp. 154ff.

Ultimately the theory of law as a *science* waned and suffered a natural death. It left as its substantial legacy not only the extensive use of legal casebooks, but also an allied belief in the importance of case analysis and synthesis in the training of the legal mind. Its most enduring value is probably found in the way it teaches students to distinguish the nature of principles and evidence at work in one case as opposed to another. By examining cases students learn which courts are considered most adept at legal reasoning and where "the weight of the evidence" lies. The case method has come to stand above all else for a way of learning how to assemble facts and judge the weight of evidence so as to transfer that weight elsewhere in new cases. It is generally (though not uniformly)[4] agreed that it offers substantial benefits in the training of lawyers, whatever its pitfalls and shortcomings.

THE CASE METHOD
IN BUSINESS SCHOOLS

When the case method at the Harvard Law School enjoyed its peak of influence, it spawned a new infant across campus at the Harvard Business School, which opened its doors in 1908. The first Dean of the school, Edwin F. Gay, determined that courses on Commercial Law would use only the case method, with other courses using it in conjunction with lectures and reports. Dean Gay specifically stated that "the example of the Harvard Law School"—greatly prized in academic business circles—was responsible for this decision.[5] Cases and reports were then introduced gradually into Business Policy and Marketing courses. In a faculty acclimated to lecturing, Gay pushed hard for more extensive use of the case system (though he never used the method in his own courses, which were in Economic History).

The method began to flourish throughout the curriculum under Dean Wallace B. Donham, who took office in 1919. His training in law at the Harvard Law School was instrumental, as the following account by a later Dean of the Business School, Donald K. David, makes clear:

> Dean Donham's training in the law and his own wide business experience gave him the conviction that the case method was the sound approach for instruction in the Harvard Business School. . . . Dean Donham recognized that the development of the case system for teaching business would be a slow and expensive process. The law schools had the decisions of the courts, the medical schools had hospital cases and clinical records,

[4]For a sharp criticism of the method and its milieu in the training of lawyers, see the *Report of the Dean* of the Maryland Law School, Michael J. Kelly, "The Scandal of American Legal Education" (Baltimore: University of Maryland School of Law, 1979).

[5]Melvin T. Copeland, "The Genesis of the Case Method in Business Instruction," in M. P. McNair, ed., *The Case Method at the Harvard Business School* (New York: McGraw-Hill, 1954), p. 25.

5

and the scientific schools had their laboratories and records of experiments. In contrast, there were nowhere any records of the process of making business decisions. Therefore the development of the case system in the Business School had to take the slow and hard way; . . . those who gathered cases had to go out to the businesses themselves to record the actual situations.[6]

Following Langdell's example, Donham pushed his faculty members to develop casebooks for use in courses. These cases were gradually collected from sources in government, business research, and journalism. After a small donation was made to the school, faculty began collecting the best materials through systematic and comprehensive searches, at first emphasizing Industrial Management. Businessmen were in many cases actively pursued and persuaded to provide accounts of their own practices and experiences. This pursuit was called "fieldwork" done on "field trips."[7] There was no attempt to present either good or bad, successful or unsuccessful practices; rather, the intent was to present the typical and significant problems faced by business administrators. Over the subsequent 1920–1940 period, over $2,000,000 was spent solely for the purpose of case development. It seems that Dean Donham had achieved the same level of commitment to the case method as Langdell had at the Law School.

It was never anticipated that the case method in business schools would be a science, or even that the cases would be treated in a uniform way. The more typical view has emphasized a broad common-sensical perspective: "The case method is so varied, so diverse, so adaptable to the nature of the individual course and to the personality of the individual instructor, that no single person can portray it accurately. Indeed, the only discernible common thread . . . is the emphasis on student participation in the educational process . . . —assessing the facts, making the analysis, weighing the considerations, and reaching a decision."[8] The cases collected for courses are therefore chosen with two criteria in mind: (1) that the case requires reflection and administrative decision under circumstances of great complexity, and (2) that the case can be expected to promote vigorous classroom discussion. As the first criterion suggests, cases that involve dilemmas without a clear solution are preferred over those that fail to present a difficult dilemma. As both the first and second suggest, any case that promotes mere passive recounting rather than reflective involvement in a problem is not acceptable. Accordingly, the presuppositions of teachers in business schools often seem directly opposite to those of teachers in

[6]Donald K. David, "Foreward," in McNair, ed., p. 11.
[7]Copeland, "The Genesis of the Case Method," p. 32.
[8]McNair, "Editor's Preface," in McNair, ed., p. 11.

law. Cases are not primarily used to illustrate principles or rules. The whole idea is to develop a capacity to grasp problems and their solutions clearly.

As at the law school, so at the Harvard Business School, the curriculum innovations required for a case-based curriculum generated considerable controversy, even hostility. At stake was a clash in educational philosophies. On one hand were those who believed in distilled wisdom and facts through lecturing. When done well, lecturing can be a highly efficient way of transmitting valuable material to students, who feel comfortable in the controllable facts and general orientation such a system provides. On the other hand, a different ideal of learning views education as a medium that affords the student an understanding of an environment where *decisions* must be taken (usually an environment under constant change and innovation). To invoke a distinction of Gilbert Ryle's, the difference in training and educational philosophy reflects a difference in knowing *that* as distinct from knowing *how*.[9] The direct purpose of the case method at the Harvard Business School was to train students in how to think and act in highly complex and shifting business environments. Those who pushed hardest for the case method knew that facts and general principles were sacrificed to train thought and decision. Thus, one might know little about probability theory but a great deal about how to think under circumstances of merely probable outcomes.

Despite the above warnings about diversity in approaches to cases, there is something of an essence to the technique of the case method as practiced in business schools. This essence is nicely recounted in a classic article on the case method by Charles I. Gragg:

> A case typically is a record of a business issue which *actually* has been faced by business executives, together with surrounding facts, opinions, and prejudices upon which executive decisions had to depend. These real and particularized cases are presented to students for considered analysis, open discussion, and final decision as to the type of actions which should be taken. Day by day the number of individual business situations thus brought before the students grows and forms a backlog for observing coherent patterns and drawing out general principles. In other words, students are not given theories or hypotheses to criticize. Rather, they are given specific facts, the raw materials, out of which decisions have to be reached in life and from which they can realistically and usefully draw conclusions. . . .
>
> There is no single, demonstrable right answer to a business problem. For the student or businessman it cannot be a matter of peeking in the back of books to see if he has arrived at the right solution. . . .

[9]G. Ryle, "Knowing How and Knowing That," *Proceedings of the Aristotelian Society,* Vol. XLVI (1945–46), pp. 1–16.

> The instructor's role is ... to provoke argumentative thinking, to guide discussion, ... and if he chooses, to take a final position on the viewpoints which have been threshed out before him. . . . But *authoritarian* use of the cases perverts the unique characteristics of the system. The opportunity which this system provides the students of reaching responsible judgments on the basis of an original analysis of the facts is sacrificed.[10]

One conviction underlying this pedagogical viewpoint is that students have generally been trained in universities as if they were immature journeypersons. Implicitly transmitted is the assumption that they are not equipped to make decisions, for they lack basic facts and principles. Decisionmaking is presented as an adult function into which they will gradually grow, upon first learning accepted theories and techniques. Those who initiated the case method at Harvard thought this an entirely wrong-headed assumption about student abilities and training. As Gragg saw it, the Harvard Graduate School of Business Administration has as one of its premiere functions "to achieve the transition from what may be described as a childlike dependence on parents and teachers to a state of what may be called dependable self-reliance."[11] The case method was the cornerstone of this shift and advance in pedagogy.

However, the method has never convinced everyone in the business community that it is *solely* sufficient as a mode of instruction. Many believe that business is too diverse and requires detailed knowledge unobtainable from case studies alone. For example, in 1982 CBS Inc. decided to sell Fawcett Books and the Popular Library. CBS had not done well in the mass market paperback book industry with these subsidiaries. When it came time to lay blame for failure, the case method at Harvard suffered much of the criticism. "Fawcett and Popular were ruined by Harvard MBAs," said Patrick O'Connor, who had moved from Fawcett to Pinnacle Books. He added: "Book publishing is a unique business, it can't be done with case studies."[12]

TWO CONCEPTS
OF "THE CASE METHOD"

The analysis thus far suggests an important difference between case analysis in law and business. Cases in law are based on the reasoning of judges. A court's reasoned opinion, we might say, is the *form* of the

[10]Gragg, "Because Wisdom Can't be Told," as reprinted in McNair, ed., pp. 6–7, 11–13 (italics added).

[11]Gragg, "Because Wisdom Can't be Told," p. 8.

[12]John F. Berry, "CBS Decides It Wants Out of the Paperback Business," *The Washington Post,* February 7, 1982, sec. G, pp. 1, 4.

case, the facts the mere *matter*. In any attempt to extract evidence or other useful parallels from the case, the facts alone are sterile and uninteresting; but in business, the cases present no parallel form, no reasoned opinion or precedent case to be studied for its controlling principles and weight of evidence. The cases themselves are nothing but "the facts of the case." Any reasoned opinion is an additional overlay; therefore it could not reasonably be hoped that from a study of the facts, even in related cases, principles could be *generalized*. There are no principles because there is no reasoning and no common law. To this extent legal methods are peculiar to law and impossible to transfer to other professional-school contexts.

There thus are at least two concepts of the "case method," both deriving historically from Langdell's vision at the Harvard Law School. Let us call these two methods the "problem-based case method" and the "authority-based case method." The problem-based orientation is the governing ideal in business, though it is used by teachers of both philosophy and law. This method focuses critical thinking on a problem; it stimulates reflection on what ought to be done, and the problems provoke personal and social decisionmaking. In the use of this method there is (usually) no ultimate authority, and disagreements are expected to abound without final resolution.

The authority-based "case method" contrasts noticeably. Here the facts of the case are merely instrumental; how the judge reasons is essential. Students learn how judges think, and it is this thinking they must grapple with—not the social or moral problems presented by the case. Of course these same cases *can* be examined by the problem-based method; and some of the best cases in this volume are from court opinions. But to employ a problem-based approach is to abandon the authority-based approach. At the heart of the latter is authoritative decisionmaking by judges who set authoritative precedents. Then lawyers take those decisions and apply them to similar cases. Predictability in transferring the reasoning from one case to another is a virtue, for what one seeks to learn in using the authority-based method is what *will happen* in the courts. This is clearly distinct from the problem-based approach, where predictability of this sort plays no significant role.

THE CASE METHOD
IN PHILOSOPHY

Philosophy is oriented toward the problem-based approach, although the idea of personal decision by case analysis has not always flourished in this field. The philosopher R. B. Perry once tendered the following reflection on education in the humanities generally:

> [I]n subjects such as philosophy and literature, in which it is likewise respectable to entertain different opinions, teachers hesitate to teach their students how to choose among them, and hesitate themselves to choose.
> But thought is applied to action through *decision*. Giving students ideas without enabling them to draw conclusions is like giving them sharpened tools without teaching them what to do with them.[13]

Perry's perspective has become a powerful but not ascendant view in philosophy over the last 30-year period. In theoretical ideal, if not in classroom practice, it has assumed powerful influence. Even so, until quite recently this ambition has never been connected to the case method or to professional practice in fields such as business. Philosophy has no history of the case method parallel to those in law and business schools. There has been scarcely any detailed discussion, paralleling that in law and business, as to whether case-based teaching more adequately prepares a student for (professional or other) judgment and practice than conventional textbook and lecture approaches.

This hiatus is surprising, as a related dispute in philosophy dates from Aristotle, who discussed the role of "practical wisdom" and "practical judgment" in directing human activities. He depicted a person of practical wisdom as one who envisions what should be done in particular circumstances, a capacity he thought distinct from mere intellectual abstraction and cleverness. Centuries later Immanuel Kant discussed the study of "cases" and "examples" in the training of practical judgment. Kant did not make comments as flattering as Aristotle's about a person *merely* of good practical judgment, but Kant did argue that the study of case examples is important for the training of practical decisionmaking.

Recently in philosophy these traditional views have been refocused on the use of case studies. Although philosophy must deal with moral and social problems at the level of abstract theory, these problems can be seen to emerge from cases, and philosophical arguments are often dramatically present in the flow of dialogue in cases. It is mainly for these reasons that the advice is now commonly heard that "case studies are employed most effectively when they can readily be used to draw out broader ethical principles and moral rules . . . [so as] to draw the attention of students to the common elements in a variety of cases, and to the implicit problems of ethical theory to which they may point."[14] The analogy to some legal uses of the case method is obvious; and, as in the case of law, it is not obvious how this goal might be accomplished.

---

[13]R. B. Perry, *The Citizen Decides: A Guide to Responsible Thinking in Time of Crisis* (Bloomington, Ind.: Indiana University Press, 1951), Ch. 6.

[14]Daniel Callahan and Sissela Bok, *The Teaching of Ethics in Higher Education* (Hastings-on-Hudson, N.Y.: The Hastings Center, 1980), p. 69.

Possibly the best use of cases in both philosophy and business is not as a *source* of generalizations, but rather as a *test* of generalizations. By this criterion cases help sharpen and refine theoretical claims, especially by pointing out the applications, inadequacies, or limitations of theories. As one business-school faculty member expresses this point of view, "In discussing [basic ethical concepts such as] Justice or Freedom, relevant cases or incidents should be introduced to make clear how the principle looks in real world situations."[15] From this perspective, cases illustrate the application of fundamental ethical notions, rather than serving as a medium from which they can be extracted. Cases illustrate principles at work and exhibit how informed judgments are expressed.

Of course nothing so fancy as an entire ethical theory or a firm set of fundamental principles needs to precede or emerge from such analysis to make it successful. Case analysis could be used largely for bringing a general principle, proposal, or procedure under scrutiny to see how well it applies to one or more particular circumstances. A related maneuver is the use of cases as counterexamples to proposed general principles.

A somewhat grander vision of case analysis is found in John Rawls's proposal that in developing a normative ethical theory it is appropriate to start with the broadest possible set of our considered judgments about a subject such as justice, and then erect principles that reflect them. These principles can then be pruned and adjusted by bringing cases under them. Suppose, for example, that some problems of deceptive advertising and environmental responsibility are selected for examination. Some widely accepted principles of right action might be taken, as Rawls puts it, "provisionally as fixed points," but also as "liable to revision."[16] Paradigm cases of what we all agree are right courses of action might be listed and examined, and a search would then be undertaken for principles consistent with our judgments about these paradigm cases. These principles could be tested by reference to other paradigm cases, and other considered judgments found in similar cases, in order to see if they yield counter-intuitive or conflicting results. The hope is that through this process moral theories and principles can be made to cohere with all our considered judgments about particular cases. That is, they can be brought into equilibrium.

Although we have now seen that there is no single consensus method delineating how cases are used in either philosophy or business, the

[15]Henry Eilbirt, "Evaluation of Experimental Courses in Business Ethics," in *Report of the Committee for Education in Business Ethics,* a monograph sponsored by a grant from the National Endowment for the Humanities (Newark, Dela.: CEBE—American Philosophical Association, 1980).

[16]John Rawls, *A Theory of Justice* (Cambridge, Mass.: Harvard University Press, 1971), pp. 20f.

matter is probably no more decided in law. Indeed there is currently some discussion among law professors of modeling case studies of ethical issues in law firms on "the business-school model" of case studies of ethical issues in management, with the intent of exposing lawyers to the business-school model of training in judgments professional practice requires.[17]

HARD CASES: THE PROBLEM OF DILEMMAS

We noted above that cases may be examined not for the purpose of extracting general principles, but rather to have a concrete forum for testing the authority or "weight" of principles when they conflict. Such testing can be most illuminating when a dilemma is present and a hard choice must be made. We have seen previously that many cases in legal and business texts involve dilemmas. Some of the legal cases have led to the saying "hard cases make bad law." Yet bad law is not always made from legal dilemmas, and hard choices need not entail tragic choices. Such cases can improve and clarify the law. Since this volume is filled with cases involving moral and social dilemmas—ones that hopefully do not make for bad decisions or confusing generalizations— it is important to understand the nature of dilemmas and their analysis.

We may note first that it is misleading to assume that the only dilemmas of importance in these cases are moral or social. Many involve personal dilemmas, especially where one is confronted with moral reasons for performing acts that may not be in one's own self-interest. Whistleblowing cases often assume this character—as, for example, an engineer named Dan Applegate illustrates in the DC-10 case. Similarly, in the Interscience Publishing case, a manager must make a decision that pits the financial interests of a small company against the privacy rights of employees by introducing a lie detector examination for all persons employed. In such dilemmas two or more conflicting but reasonable judgments can often be made—as anyone who makes hard choices (managerial, moral, personal, or whatever) will understand. Most dilemmas present a need to balance competing ideal claims in untidy circumstances, and most decisions require such balancing.

As we reflect on disagreements, we may be increasingly tempted to declare them *irresolvable* dilemmas, for even if rational deliberation plays a critical role in our argument, reason alone is insufficient to resolve dilemmas with equally plausible solutions. It is thus understand-

[17]Michael J. Kelly, "Notes on the Teaching of Ethics in Law School," *The Journal of the Legal Profession* **5** (1980), pp. 28f; and *Legal Ethics and Legal Education* (Hastings-on-Hudson, N.Y.: The Hastings Center, 1980), p. 47.

able why there seem to be intractable social controversies over many cases. Nevertheless, we must not make too much of this intractability. Many apparent dilemmas turn out to be at least partially resolvable, and it is important to study cases with an eye to ways in which dilemmas can be avoided. Dilemmas found in this volume—perhaps the majority—could have been avoided or minimized through more skillful management. Good management is rarely present in situations where persons face agonizing dilemmas about whether to blow the whistle or pledge allegiance. A study of these cases in order to reveal actual steps that management could have taken (but did not) can be profitable, as can reflection on procedures that might have deflected or defused a problem. For example, as the cases on conflict of interest illustrate, many problems arise because a manager failed to consult with others or because no peer or employee review committee existed.

This point about sound management and sound procedures suggests the need to examine cases in terms of alternative strategies and actions. There will invariably be many alternatives that might have been employed. Indeed, there is such a rich possibility of alternatives that it will generally not prove feasible to agree on the single most acceptable alternative. Of course such agreement need not be the goal of case analysis, any more than reaching consensus or agreement on "*the* problem" in a case should be the goal. It is *learning how* to spot problems and create alternative maneuvers that is of chief importance. The criterion of excellence in case analysis is the preparation such analysis provides for dealing with similar situations.

Philosophers have been far more reluctant to accept this point of view about ethical dilemmas than have lawyers and business persons about dilemmas in their fields. This perhaps indicates that philosophers have often been too far removed from practice. In ethics as elsewhere it is difficult to escape the view that reasonable and informed persons differ concerning both actions that should be taken and justifying principles invoked as grounds for such actions. They can disagree vigorously over the proper interpretation of cases, and nowhere will they disagree more than in dilemmatic cases. One person's clinching paradigm will often be the butt of another's attack. In such cases, we often say that two disputants simply cannot bring their intuitions into harmony.

Reliance upon intuition and quasi-legal notions such as the "outweighing" of one right or principle by another will ultimately fail to resolve many important dilemmas. Moreover, argument from analysis of cases is not commonly purely descriptive of shared evaluative beliefs, and hence is not simply a matter of systematically bringing general intuitions into harmony. Often such argument is revisionary of our beliefs. Cases shock intuition and alter belief. Disagreements, then, may largely reduce to arguments concerning why some beliefs and principles *ought* to be *readjusted*. Cases can be a blunt instrument for suggesting the need for such readjustment.

"THE 'FACTS' OF THE CASE"

The great majority of cases in this volume are actual rather than hypothetical, and most use actual names rather than fictitious names that mask identities. What is reported about the role of McDonnell Douglas in producing the DC-10, or about Kellogg Cereals in advertising its product, are presumably the facts of the case—what really occurred in a certain time slice across history. It is prudent, however, to have reservations about the notion that the facts as presented simply are the facts of the case. Several considerations suggest the need for a modestly skeptical attitude about reported facts.

First, analysis of the notion of a fact has itself proved an elusive task. A fact is generally assumed to be an empirically confirmable or falsifiable statement that describes some event or object. Factual statements are thus either true or false. A value, by contrast, is presumably an evaluative statement or judgment concerning what is good, right, or virtuous. (In many, but not all, cases, value judgments also determine what ought to be the case.) Evaluative statements appraise and assess events, while factual statements describe some aspect of the event and do not appraise or assess.

Unfortunately, this noble ideal of neutrality can quickly dissipate at the level of concrete reports of facts. In criminal trials, for example, it is notorious that different eyewitnesses report the facts differently— often because of biases or prior opinions. Similarly, journalists often provide substantially different accounts of a press conference or an athletic event. Even scientists operate with different theories that direct them to see the facts differently. For these reasons, and a hundred like them, the notion of neutral facts has come under severe attack.

Second, the facts as presented are always selected for a purpose. From an infinity of events in a given day, the nightly national news is condensed to less than thirty minutes. Such selectivity does not itself entail a distorting bias; selection may be an intelligent and revealing structuring of an otherwise massive and baffling array of events and relationships. The Love Canal case in this volume is an example of a case that requires careful historical selection and reconstruction. Moreover, the goal of a *complete* set of facts is a mythical ideal. Whole volumes have been written on some of the cases in this text, and these volumes omit many possible descriptions of what occurred. On the other hand, selectivity and sheer lack of available information *can* introduce bias in the writing of cases. While the cases in this volume have been carefully scrutinized to keep the problem of bias to a minimum, the cautious reader will never forget the possibility that circumstances are commonly described and evaluated in starkly different terms by different individuals.

This reminder is especially important when companies and individuals are named. The picture of management at McDonnell Douglas, for example, is not favorable in the DC-10 case, but we also lack many facts about what transpired at that company over a multi-year period. What is emphasized in these descriptions may be deemphasized or even ignored in other accounts. In the end there is no mirror of history; there are human actors interpreting the actions of others. A useful rule is to try to put aside the identities of individuals and companies, while *assuming* the correctness of the facts. One can then more easily criticize decisions and strategies, rather than individuals or corporate groups. That is, a charitable approach analyzes cases *as if* they occurred in the way described, but without fervent commitment to the precision of the account as reality.

Third, in cases such as those presented in this volume, corporations have often been treated harshly by journalists who present the facts of the case to the public. As a result, corporations have become leery of opening their files and office doors to journalists. Indeed, at present there is something of a cold war between journalists and many corporations. Journalists tend to view corporations as inherently secretive and as presenting facts with the same objectivity with which they prepare advertising for public consumption. Management, in turn, sees journalists as biased and even sensationalistic distorters of the truth who investigate cases with the thoroughness of someone who picks horses on a friend's tip. They also see reporters as unqualified for the range of issues their newspapers commission them to study, since news coverage from a single reporter can cover such diverse matters as new products, embezzlement schemes, plant relocations, labor relations, securities, investments, price hikes, company growth, salaries, profits, etc.

This is not the place to arbitrate such a dispute, but it is the place to note that the press is frequently a major source of information about the "facts of the case." The reports of journalists *alone* are rarely used in this volume, and attempts to incorporate divergent views of corporate officials have been maximized in cases where there has been a reliance on the press. However, the use of journalistic material in researching and writing cases is not uncommon and provides one more reason to place some distance between the facts of the case as presented and the actual circumstances from which they arose. "The facts as reported" or "the facts as they have thus far emerged" are more guarded but fairer descriptions.

There is a final reason for caution about the facts of the case. Those who study cases invariably want more facts. The belief is insistent that if only more facts were known, dilemmas and uncertainties would disappear. A temptation is to doctor the case by adding hypothetical facts. This move is usually prefaced by someone's saying, "But what if. . . ?" These retreats to new or different facts are understandable reactions, but it is desirable to suppress them in the analysis and discussion of cases in this volume, which have been selected *because* of the way they present difficult problems. Most important is to come to grips with the problems as presented, not to alter the circumstances or shelve the problems on grounds of an insufficiency of facts. Understanding the dilemmatic nature of situations faced in professional practice is a prime reason for studying the cases. Moreover, presenting more facts may not waive the problem away; rather, it increases the complexity of the situation, and this added complexity increases the problems in case analysis.

This position does not imply that it is never a useful exercise to modify the conditions and then think through problems under these new conditions. To the contrary, this method can be quite valuable, and skillful teachers use it with profit. Furthermore, these warnings are not intended to discredit the careful reader who looks for pertinent missing facts. One should sleuth for missing facts as well as for facts subject to alternative description. But just as one must make decisions every day on incomplete and uncertain information, so must the cases in this volume be studied under conditions of uncertainty. To do otherwise would be to distort "the 'facts' of the case."

chapter 1

The Employee

INTRODUCTION   The dominant model of the employee/employer relationship in large businesses has for many years been "labor and management." This model has been generally understood as adversarial— a model placing conflicting goals and interests at the center of the relationship. Traditionally this model (as cultivated in the history of common law) has awarded the balance of power to management. As with the military, an employee must be loyal, obey the orders of superiors, and keep confidential information secret—unless some clear moral wrong or illegal act is involved. Of special importance has been a body of law governing corporations known as the "law of agency." This law, fashioned largely from legal precedents, deals with the duties of loyalty and obedience of an employee and generally has functioned to protect corporations. For example, in conflicts of obligation, corporate executives and lawyers owe their allegiance and legal duty to the corporation and *not* to stockholders, the public, other employees, etc. In some influential cases it has been held that disloyalty by an employee to the corporation or to its interests is in effect "private treason."

Recently this model of the employer/employee relationship has been under careful scrutiny, with much discussion focusing on the rights of employees and workplace conditions. Thus, the rights of employees to privacy, to information about hazards in the workplace, to "blow the whistle," to security, to avenues of complaint, and to due process have all been seriously discussed. The ancient theory that management's loyalty and responsibility are owed to the corporate entity rather than to employees or the public has been eroded by these changes. The older body of law and the new trends have thus combined to form a new set of moral and legal controversies over what ought to be done in the corporate setting when conflicts of interest, conflicts of duty, and conflicts of role-responsibility arise. There is a great deal of ferment as to the nature and strength of such rights claims. This ongoing discussion of employee rights and employer responsibilities should not be understood as a unilateral movement wholly redounding to the benefit of the employee. The idea is rather to rectify past injustices in the conception and functioning of the employer/employee relationship, including those that may have negatively affected the employer.

Virtually none would deny that employees owe important obligations to employers, and that employers themselves have rights. One of these rights, for example, is the protection of business interests and investments. Employees can function as spies, can use company resources for private gain, and can easily secure confidential information when moving from one firm to another (information they possess only because of their relationship with an employer). Because employers have a right to the protection of property, and employees a right to accept new positions, the protection of "trade secrets," for example, has become a sticky problem. Other questions of comparable importance about the limits of valid company control of employees are found in the Bethlehem Steel and Interscience Publishing cases in this chapter.

Most of the cases in this chapter, however, focus more prominently on employee rights. One issue of current interest raised in the Du Pont Female Exclusion case is the increased protection for workers in hazardous environments. Flimsy scaffolding, exposed saw blades, careless dynamiting, and thousands of similar dangers in the workplace have long been known, and precautions have been taken to minimize these hazards. However, many have argued that an unprecedented and unanticipated situation now prevails. We are beginning to understand the dangers of various toxic agents and airborne dangers in the work environment, and yet do not have enough information to assess the actual seriousness of the threat. This raises questions about the nature of a "safe workplace" and about the notion of an "acceptable risk." Obviously a workplace cannot be guaranteed safe, but what counts as an adequate precaution? Can a company treat employees paternalistically by protecting them against their decisions to assume risks? And what counts as providing adequate information to employees so that they can protect themselves against or assess the dangers of their workplace? This question plays a central role in the Du Pont case, which features a policy to prevent fertile women employees from exposure to certain chemicals by banning them from the environment.

A series of important issues also surrounds conflicts of interest, and there are conflicts among the roles the employee must assume. The best known among these problems is "whistleblowing," which involves questions about whether employees ought to blow the whistle on presumed corporate wrongdoing by revealing information or encouraging inspections by responsible parties outside the corporation. Usually a whistleblower believes that his or her conscience compels action in "the public interest." This justification could simply be a cover for various inadequacies or self-interested goals on the part of the employee;

and management has generally denounced whistleblowing as a practice involving despicable acts of disloyalty. On the other hand, loyalty to the corporation is no more an absolute obligation than it is in the military. Thus, cases of whistleblowing generally involve balancing the duty of loyalty with the duty to protect the public interest by revealing presumably wrongful actions. Such cases also raise interesting questions of management practices that could have avoided this kind of conflict. The Fumio Matsuda and DC-10 cases in this chapter feature the issue of whistleblowing. The latter two cases stimulate reflection on whether, by whom, and (very centrally) *when* the whistle should have been blown; the Matsuda case provokes discussion of techniques whistleblowers may employ.

Whistleblowing cases are not the only difficult problems involving employer and employee conflicts. Conflicts of interest arise when an employee (or employer) has a personal interest that conflicts with the interests of the firm. Generally, the pertinent interests are found in contexts where reasonable objectivity and impartiality are expected. Thus, for example, a manager who wants to promote his daughter instead of more experienced and senior employees has two interests (at least potentially) in conflict: his interests in his family's welfare (including his own pride and satisfaction) and his company's welfare. Doctors who serve on boards of directors of health insurance companies can have a similar conflict of interest: They have an interest in their personal income and the income of hospitals in which they work, but they are also charged to keep payments low to protect those who take out company policies. As in the whistleblowing cases, many conflict-of-interest situations raise questions about an employee's loyalty to an employer. Must an employee always put the employing firm's interest above his or her own personal, familial, or social interests? This question raises further questions about the extent to which an employee can be excused for the performance of an immoral or illegal action on grounds that "my boss told me to" or "I thought it was in the company's best interest." These and other questions are probed in the Bethlehem Steel case in this chapter.

Polygraph Tests at Interscience Publishing

In January of 1982 Dick Snell, president of Interscience Publishing Company of La Jolla, California, faced a difficult decision about the control and monitoring of his employees. Ever increasing thefts and dishonesties—complicated by declining sales and profits in the entire college textbook market—threatened the publishing business that he had founded (originally as a largely independent subsidiary of a major publisher located in the Eastern United States). His company was now on such shaky financial ground that its parent company was considering absorbing it into their much larger editorial and marketing operations. In order to combat increasing employee dishonesties, Snell was now considering instituting polygraph (lie detector) examinations for all employees.

The use of the polygraph had become routine in a number of California companies of comparable size and problems. Its success in increasing revenues by decreasing costs had been documented to Snell's satisfaction. Nonetheless, Snell still resisted using this new technology. He found himself paradoxically horrified at the idea, though attracted to its benefits. He had just read about a serious strike at the Adolph Coors Brewery in Golden, Colorado (in April, 1977) in which 1,000 workers left their jobs in a bitter walkout partially caused by the use of lie detectors for screening job applicants. He had also just watched a television documentary on "The New Era" of industrial spying that examined the new wave of polygraph examinations and so-called "monitoring devices," which were principally wiretaps placed on office phones. The documentary showed supervisors listening to long-distance "private" calls made clandestinely by employees to friends, parents, and sometimes rival firms to which they were passing on information as "industrial spies." The documentary pitted the "private interests" of employees against the company's interest. Employees who were interviewed in the documentary expressed strong reservations about wiretaps and polygraph examinations, on grounds that their privacy was invaded and their personal integrity challenged without cause. The executives interviewed (all of whom had instituted polygraph testing) denied all violations of privacy rights on grounds that company time and phones, not private resources, were in question. As one executive put it, "We would never tap an employee's home phone, even if we thought the person was spying on us; but during working hours you are not a private person."

Snell was struck by the powerful feelings demonstrated by employees and management alike. The documentary made an excellent case that the use of wiretaps and polygraph examinations raised productivity, cut costs dramatically, and reduced waste at a number of levels. And thus far no one had been able to show that employee morale was actually lowered—so long as executives and employees at all levels were treated similarly. Still, employees *complained* of lower morale, and some court cases were pending. Snell felt sick to his stomach watching the president of one company listening to tape recordings monitored by a supervisor, as a happy employee on Christmas Eve morning spoke to the man to whom she was engaged. This long distance call to Alaska had cost the company $20.94, and when a consistent pattern of such calls from this employee was detected, she was fired. Snell was so bothered by the idea of wiretapping that he had ruled out its use. But he saw polygraph tests as quite a different matter. He viewed them as less invasive, for everyone could be treated similarly and it would all be out in the open.

Interscience Publishing had been established in 1963 when a major Eastern publisher wished to venture further into science textbook publishing—a market that was then rapidly expanding. Snell had been made president of the new satellite, and under his management the company had slowly grown from a four-editor, one-sales-manager operation to a large sales staff and separate editors for each scientific field in which they published. There were also a number of production editors, technical and clerical assistants, and secretaries at the main office.

Snell had been a superb editor before becoming president of Interscience, and he had built up the company through long hours of patient training of new editors. He taught them skills of manuscript acquisition and sales, but several editors had left for larger companies as soon as they were thoroughly experienced and could learn no more from Snell. He shrugged off these losses as the ways of the industry, yet he was shocked at the absolute nonexistence of employee loyalty—

a far distance from his early years with the parent company. Company and personal loyalties had been institutionalized in those days, and one thought much more about moving up to higher management positions in the company than about moving to a competitor (in some cases taking the entire editorial staff along to the new employer).

Nonetheless, both then and now the major management challenge in textbook publishing was to attract and develop promising editors with strong individual initiative and the ability to work with the sales staff in the field. This staff is composed of a number of company "representatives" or "travelers" who "work" various science departments in universities and colleges in the region in which they live. "Working" involves calling on professors to promote books, shopping around for manuscripts in preparation, making phone calls to encourage the adoption of texts, and in some cases gathering data for direct-mail campaigns. This sales staff cannot be supervised on a day-to-day basis, because they work independently in distant cities. Such persons tend to move from company to company even more frequently than do editors. Over the years Snell had developed an efficient and effective system of managing editors and sales staff—a system of which he was justifiably proud.

However, in spite of his efforts, minor thefts and various forms of dishonesty plagued Snell, and matters were clearly getting worse. Snell had long known about the problem of private long-distance phone calls made at company expense. This had been easy to control when they were a smaller operation, but now it was almost impossible to trace if an employee was at all clever. He had also uncovered some petty theft, and had his suspicions about two expensive word processors that had mysteriously vanished at considerable expense to the company. He was also shocked to discover recently that several members of the sales force had been selling large numbers of promotional copies of new books to bookstores as "used books" at campuses they worked. This doubly affected profits and sales: First, the books did not get in the hands of professors, and, second, the bookstores would sell the "used copies" directly to students and would order fewer copies (perhaps none) from the publishing company.

Snell had also discovered a pattern of "cheating on company time" by members of the sales force. The representative in Tacoma, Washington, for example, had taken the job of apartment manager in the 190-unit apartment house in which he lived. This was allegedly only a "weekend job," but in fact the employee was now spending over 80% of his time managing the apartment house. The employee had been clever at concealment, and it took over three years to discover why sales had been declining in the region. (In fact, it might never have been discovered had not suspicion been aroused when several phone calls were placed to the publishing company about various apartment disasters while the representative was on vacation.)

While Snell was trying to figure out how to solve this problem, he was confronted with the embezzlement of over $10,000 by his highly trusted sales manager. Because the sales manager was married to the company's accountant, Snell was unsure how aggressively to pursue the matter and how much proof he could muster. He was only certain from his examination of the books that the company was out the $10,000 and that it could not be explained.

After this disastrous series of events, Snell became convinced over a six-month period that he had to protect the company through new initiatives. He was now generally angry, upset, and depressed about the company's future. He always had felt keenly his responsibilities to his employees, but now he felt betrayed by the disloyal employees. He was convinced that he had many conscientious, loyal, honest, hard-working employees, and he knew that they too would be subjected to polygraph tests. Snell had searched about for other solutions but was unconvinced they would succeed. His consultants and other executives strongly supported his hypothesis that the polygraph would be successful. One executive had reported an amazing cost reduction after instituting polygraph tests, as well as no complaints from employees once the examinations had become routine, and no attempts at unionization. "The very threat of possible detection by a polygraph," he argued, "deters most employees."

Snell had hired a polygraph consultant from New York, who proposed a scheme whereby employees would not be tested for past dishonesties. No question would be asked about any event that might have occurred prior to the time of the tests. Snell would therefore never learn about past dishonesties, and employees would not have to worry about their disclosure. (Potential new employees would, however, be asked about their records with other companies.) Employees would also not be asked about the behavior of other employees, until some legitimate suspicion had been detected about a specific employee. The tests would be administered to potential employees prior to employment—and annually to all employees, including Snell. Only ten questions would be asked, and these questions would be handed out on a typed sheet to the examinee prior to examination. The most offensive of the ten questions to Snell were: (1) "Do you believe it is all right to cheat if no law is broken?" and (2) "Have you been refused a loan or credit in the past three years?" Yet Snell himself did not mind answering such questions.

Although Snell felt strongly attracted to this consultant's program, which had worked effectively elsewhere, he still had that nauseous feeling in his stomach.

Du Pont's Policy of Exclusion from the Workplace

In January 1981 the *New York Times* reviewed a new and startling development in the workplaces of the nation. Some fertile women workers chose to undergo voluntary sterilization rather than give up high-paying jobs that involved exposure to chemicals potentially harmful to a developing fetus. Disclosure of this practice precipitated discussion of a new civil rights issue with "questions . . . raised about whether a company should be allowed to discriminate against a woman to protect her unborn child, or whether the practice of keeping a woman out of certain well-paying jobs because she was fertile was simply another form of sex discrimination in the workplace."[1]

Some background information is necessary for understanding this issue. The causes of congenital (or "birth") defects in humans are not well understood. Four to six percent are known to be caused by specific drugs and environmental chemicals, but the causes of at least 65 to 70 percent are unknown. It *is* known, however, that of the 28,000 toxic substances listed by the National Institute of Occupational Safety and Health (NIOSH) 56 are known animal mutagens (that is, they cause chromosomal damage to either the ova *or* the sperm cells), and 471 are known animal teratogens (that is, they can damage the developing fetus).[2] As the 1960s' thalidomide tragedy showed, a substance can be perfectly harmless to the mother, while at the same time having devastating effects on the developing fetus. (Doctors prescribed thalidomide for pregnant women as a tranquilizer, but found that the drug caused such fetal defects as severely shortened and often useless arms and legs.)

[1]Philip Shabecoff, "Industry and Women Clash over Hazards in the Workplace," *New York Times,* January 3, 1981.

[2]Earl A. Molander, "Regulating Reproductive Risks in the Workplace," in his *Responsive Capitalism: Case Studies in Corporate Social Conduct* (New York: McGraw-Hill Book Co., 1980), p. 9.

This case was prepared by Martha W. Elliott and Tom L. Beauchamp and revised by Linda Kern. **Not to be duplicated without permission of the authors and publisher.**

Exposure to mutagenic or teratogenic substances in the workplace is complicated by the fact that chemicals and other toxic substances usually do not occur singly, but in combination. Also, the average worker does not have knowledge of the chemical makeup of many products. Furthermore, the period of maximum hazard of the developing fetus occurs during the third and fourth weeks of pregnancy, which is often before the woman is even aware of her pregnancy. The United States government (FDA and EPA, in particular) requires animal testing of drugs to insure that any new product to which pregnant women may be exposed is harmless to the fetus.

Industries such as chemical plants and zinc smelters with high concentrations of lead have coped with this potential threat to the fetus in various ways. The most common strategy is simply to make jobs that involve the risk of exposure "off limits" to women "of child-bearing potential." That is, fertile women in their late teens, twenties, thirties, and forties are banned from those particular positions. (Ironically, lead poses an equal danger to the male reproductive system.) Since a woman is assumed fertile until proven otherwise, this sweeping policy affects a large portion of the female workforce.[3] This policy, entitled "protective exclusion," has aroused the ire of the women's movement and civil libertarians, who see these policies as one more form of sex discrimination.

Charges of discrimination are made credible for several reasons. Jobs that *are* open to "women of child-bearing potential" are almost always lower-paying jobs. In addition, women's groups have noted a shortage of well-supported evidence about exposure to certain alleged toxic hazards and a general lack of consensus in government and industry about proper levels of unsafe exposure. The most significant charge of discrimination rests on evidence of the *male's* contribution to birth defects. As noted earlier, mutagenic substances affect the sperm as well as the egg. This can result in sterility for the man, but also can produce mutated sperm and ultimately a malformed fetus. (See pp. 28–29 for a table of chemicals known to affect the male reproductive system.) Thus, any policy designed to protect the fetus must include considerations of the sperm and egg that form it. This would logically include a more expansive protective policy than the mere exclusion of women from the workplace.

Du Pont de Nemours & Co., the largest chemical manufacturer in the United States, has been concerned about these issues since a high

---

[3] Albert Rosenfeld, "Fertility May be Hazardous to Your Job," *Saturday Review* **6** (9), p. 12.

incidence of bladder tumors appeared at its large Chambers work plant in Southern New Jersey in the 1930s. Du Pont has issued perhaps the most explicit policy statement about hazards to women and fetuses. If a chemical is found to be or is suspected of being an "embryotoxin" (toxic to the fetus), the first step is to use engineering and administrative procedures to eliminate the risk or to reduce it to an acceptable level. Engineering procedures might, for example, involve special ventilation equipment; administrative procedures might involve management of the length of exposure time or the required use of protective clothing. However, where no "acceptable exposure level" has been determined or where engineering and administrative procedures are inadequate to control exposure, the Du Pont policy reads: "females of child bearing capacity shall be excluded from work areas."[4]

Du Pont has rejected the suggestion that a woman be apprised of the health risk and sign a waiver if she chooses to accept the risk. The Du Pont position is that the exclusionary policy is to protect the fetus, not the woman. Bruce Karrh, medical director of Du Pont, holds that "the primary issue . . . is not whether the exclusion from the workplace is necessary to protect the adult female or male, but whether it is a necessary step to protect the embryo or fetus."[5] Karrh has developed a specific procedure for management and employees upon determination that a substance presents a risk to the fetus:

1. Employees who may be affected shall be informed of the possible consequences of exposure to such substances and appropriate safe handling procedures shall be established and communicated.
2. Engineering controls shall be used to the extent practical to reduce and maintain exposure to embryotoxins to acceptable levels. Such controls shall be augmented by administrative controls as appropriate.
3. Whenever engineering and administrative controls are not practical to keep exposure at or below acceptable levels, personal protective equipment, where appropriate, and training for its proper use shall be provided to and required to be used by employees who may be affected by such compounds.
4. Females of childbearing capability shall be excluded from work areas where:
   a. There is potential for exposure to an embryotoxin for which an acceptable exposure level cannot be set, or

[4]Bruce W. Karrh, "A Company's Duty to Report Health Hazards," *Bulletin of the New York Academy of Medicine* **54** (September 1978), esp. pp. 783, 785, and Molander, "Regulating Reproductive Risks," p. 16.

[5]Bruce W. Karrh, "Occupational Medicine," (Editorial) *Journal of the American Medical Association* **245** (June 5, 1981), p. 2207; see also his "Evaluation and Control of Embryotoxic Agents" (1979), available from Du Pont.

      b. whenever engineering and administrative controls augmented as appropriate by personal protective equipment, are determined to be inadequate to insure acceptable levels of exposure.[6]

Du Pont also holds that ". . . the waiver of subsequent claims by the female worker would be of no legal significance because the deformed fetus, if born, may have its own rights as a person which could not be waived by the mother."[7]

Women's groups continue, however, to view "protective exclusion" as sex discrimination, especially since there is growing evidence that the reproductive systems of men are also adversely affected by certain industrial chemicals. A discussion between Dr. Donald Whorton, one of the first to study testicular toxins in the workplace, and Dr. William N. Rom illustrates the problem many women's groups find with policies of female exclusion:

DR. WHORTON: . . . In a situation in which there is testicular toxicity, why would you be removing the women?

DR. ROM: Because it may affect both sexes.

DR. WHORTON: But you would remove the men before the women, wouldn't you?

DR. ROM: Somebody has to work there.[8]

The Coalition for the Reproductive Rights of Women, a group organized to fight discrimination against women of childbearing age, points out that exclusionary protections are unusually broad, especially since not all women want or plan to have children. An attorney for the women's rights project of the American Civil Liberties Union has criticized the notion that women should be protected "against their wishes" and states that "we insist that the cost of safety cannot be equality. Another solution should be found."[9]

Du Pont sees the sex of the excluded party as irrelevant, on grounds that the sole issue is that of protecting the susceptible fetus. The company also notes that implementation of the above four-step procedure is far more costly to the company than a policy that would allow women to make their own choices. However, women's advocates take

---

[6]Bruce W. Karrh, "Women in the Workplace," an address on May 2, 1978, as quoted in Molander, "Regulating Reproductive Risks," p. 16.

[7]Molander, "Regulating Reproductive Risks," p. 16.

[8]M. Donald Whorton, "Considerations about Reproductive Hazards," in Jeffrey S. Lee and William N. Rom, eds., *Legal and Ethical Dilemmas in Occupational Health* (Ann Arbor: Butterworth Group), p. 412.

[9]Shabecoff, "Industry and Women Clash."

TABLE 1

MALE REPRODUCTIVE EFFECTS: ENVIRONMENTAL AGENTS, HUMAN STUDIES

Agent	Exposure Conditions	Species	Type of Study	Effects
Anesthetic gases	Occupational	Male workers	Reproductive history	Increased incidence congenital anomalies offspring
Chloroprene	Occupational	Male workers	Semen analysis; reproductive history	Decreased motility and number of sperm; threefold excess miscarriages in wives
Dibromochloro-propane	Occupational	Male workers	Semen analysis; reproductive history	Decreased sperm count; infertility
High altitude	14,000 ft	Male	Semen analysis	Decreased sperm count and motility; increased number abnormal sperm
Hydrocarbons	Occupational	Male workers	Reproductive history	Twofold increased incidence childhood cancer with occupational hydrocarbon exposure of father
Kepone	Environmental	Male	Reproductive history	Decreased fertility males
Lead	Occupational	Male workers	Semen analysis	Decreased sperm count and motility; increase abnormally-shaped semen
Microwaves	Occupational	Male workers	Semen analysis; reproductive history	Decreased libido; decreased sperm count and motility, increase abnormally-shaped sperm
Carbon disulfide	Occupational	Male workers	Semen analysis; reproductive history	Impotence, loss of libido
Irradiation	Occupational	Male workers	Gonadotropic hormone and semen analysis	Depression gonadotropic hormone levels; alterations in spermatogenesis

Oral contraceptives	Occupational manufacture	Male workers	Reproductive history, physical exam, blood analysis	Gynecomastia, decreased libido, infertility
Vinyl chloride	Occupational	Male workers	Reproductive questionnaire	Adverse pregnancy outcome wives; excess fetal loss
Cigarette smoking	Environmental	Male	Semen analysis	Increase in abnormally-shaped sperm
Elevated temperature	Occupational, environmental 30 → 37°C	Male	Semen analysis; histology	Inhibition spermatogenesis, testicular pathology

Source: Vilma Hunt, *Work and the Health of Women* (Boca Raton, Fla.: CRC Press, Inc., 1979), pp. 158–159.

the view that companies such as Du Pont are simply remiss in developing technological solutions for the control of embryotoxins. A common union complaint is that industry makes the worker safe for the workplace, even to the point of exclusion, rather than making the workplace safe for the worker. These women view with suspicion management contentions that acceptable levels of exposure cannot be achieved.

Growing evidence that toxic substances pose a threat to the *future* fetus, as well as to the *existing* one, through mutation of the sperm and egg, indicates that this issue is not likely to prove amenable to simple solution.[10]

All these issues are further complicated because information that a chemical may be embryotoxic often is not available well in advance of policy decisions. In the case of a chemical used by Du Pont in some resins and elastomers, Du Pont was informed by a supplier in March 1981 that it was possibly teratogenic. The data was preliminary and needed corroboration by a study designed to show if teratogenicity occurs. Rather than wait for such a study to be completed, Du Pont immediately determined a level of exposure considered to pose "no risk." Du Pont then promptly advised all employees working with the chemical of the preliminary findings and determined that the jobs of about fifty women involved unacceptable levels of exposure. About one-half were found to be of childbearing capability and were excluded. All excluded women were moved to comparable positions without penalty in wages or benefits.

Du Pont's Haskell Laboratory simultaneously instituted an animal study to corroborate the preliminary work. The supplier's follow-up study and the Du Pont study both found no teratogenic effect in the animals studied. The supplier's earlier study results apparently contained experimental error. Du Pont notified its employees of the new findings and no longer excluded women of childbearing capability. Return preference was given to women formerly removed from these jobs. During this period, Du Pont made its plant physicians available for counseling employees and for consultations with the personal physicians of employees.[11]

[10]Sources: M. Donald Whorton, *et al.*, "Testicular Function among Cabaryl-Exposed Employees," *Journal of Toxicology and Environmental Health* **5** (1979), pp. 929–941; H. Northrop, "Predictive Value of Animal Toxicology," a paper presented at the "Symposium on Reproductive Health Policies in the Workplace," Pittsburgh, Pennsylvania, May 10, 1982; Vilma R. Hunt, "The Reproductive System Sensitivity through the Life Cycle," a paper presented at the American Conference of Governmental Industrial Hygienists, "Symposium: Protection of the Sensitive Individual," Tucson, Arizona, November 9, 1981.

[11]The final two paragraphs are based on personal correspondence of August 24, 1982, from Nancy K. Tidonia of Du Pont's Public Affairs Department to Tom L. Beauchamp.

The DC-10's Defective Doors

The Douglas Company had always held the lead in commercial avia-
tion until the Boeing Company captured a significant portion of the
commercial jet market in the late 1950s with its 707. (The 707 was actually similar to Douglas's DC-8, which already was in service.) The
Douglas Company, keenly aware of new and stiff competition, hoped
to supply a wide-bodied jet that would be attractive to international
commercial markets. To bring an "airbus" into service soon became
viewed by top management as crucial to long-term economic well being
(although in fact no wide-bodies were actually produced for another
ten years).[1]

Douglas was taken over by McDonnell Aircraft in 1967. By this time,
pressure to produce a wide-bodied jet had intensified. The Boeing
Company had already introduced its 747, and neither Douglas nor the
FAA wished Boeing to have exclusive control over this aspect of the air
travel market. The McDonnell Douglas firm then searched for a structural design subcontractor capable of sharing short-term financial burdens of a program building wide-bodied jets that would realize long-
term profits. The Convair Division of General Dynamics was such a
subcontractor, and it possessed an excellent reputation for structural
design. The understanding between the two companies was that Mc-
Donnell Douglas had the primary authority to furnish design criteria

---

[1]This paragraph was constructed from information provided by three unpublished
sources: Fay Horton Sawyier, "The Case of the DC-10 and Discussion" (Chicago: Center
for the Study of Ethics in the Professions, Illinois Institute of Technology, December 8,
1976), mimeographed, pp. 2–3; correspondence with John T. Sant of the McDonnell
Douglas Corporation's Legal Department in St. Louis; and correspondence with Professor Homer Sewell of George Washington University (see his article in note 5 below).

and to amend design decisions. Convair's role was primarily to create a design that would satisfy the stipulated criteria.[2]

In August 1968, McDonnell Douglas awarded Convair a contract to build the DC-10 fuselage and doors. The lower cargo doors became the subject of immediate discussion. These doors were to be outward-hinging, tension-latch doors, with latches driven by hydraulic cylinders—a design already adequately tested by DC-8 and DC-9 models. In addition, each cargo door was to be linked to hydraulically actuated flight controls and was to have a manual locking system designed so that the handle or latch lever could not be stowed away unless the door was properly closed and latched. McDonnell Douglas, however, decided to separate the cargo door actuation system from the hydraulically actuated primary flight controls. This involved using electric actuators to close the cargo doors rather than the hydraulic actuators originally called for. Fewer moving parts in the electrical actuators presumably made for easier maintenance, and each door would weigh 28 pounds less.

However, the Convair engineers had considered the hydraulic actuators critical to safety. They were not satisfied with these changes, and they remained unsatisfied when still further modifications were introduced. As Convair engineers viewed the situation, the major difference between the two actuator systems turns on the way each would respond to the buildup of forces caused by increasing pressure. If a hydraulic latch was not secured properly, the latches would smoothly slide open when only a small amount of pressure had built up in the cabin. Although the doors would be ripped off their hinges, this would occur at a low altitude so the shock from decompression would be small enough to land the plane safely. By contrast, if an electric latch failed to catch, it would not gently slide open due to increasing pressure. Rather, it would be abruptly and violently forced open, most likely at a higher altitude where rapid decompression would dangerously impair the structure of the plane.

Convair's Director of Product Engineering, F. D. "Dan" Applegate, was adamant that a hydraulic system was more satisfactory. However, McDonnell Douglas did not yield to Convair's reservations about the DC-10 cargo door design.

Once a decision had been made to use an electrical system, it was still necessary to devise a new and foolproof backup system of checking and locking. McDonnell Douglas asked Convair in the summer of 1969 to draft a Failure Mode and Effects Analysis, or FMEA, for the cargo

[2]See Paul Eddy, et al., Destination Disaster: From the Tri-Motor to the DC-10 (New York: Quadrangle Books, The New York Times Book Co., 1976), as reprinted in Robert J. Baum, ed., Ethical Problems in Engineering, 2nd ed. (Troy, N.Y.: Rensselaer Polytechnic Institute, 1980), Vol. II, pp. 175–185.

door system. An FMEA's purpose is to assess the likelihood and consequences of a failure in the system. In August 1969, Convair found nine possible failure sequences that could result in destruction of the craft, with loss of human lives. A major problem focused on the warning and locking-pin systems. The door could close and latch, but without being safely locked. The warning indicator lights were prone to failure, in which case a door malfunction could go undetected. The FMEA also indicated that the door design was potentially dangerous and lacked a reliable failsafe locking system. It could open in flight, presenting considerable danger to passengers.[3]

The FAA requires that it be given an FMEA covering all systems critical to safety, but no mention was made of this hazard to the FAA prior to "certification" of the DC-10 model. McDonnell Douglas says that the reason no such report was filed was that this cargo door design was never implemented until all defects expressed in the FMEA were removed. The FMEA *submitted*, they contend, was the *only final* FMEA, and did not discuss past defects because they had been removed.[4]

As lead manufacturer, McDonnell Douglas made itself entirely responsible for the certification of the aircraft and, in seeking the certification, was expressing its position that all defects had been removed. Convair, by contrast, was not formally responsible, because its contract with McDonnell Douglas forbade Convair from reporting directly to the FAA.

During a model test run in May 1970, the DC-10 blew its forward lower cargo door, and the plane's cabin floor collapsed. Because the vital electric and hydraulic subsystems of the plane are located under the cabin floor (unlike the 747 where they are above the ceiling), this collapse was doubly incapacitating.[5] A spokesperson at McDonnell Douglas placed the blame for this particular malfunction on the "human failure" of a mechanic who had incorrectly sealed the door. Although no serious design problems were contemplated, there were some ensuing modifications in design for the door, purportedly to provide better checks on the locking pins. As modified, the cargo door design was properly certificated and authorities at McDonnell Douglas believed it safe. Five DC-10s were flight tested for over 1500 hours prior to certification of the craft.

Certification processes are carried out in the name of the FAA, but the actual work is often performed by the manufacturers. As a regu-

---

[3]*Ibid.*, pp. 176–77; and Peter French, "What is Hamlet to McDonnell-Douglas or McDonnell-Douglas to Hamlet: DC-10," *Business and Professional Ethics Journal* **1** (Winter 1982), pp. 1, 5–6.

[4]John T. Sant, personal correspondence.

[5]See Homer Sewell, "Commentary," *Business and Professional Ethics Journal* **1** (Winter 1982), pp. 17–19.

latory agency, the FAA is charged with overseeing commercial products and regulating in the public interest. However, the FAA is often not in an independent position. The FAA appoints Designated Engineering Representatives (DER) to make inspections at company plants. These are company employees chosen for their experience and integrity, who have the dual obligations of loyalty to the company that pays them (as design engineers) and of faithful performance of inspections to see that the company has complied with Federal Airworthiness Regulations. The manufacturers are in this respect policing themselves, and it is generally acknowledged that conflicts of interest arise in this dual-obligation system.[6]

During the months surrounding November 1970, a number of internal memos were written at McDonnell Douglas and Convair that cited old and new design problems with the cargo door. New structural proposals were made, but none was implemented. McDonnell Douglas and Convair quarreled about cost-accounting and about pinning fault for remaining design flaws. The FAA finally certificated the DC-10 on July 29, 1971, and by late 1971 the plane had received praise for its performance at virtually all levels. Under rigorous conditions its performance ratings were excellent. The company vigorously promoted the new aircraft. But on June 12, 1972, an aft bulk cargo door of a DC-10 in flight from Los Angeles to New York separated from the body of the aircraft at about 11,750 feet over Windsor, Ontario. Rapid cabin decompression occurred as a result, causing structural damage to the cabin floor immediately above the cargo compartment. Nine passengers and two stewardesses were injured. A National Transportation Safety Board (NTSB) investigation found that the probable cause of the malfunction was the latching mechanism in the cargo door and recommended changes in the locking system. The NTSB's specific recommendations were the following:

1. Require a modification to the DC-10 cargo door locking system to make it physically impossible to position the external locking handle and vent door to their normal locked positions unless the locking pins are fully engaged.
2. Require the installation of relief vents between the cabin and aft cargo compartment to minimize the pressure loading on the cabin flooring in the event of sudden depressurization of the compartment.[7]

Fifteen days *subsequent* to the blowout over Windsor (June 27, 1972), Dan Applegate wrote a stern memo to his superior at Convair that expressed his doubts about the entire project and offered some reflec-

---

[6]Eddy, *Destination Disaster*, p. 179.

[7]National Transportation Safety Board, Aircraft Accident Report No. NTSB-AAR-73-2 (February 28, 1973), p. 38.

tions on "future accident liability." The following excerpts from the memo reveal Applegate's anguish and concerns:[8]

> The potential for long-term Convair liability on the DC-10 has caused me increasing concern for several reasons.
>
> 1. The fundamental safety of the cargo door latching system has been progressively degraded since the program began in 1968.
> 2. The airplane demonstrated an inherent susceptibility to catastrophic failure when exposed to explosive decompression of the cargo compartment in 1970 ground tests.
> 3. Douglas has taken an increasingly "hard-line" with regards to the relative division of design responsibility between Douglas and Convair during change cost negotiations.
> 4. The growing "consumerism" environment indicates increasing Convair exposure to accident liability claims in the years ahead. . . .
>
> In July 1970 DC-10 Number Two was being pressure-tested in the "hangar" by Douglas, on the second shift, without electrical power in the airplane. This meant that the electrically powered cargo door actuators and latch position warning switches were inoperative. The "green" second shift test crew manually cranked the latching system closed but failed to fully engage the latches on the forward door. They also failed to note that the external latch "lock" position indicator showed that the latches were not fully engaged. Subsequently, when the increasing cabin pressure reached about 3 psi (pounds per square inch) the forward door blew open. The resulting explosive decompression failed the cabin floor downward rendering tail controls, plumbing, wiring, etc. which passed through the floor, inoperative. This inherent failure mode is catastrophic, since it results in the loss of control of the horizontal and vertical tail and the aft center engine. We informally studied and discussed with Douglas alternative corrective actions including blow out panels in the cabin floor which would provide a predictable cabin floor failure mode which would accommodate the "explosive" loss of cargo compartment pressure without loss of tail surface and aft center engine control. It seemed to us then prudent that such a change was indicated since "Murphy's Law" being what it is, cargo doors will come open sometime during the twenty years of use ahead for the DC-10.
>
> Douglas concurrently studied alternative corrective actions, inhouse, and made a unilateral decision to incorporate vent doors in the cargo doors. This "bandaid fix" not only failed to correct the inherent DC-10 catastrophic failure mode of cabin floor collapse, but the detail design of the vent door change further degraded the safety of the original door latch system by replacing the direct, short-coupled and stiff latch "lock" indicator system with a complex and relatively flexible linkage. (This change was accomplished entirely by Douglas with the exception of the assistance of one Convair engineer who was sent to Long Beach at their request to help their vent door system design team.)
>
> This progressive degradation of the fundamental safety of the cargo

---

[8]Eddy, *Destination Disaster*, pp. 181–183.

door latch system since 1968 has exposed us to increasing liability claims. On June 12, 1972 in Detroit, the cargo door latch electrical actuator system in DC-10 number 5 failed to fully engage the latches of the left rear cargo door and the complex and relatively flexible latch "lock" system failed to make it impossible to close the vent door. When the door blew open before the DC-10 reached 12,000 feet altitude the cabin floor collapsed disabling most of the control to the tail surfaces and aft center engine. It is only chance that the airplane was not lost. Douglas has again studied alternative corrective actions and appears to be applying more "band-aids." So far they have directed us to install small one-inch diameter, transparent inspection windows through which you can view latch "lock-pin" position, they are revising the rigging instructions to increase "lock-pin" engagement and they plan to reinforce and stiffen the flexible linkage.

It might well be asked why not make the cargo door latch system really "fool-proof" and leave the cabin floor alone. Assuming it is possible to make the latch "fool-proof" this doesn't solve the fundamental deficiency in the airplane. A cargo compartment can experience explosive decompression from a number of causes such as: sabotage, mid-air collision, explosion of combustibles in the compartment and perhaps others, any one of which may result in damage which would not be fatal to the DC-10 were it not for the tendency of the cabin floor to collapse. The responsibility for primary damage from these kinds of causes would clearly not be our responsibility, however, we might very well be held responsible for the secondary damage, that is the floor collapse which could cause the loss of the aircraft. It might be asked why we did not originally detail design the cabin floor to withstand the loads of cargo compartment explosive decompression or design blow out panels in the cabin floors to fail in a safe and predictable way.

I can only say that our contract with Douglas provided that Douglas would furnish all design criteria and loads (which in fact they did) and that we would design to satisfy these design criteria and loads (which in fact we did). There is nothing in our experience history which would have led us to expect that the DC-10 cabin floor would be inherently susceptible to catastrophic failure when exposed to explosive decompression of the cargo compartment, and I must presume that there is nothing in Douglas's experience history which would have led them to expect that the airplane would have this inherent characteristic or they would have provided for this in their loads and criteria which they furnished to us.

My only criticism of Douglas in this regard is that once this inherent weakness was demonstrated by the July 1970 test failure, they did not take immediate steps to correct it. It seems to me inevitable that, in the twenty years ahead of us, DC-10 cargo doors will come open and I would expect this to usually result in the loss of the airplane. [Emphasis added.] This fundamental failure mode has been discussed in the past and is being discussed again in the bowels of both the Douglas and Convair organizations. It appears however that Douglas is waiting and hoping for government direction or regulations in the hope of passing costs on to us or their customers.

If you can judge from Douglas' position during ongoing contract change negotiations they may feel that any liability incurred in the meantime for loss of life, property and equipment may be legally passed on to us.

It is recommended that overtures be made at the highest management level to persuade Douglas to immediately make a decision to incorporate changes in the DC-10 which will correct the fundamental cabin floor catastrophic failure mode. Correction will take a good bit of time, hopefully there is time before the National Transportation Safety Board (NTSB) or the FAA ground the airplane which would have disastrous effects upon sales and production both near and long term. This corrective action becomes more expensive than the cost of damages resulting from the loss of one plane load of people.

F. D. Applegate
Director of Product Engineering.

If this memo had reached outside authorities, Applegate conceivably might have been able to prevent the occurrence of events that (to some extent) he correctly foresaw. However, this memo was never sent either to McDonnell Douglas or to the FAA. Applegate received a reply to his memo from his immediate supervisor, J. B. Hurt. By now it was clear to both Applegate and Hurt that such major safety questions would not be addressed further at McDonnell Douglas. Hurt's reply to Applegate pointed out that if further questions were now raised, Convair, not McDonnell Douglas, would most likely have to bear the costs of necessary modifications. Higher management at Convair subsequently agreed with Hurt. Without taking other routes to express his grave misgivings about the DC-10, Applegate filed away his memo.

In 1974 a DC-10 crashed near Paris killing all 335 passengers and 11 crew members. Experts agreed, according to the *New York Times,* that a cargo door failure caused the crash. The *Times* further maintained that airline personnel had not been adequately trained in the control and maintenance of the craft at the time it was sold.[9] It was alleged by McDonnell Douglas that the Turkish airline involved in the crash had attempted to "rework" the door rigging or latching mechanism, was working with an inadequately trained ground crew, and failed to follow specified procedures for proper latching. The Turkish airline denied the charges, and the official French investigatory body never made a public statement as to the likely cause of the crash.

In 1980 the McDonnell Douglas Corporation issued a special report addressing the public's growing fears about the design of the DC-10. The facts presented in the corporation's report were aimed at proving "that the DC-10 meets the toughest standards of aerospace technology."[10] The report does not mention the problems with the cargo

[9]See "The DC-10 Cargo Door Dilemma," in Richard M. Hodgetts, *The Business Enterprise: Social Challenge, Social Response* (Philadelphia: W. B. Saunders Co., 1977), pp. 107–108, quoting the *New York Times* (March 17, 1974), p. 48.

[10]McDonnell Douglas Corporation, *The DC-10: A Special Report* (Long Beach, Calif.: McDonnell Douglas Corporation, 1980).

doors. This omission is perhaps understandable in that a cargo door malfunction did *not* cause the American Airlines DC-10 crash at Chicago's O'Hare Airport on May 25, 1979, which killed 275 people and was the nation's worst air disaster. Subsequent examination by the FAA revealed that this DC-10, whose floor-venting problems (mentioned by Applegate) was corrected, suffered from different defects,[11] and it was these defects that were focused upon in the special report issued by McDonnell Douglas.

[11]*New York Times*, June 7, 1979, sec. B, p. 13, and *New York Times*, June 19, 1979, sec. D, p. 19; see also "New Testing Methods Could Boost Air Safety," *Science* **205** (July 6, 1979), pp. 29–31.

Fumio Matsuda's Automobile Users Union

In 1957 Fumio Matsuda achieved his goal of entering private industry by getting a job as a service engineer with Nissan Motors. His first choice was design, but because he had no experience in the field he was assigned to the service department. . . . His duties included writing a technical manual for dealers and users, receiving complaints from dealers and users, and servicing automobile parts.

His concern with safety grew gradually. His first major discovery was that many consumer complaints could be traced to faulty design or to inferior material in parts. Subsidiary companies manufactured parts for Nissan and they were inspected by "lot tests." Matsuda realized that there was a difference in the quality of the items that composed the lots. Other defects occurred in the process of assembling the parts.

His list of discoveries grew longer. A transmission gear lacked the proper strength. A rear axle shaft broke because of a defect in design. A bad dust cover for the ball joint of the steering linkage tie rod allowed dust to get inside and wore out the ball joint quickly. "I began to find defects in all of the parts," he says, "in suspension, brakes, steering, everything."

At least twice a month in meetings with designers, Matsuda talked about these defects. He pointed out, for example, that inadequate coating on a brake tube allowed the tube to become rusted and cause crashes. These were the kind of defects, he says, that would only be found by service engineers, the people who heard the consumers' complaints.

The difference between Matsuda and his superiors soon hinged on the extent to which the company was willing to inform customers of defects. He found that the policy was never to let them know—except in special cases when the user himself spotted the defects and the manufacturer allowed the service department to repair them. In cases where there were complaints of defects and a crash occurred, the policy was to "recall" the defective vehicles by secretly requiring repair when the consumers brought their cars for the regular two-year inspection required in Japan. This was accomplished by collusion with the Japanese government. One of several flaws Matsuda saw in this system was that not all cars made their way to the inspections. The rest continued with the unacknowledged defects.

The picture Matsuda began to see unfolding was one in which the automobile user was generally ignorant of serious defects and, even when he was aware of them, was unable to call the manufacturer to account and receive free repair or compensation for injuries in auto crashes. "After the car had crashed, no one could see the original defect and even if the owner knew about the defect, he was unable to prove it without assistance."

The next realization was that the service engineer was the best—or even the only—person equipped to aid the auto consumer. But he found little support among his fellow service engineers. "Their attitude was not to do anything that would jeopardize the company," he says.

As a service engineer, Matsuda did not belong to any automotive engineering societies. The employee union was "so close to the company" that he found no support from its ranks.

The pressure to act became intense as Matsuda saw drivers being held responsible for crashes that he believed stemmed from defects. Drivers were judged guilty of negligence that he knew was not theirs. His colleagues repeated the phrase "do nothing that will hurt the company." But Matsuda was evolving the theory that the best he could do for the company was to urge practices and policies that would win the trust of auto consumers. "I believed that the best policy for the company was to inform users about defects and repair the defects," he says.

Five years after he began working for Nissan, Matsuda suggested that the company publish a list of a thousand defects which he had documented. At that time, secret repairing of serious defects was costing Nissan some 1–2 billion yen a month. Publication of the defects could cost the company two or three times as much money. The company rejected his suggestion.

Next Matsuda suggested that the company recall all cars of a model that had been involved in an accident when a defect was recognized. His immediate boss rejected the suggestion; Matsuda went to his superiors, which infuriated his own supervisor. Again and again he went over his own superior to higher officials in the company until the relationship between him and his supervisor became strained. The supervisor began making damaging reports about Matsuda to the main office, falsely charging him with accepting bribes from dealers and leaking information to the press.

At the same time Matsuda was involved in a fight with the employee labor union, which he had charged with corruption. Specifically, he charged union leaders with spending union money on personal entertainment. He was also frustrated because the union failed to support his reform efforts.

Finally, discouraged by his attempts to help the automobile consumer within the company and by his rapidly deteriorating relationship with his superiors, he resigned in August, 1968.

He was now free to do what he wanted to do: to give automobile owners all the information they needed about defects. He developed a plan for an organization through which he could become an effective critic of the industry. But he knew that he faced tremendous difficulties. For over a year he did nothing but study auto design, earning a living by writing articles for magazines and newspapers and doing consulting work. Most of his acquaintances, even those who supported his ideas, believed then that his project would fail and he would never "beat the manufacturers." His family was skeptical and his wife complained as he began to spend more and more time in the one-room office he rented in Tokyo. Some publishers refused to print his articles, but reporters began coming to him for assistance and gradually he began getting his ideas into the public media.

During this time, he formed an important alliance with Masataka Itoh, a top reporter for the prestigious newspaper *Asahi Shimbum* in Tokyo. In June, 1969, Itoh broke a story that caused a furor in Japan. He reported that Japanese auto makers were recalling defective automobiles in the United States under the United States safety law requirements, but were not recalling the same autos sold in Japan, which had no recall law. After substantial newspaper publicity and public hearings in the Diet, a voluntary recall system was instituted for Japanese owners by the companies. Itoh followed this story with other reports on the Japanese auto industry, often using tips from Matsuda whose reliability he came to respect. Itoh in turn helped Matsuda with plans for his auto users union and became an invaluable source of support. . . .

An essential part of the union's effectiveness has been Matsuda's network of contacts inside the auto industry, with salesmen and dealers, customers and service engineers. This network is carefully guarded, and Matsuda contacts them secretly. Professors in five universities work for him regularly without pay, he says, doing research and tests and writing articles for the magazine and feeding him information.

From his informants Matsuda has obtained lists of defects still kept by auto companies and given to dealers who make secret repairs, that is, repairs the customers pay for when they have their cars inspected without knowing that the defects existed when they bought the cars. Matsuda has charged that most auto defects are still handled secretly in Japan. He has also directed lawyers and police investigators to sources of information within the companies of which they were previously unaware, for example, manufacturer drawings and durability tests and receipts at servicing plants for repair fees.

Whenever Matsuda has made a new discovery he has approached the auto manufacturer first. If the manufacturer is unresponsive, the union has taken its case to the press. The result has been, says Matsuda, that every manufacturer except one has begun to respond to his requests for repair and redesign.

Bethlehem Steel's Policy on Conflict of Interest

On March 16, 1964, the Bethlehem Steel Company fired Philip B. Woodroofe. The charge was that Woodroofe and his wife refused to comply with a company demand to resign from the Community Civic League. . . .

When pressed for an explanation, the company simply stated that Woodroofe had resigned and that it was not company policy to make statements on an individual employee's resignation. Woodroofe himself denied having resigned:

> I have never submitted my resignation, nor have I been asked to submit one. . . . I was told I was through. . . . I was told I couldn't act as a private citizen, nor could my wife.[1] . . .

Bethlehem Steel, the second largest steel company in the United States, dominates the economic and social life of the Lehigh Valley and the city of Bethlehem, Pennsylvania. It furnishes nearly 50 percent of the entire payroll of the town. Of Bethlehem's population of 77,000, about 1,000 are blacks and a very small number are Puerto Ricans. (In the Lehigh Valley as a whole, with a population of 250,000, about 2,500 are blacks.) Schools have not been segregated, and there have been no civil rights demonstrations. There has been a problem of inadequate housing for the poor and a high rate of Negro school dropouts.[2]

[1]Joseph A. Loftus, "Bethlehem Puzzled by Dismissal of Steel Aide over Racial Stand," *The New York Times,* March 22, 1964, p. 10.

[2]*Ibid.*

This case was prepared by S. Prakash Sethi, *Up Against the Corporate Wall: Modern Corporations and Social Issues of the Seventies* (Englewood Cliffs, N.J.: Prentice-Hall, 1977), pp. 342–350. Reprinted with permission of the publisher. **Not to be duplicated without permission of the author and publisher.**

> Over the years [Bethlehem Steel] has demonstrated its consciousness of the civic well-being of its home office city in many ways. It has invested heavily, without any prodding, in air pollution controls, in neutralizing the manufacturing effluents which it dumps into the Lehigh River, and in expending heavy sums to beautify the city by buying up eyesores and staving off blight along approaches or property not used for steel manufacturing. Besides, it has increasingly encouraged its people to participate in a wide range of civic activity, even to the point of giving one of its junior executives a leave of absence to run for Congress last year.[3]

In its management policies, however, the company has long been regarded as one of the "most withdrawn and individualistic companies in a conservative industry."[4]. . .

The style of management has been strictly individual and authority has clearly been centralized at the top. In its fifty-nine-year history the company has had only three chief executives. . . .

In May 1963 the Right Reverend Arthur Lichtenberger, presiding bishop of the Protestant Episcopal Church in the United States, appealed to his church members to take positive action and assume responsibility in solving this country's racial problems. Woodroofe [supervisor of municipal services at the Bethlehem Steel Company's home office], an Episcopalian, took this appeal seriously and initiated informal meetings between local white and black leaders to develop the framework for an organization that could provide a forum where community problems could be brought into the open and discussed, thus avoiding the possibility of violent confrontation between various groups. Woodroofe took a leading role in mobilizing community support. As a result, the Community Civic League was formally organized on March 15, 1964, at the local YWCA. Participating were more than two hundred local citizens, including Bethlehem's mayor, H. Gordon Payrow, and a number of clergymen. . . .

The story [of Woodroofe's resignation] made the national newspapers. The local papers during the next few days were full of angry letters from readers and editorials condemning Bethlehem Steel's action. Not a single word could be found in either the local or the national news media justifying or supporting the company's action.[5]

Bethlehem's press statement that Woodroofe had resigned was clearly unsatisfactory to the community. It refused to accept the company's statement in view of Woodroofe's charge that he was indeed fired. Consequently, in response to local inquiries, the company issued

---

[3]"The Woodroofe Incident," *Bethelem Globe-Times*, March 20, 1964, p. 6.

[4]John M. Lee, "1964: Year of Change for Bethlehem Steel," *The New York Times*, April 12, 1964, sec. 3, pp. 1, 5.

[5]See *Bethlehem Globe-Times*, March 18, 20, 23–25, 27, 30, April 10, 1964; and *Allentown Morning Call*, March 27, 1964.

two statements denying that it was against employee participation in community affairs and insisting that Woodroof's dismissal was based on a clear case of conflict of interest. . . .

[One] statement, issued on March 25, 1964, dealt specifically with Woodroofe's dismissal:

> As supervisor of municipal services of this company, Mr. Woodroofe participated as the official representative of the company in certain municipal activities. When he became identified with the Community Civic League, it was the company's belief that his position on matters coming before that organization would be viewed as an expression of the official position of the company. This type of activity did not represent an area related to his responsibilities with the company and the company believed it inescapable that misunderstandings would result.
> Therefore, although the company does encourage employees to participate in affairs of their local communities, the circumstances in this case were such—and Mr. Woodroofe was so advised—that there was a clear conflict between his official representation of the company in certain community activities and his participation in the League. Mr. Woodroofe chose to resign from the company.[6]

In a later announcement, the company stated that Woodroofe was offered two other jobs with the company prior to his dismissal but that he refused to accept either of them.[7]

When asked to comment, Mr. Woodroofe said that he found it difficult to accept the company's statement at face value since it demanded that his wife also resign from the Community Civic League.[8] Mrs. Woodroofe added, "And I am on the Red Cross Board. I don't speak for the company there."[9] . . .

On June 30, 1964, Philip Woodroofe resigned from the board of directors of the league, as he planned to move to New York where he had reportedly accepted a real estate job. However, he retained his membership in the league.[10]

EPILOGUE—TEN YEARS LATER

On October 16, 1975, at the invitation of Bethlehem Steel, the author [of this case] met with four company executives from the Industrial Relations and Public Affairs Departments to review company policies during the ten years since the Woodroofe incident occurred. A summary of their remarks follows:

[6]"Steel Blames 'Conflict' in Woodroofe Case," *Bethlehem Globe-Times,* March 26, 1964.

[7]"Woodroofe Vetoed Two Other Jobs," *Bethlehem Globe-Times,* April 15, 1964, p. 1.

[8]*Bethlehem Globe-Times,* March 26, 1964.

[9]Loftus, "Bethlehem Puzzled by Dismissal of Steel Aide."

[10]"Woodroofe Resigns Seat on Civic League Board," *Allentown Morning Call,* July 1, 1964.

THE EMPLOYEE

1. The executives agreed that perhaps there was overreaction to Woodroofe's participation in the Community Civic League and that it
   should have been handled differently.[11] However, they also maintained that it was not Woodroofe per se, but the political visibility of
   the minority-related issues at that time which attracted the attention
   of the national news media and turned the case into a *cause célèbre*.

2. There was indeed a potential conflict of interest situation which the
   company sought to avoid; even now, if an executive's outside activity
   runs counter to the company policy of which that executive is in
   charge, he will have to withdraw from such outside activity. Furthermore, the company would not want a high-level executive to make
   any public statements, which are clearly outside the area of his or her
   expertise and job in the company, that ran counter to the company's
   publicly stated position.

3. Notwithstanding, there have been tremendous changes in the last ten
   years that make Bethlehem a very different company. These changes
   have evolved gradually as a result of economic, social, and political
   pressures, both from within and without, and as a result of changes
   in top management and its philosophy. Some of these changes are:

   A. The company's board of directors no longer consists only of
      insiders.

   B. There is a mandatory retirement age of sixty-five which is
      strictly enforced in all cases, including the top management.

   C. The operating climate has changed: "We are a cosmopolitan
      company now." There is a great emphasis on management
      training and development. "Each year we send a number of
      our executives to Harvard Business School—and other places.
      We also conduct in-house advanced management courses with
      faculty drawn from various schools."

   D. There is more open communication between management
      and employees. "We publish 26 separate newsletters in differ-
      ent locations where none existed ten years ago. Moreover,
      these newsletters came about at the request of employees."

   E. Bethlehem has always encouraged its executives and employ-
      ees to be active in the civic affairs in the community where
      they live and work. However, because of its sheer size, the
      company often tends to be a large part of the community
      where its operations are located. "Therefore, we have to tread
      a very fine line for fear that we may be accused of dominating
      the town's life. For example, in one town, the company ap-
      plied for a re-zoning permit before the local Planning Board.
      One of the members of the Planning Board was a Bethlehem
      Steel executive. The Planning Board voted 2–1 in favor of the
      Company, with one of the two favorable votes cast by a Beth-
      lehem Steel employee. We believe that in casting the favorable
      vote, the Bethlehem employee acted as a private citizen and
      not as a Bethlehem employee. Furthermore, our view toward

[11]None of the executives participating in this meeting was directly involved in the
Woodroofe incident.

46

his vote would not have changed had his vote gone against the Company."

F.   Bethlehem's written policy defining areas of conflict of interest does not precisely cover the Woodroofe case. However, in most cases conflict situations are pretty clear. "In gray areas we tend to be conservative, i.e., when in doubt, even a possible or potential conflict of interest situation should be avoided."

G.   The company has instituted wide-ranging programs in minority and female hiring and purchasing from minority vendors, and has even gone to the extent of developing minority suppliers and helping them to set up facilities to supply the company.

H.   Bethlehem has taken vigorous steps to eliminate job discrimination based on race, sex, and age. Any infractions of company policies are swiftly punished and corrections made.

chapter 2

The Consumer

INTRODUCTION   The general subject of "business, society, and ethics" reminds us that business has a multitude of social relationships, most of which involve the obligations of some parties and the rights of others. Just as we studied the relationship between business and its employees in the first chapter, so in this chapter we shall explore the relationship business has to consumers. In particular, we shall encounter cases requiring reflection on the obligations business has to advertise its products truthfully, to sell products at reasonable and clearly identified prices, to market only "quality" products, to provide information about products to its purchasers, and to warranty a product nondeceptively. Everywhere in these cases we find perplexing questions about the limits of business's obligations, the limits of consumers' rights, and gray areas about rights and responsibilities.

The circumstances under which markets are created and goods sold and delivered are notoriously complex, yet none would deny that advertising is the primary instrument of consumer marketing—unrivalled by the use of sales representatives and other sales techniques. While misleading or information-deficient advertising has frequently been denounced, the moral and legal concepts underlying these denunciations have seldom been carefully examined. What is a deceptive advertisement? A misleading advertisement? Is it, for example, deceptive or misleading to advertise presweetened children's cereals as "nutritious" or as "building strong bodies"? Are such advertisements forms of lying? Are they coercive or manipulative, especially when children are the primary targets or when people are led to make purchases they do not need (or would not have made were it not for the advertising)? If so, is the coercion or manipulation related to the deception? For example, if Listerine advertisements about killing germs "manipulate" listeners into purchasing the mouthwash, does it follow that consumers have been deceived? Even if advertisements are manipulative, is this unjustifiable or harmful manipulation? Indeed, in light of certain theories of the free marketplace, can there be unjustifiable advertising at all: If markets shift to meet consumer demand, then is not the consumer king, and is not the role of advertising simply to provide information about the products that consumers demand? Or is this depiction merely a convenient fiction that has crept into beliefs about the market? These questions are rarely attended to, and yet they need examination in cases such as those involving Listerine and the Kellogg Cereal Company.

Similar problems in various other marketing practices do not involve advertising. For example, the way counter goods are displayed in a grocery store is featured in the Giant Food case in this chapter. One major question about most advertising and other marketing practices denounced as "misleading" is whether they can be justified by the "rules of the game" that prevail in the consumer world. Some have argued that marketing is analogous to activities in which we all engage— for example, purchasing a house or bargaining over the price of a rug in an overpriced store. Here bluffing, overstatement, and even enticement are expected and invite similar countermoves; certainly these routines involve more than mere negotiation. While abuse and contempt are not tolerated, deception is—so long as the rules of the game are known and the players are in a roughly equal bargaining position. This toleration indicates that deceptive practices need not be unjustifiable; on the other hand, there clearly are limits to such deception. For example, harmful products cannot simply be marketed as if benign—as the Rely Tampon case in this chapter illustrates.

Perhaps much advertising and marketing can be justified by a parallel rules-of-the-game model: There are more or less established, well-delineated procedures or moves for marketing a product; the consumer world is well acquainted with these rules of the game, and consumers are generally in an equal bargaining position. Only an isolated innocent wholly unacquainted with the game of advertising would think otherwise. While abuse of subliminal persuasion or ads inherently offensive to large segments of the population are not permitted, it might be argued that sexual suggestion or strong pitches to young children in toy advertisements are simply parts of the game. This defense of prevailing advertising and marketing practices has its advocates, but is scarcely universally accepted as a model of the best or even of an adequate relationship between producers and consumers.

The Federal Trade Commission and others take the view that the rules of acceptable advertising encompass more than the mere creation of a market; advertising, as the agency views it, is the dissemination of information from which consumers make an informed choice. If they are misled in the attempt to make an intelligent choice or are enticed into the choice by deception, the advertising cannot be justified—no matter what the implicit rules of the game may be. The FTC has therefore placed strict regulations on some industries that produce potentially harmful products—cigarettes being the best known example.

The two cases in the advertising section of this chapter reveal how a government response can be triggered when advertisements tend to mislead. These cases indicate how the government and consumer protection groups focus on the consumers' *response* to advertising and on its human effects, rather than on the *intention* of those who create the advertising. By contrast, those who defend controversial advertising focus more on the intentions of advertising agencies and manufacturers in marketing a product—viz., the intent to sell a "good product." These different emphases complicate the issues, especially since a product marketed with good intentions can nonetheless be misleading or have bad effects. (The cases in this chapter focus far more on the effects of advertisements than on the intention of advertisers.)

Another complicating factor is that not everyone has the same threshold of deception: What deceives one person can be laughed off by another. The so-called "reasonable consumer" is not, as federal agencies have pointed out, the same as the "ignorant consumer"; yet they are both alike the consumers to whom business relates with its advertising and marketing techniques. The earlier discussed rules-of-the-game defense of advertising and marketing practices has this same problem, for how skillfully a person understands and deals with the rules of a game is also relative to individual resistance and acceptance. The abilities of children to grasp the nature of advertising and to distance themselves from its appeal is a celebrated issue, one featured in the Kellogg Cereals case.

One related and widely discussed issue is the extent to which a consumer's desires and needs originate with the consumer, and the extent to which those desires and needs are *created* by advertising. Debates on this subject are often emotional and can be highly political. They are also hard to assess from evidence, because our desires and needs commonly derive from social causes and conventions, and thus cannot be said to be either "ours" or "created" by advertising and marketing practices. Moreover, even if a desire or need for a product does not *originate* from a consumer's choice, it does not follow that it is an *unfortunate* desire or that it has not been *freely* accepted. One who trades in an old car and buys a new Chrysler because of the advertised rebate may have had a desire stimulated, or even created, but this cause may be neither manipulative nor regrettable. In legal jargon, an influence need not be an *undue* or *coercive* influence. Naturally, this invites further reflection on the distinction between legitimate and illegitimate influence.

These debates about influence and creating a market are especially heated when a product is thought to be harmful—as some have alleged presweetened children's cereals, cigarettes, and various automobiles are. A different, but important slant on all the issues thus far discussed is that *quality control* rather than advertising or marketing practices per se is the true problem with consumer products. If cereals and cupcakes were certified as nutritious and free of harmful artificial coloring before being allowed on the market, then we would care much less about what is conveyed by advertisements or sales representatives. This is a call for higher qualitative standards in industry and regulatory branches of government as a means to resolve these issues of consumer protection. ("Consumerism" and "consumer advocates" have generally focused more on quality control than on marketing practices.) Higher standards would also protect manufacturers who produce quality products in the first place from those who produce inferior ones. There are substantial practical problems about how these standards can be established and enforced, and there are also liberty issues at stake—e.g., the freedom to put a new "junk food" on the market may be jeopardized (in theory there would no longer be junk foods), and the freedom to buy cheap but substandard products would be lost (for they could not be marketed).

These problems about quality control raise important questions about the notion of "merchantability" or a merchantable product— issues raised in this chapter in a case about manufacturer warranties: *Henningsen* v. *Bloomfield Motors*. In this case, as the judge points out, the whole premise behind "contracting" in the free market under rules of the game with bargaining among equals can be brought into question when products prove to be defective. There are also troublesome problems about the parties with whom one is contracting when there are multiple manufacturers and suppliers, and about implicit as well as explicit warranties.

The relationship between consumers and producers continues to plague the courts and the regulatory branches of government—as well as the producers and consumers themselves. This chapter is not the last one in which this problem will be manifest.

Kellogg Cereals and Children's Television Advertising

> It is both unfair and deceptive . . . to address televised advertising for *any* product to young children who are still too young to understand the selling purpose of, or otherwise comprehend or evaluate, the advertising. . . . The classical justification for a free market, and for the advertising that goes with it, assumes at least a rough balance of information, sophistication and power between buyer and seller. . . . In the present situation, it is ludicrous to suggest that any such balance exists between an advertiser who is willing to spend many thousands of dollars for a single 30-second spot, and a child who is incapable of understanding that the spot has a selling intent, and instead trustingly believes that the spot merely provides advice about one of the good things in life.[1]

The above quotation from a 1978 Federal Trade Commission (FTC) staff report presents the heart of an argument advanced by the FTC staff and others against televised advertising directed to children for pre-sweetened, ready-to-eat cereals. This report accompanied a set of proposed regulatory rules that would:

(a) Ban all televised advertising for any product which is directed to, or seen by, audiences composed of a significant proportion of children who are too young to understand the selling purpose of, or otherwise comprehend or evaluate, the advertising;

(b) Ban televised advertising directed to, or seen by, audiences composed of a significant proportion of older children for sugared food products, the consumption of which poses the most serious dental health risks;

(c) Require that televised advertising directed to, or seen by, audiences composed of a significant proportion of older children for sugared food products not included in paragraph (b) be balanced by nutritional and/or health disclosures funded by advertisers.[2]

[1]FTC, "Staff Report on Television Advertising to Children," (February, 1978), pp. 27, 29.

[2]*Ibid.*, pp. 345–346.

This case was prepared by Linda Kern, Martha W. Elliott, and Tom L. Beauchamp. **Not to be duplicated without permission of the authors and publisher.**

This broad-based attack on children's advertising was triggered by a petition with a specific intent. In 1977, Action for Children's Television (ACT) and the Center for Science in the Public Interest (CSPI) jointly petitioned the FTC. They proposed a ban on the advertising of sugary, in-between-meal (snack) foods to children. ACT and CSPI got more than they bargained for when the above-mentioned 1978 staff report called for a ban on *all* children's advertising. This discussion, however, has a prior stretch of history.

HISTORY

Circa 1970. A U.S. Senate consumer subcommittee opened hearings on the nutritional value of ready-to-eat cereals in 1970 that reflected a growing national concern about nutrition. Two separate issues were then under discussion that set the context of later debate: First, does the food industry have an obligation to market a nutritious product? Second, even if a product is highly nutritious, what limits should be placed on advertising this product to children?

Robert Choate, Jr., President of the Council on Children, Media, and Merchandising, figured prominently in the 1970 hearings. He made headlines with his nutritional ranking of sixty leading cold cereals. He stated, "I watch TV commercials on Saturday morning and get really mad. The image projected for these cereals is that they give kids muscles and energy so they can catch every football pass. But read the nutrients on the boxes, and there is little to support these claims."[3] Although his criteria for ranking the nutritional value of cereals rested on vitamin fortification and not on sugar content (later a central concern), his ranking system may have had significant impact. Top executives of the cereal companies consulted their technologists, who had long advocated nutritionally improved formulae. Within eighteen months of Choate's first Senate testimony, 26 of 40 criticized cereals had been reformulated.

At these 1970 Senate Cereal hearings, Dr. Frederick Stare, chairman of the Department of Nutrition, Harvard University School of Public Health, and Dr. W. H. Sebrell, Jr. of the Institute of Human Nutrition at Columbia University gave testimony. They agreed with the cereal industry that cereal with "milk and sugar" is a nutritionally adequate food and that evaluating the nutritional content of cereal without milk is unfair.[4] Dr. Jean Mayer, then Harvard Professor of Nutrition, agreed with industry experts that "taken in the whole breakfast context, cereals did make an important contribution." Nevertheless, Mayer

---

[3]"A Gadfly Buzzes Around the Table," *Business Week* (September 26, 1970), p. 116.
[4]Molander, "Marketing Ready-to-Eat Breakfast Cereals," p. 130.

continued, "There are wide differences in nutritional value between various types of cereals, and these differences could be easily avoided if modern technology and nutritional knowledge were used to upgrade weaker products."[5] More recently Mayer has been quoted as saying that "The nutritional value of a food varies inversely with the amount of money spent to advertise it."[6]

1973–77. In 1973, a second Congressional investigation focused on children's pre-sweetened, ready-to-eat cereals. This time the Senate Select Committee on Nutrition and Human Needs addressed the twin issues of nutritional value and advertising fairness. Some of the 1970 testimonies were simply reiterated. Action for Children's Television presented evidence that a child watching a particular Boston station from 7:00 a.m. to 2:00 p.m. on Saturday, October 28, 1972, would have seen 67 commercials for sugary foods, including ready-to-eat cereals. Representatives of the cereal companies, including Kellogg and General Mills, testified at the hearings.[7] Executive vice-president of the Kellogg Company, William E. LaMothe, stated: "Our company is very conscious of the fact that social responsibilities go hand-in-hand with business responsibilities. The steps that we are taking to contribute to the improvement of the understanding of the need for breakfast and a complete and adequate breakfast reflect this consciousness."[8]

In March of 1973, the FDA introduced the USRDA standards (recommended daily allowance), replacing the older minimum daily requirement (MDR). The cereal companies had to reset their standards at this more stringent level. Also in 1973, FTC chairman Louis Engman set up a task force in the Division of Special Projects to investigate the issues of children's advertising further. During his term of office, the FTC staff was granted the use of a compulsory process that gave them the right to subpoena cereal companies for access to their market research data, and thus to examine their advertising strategies.

In 1974, the FTC staff proposed a guide for advertising premiums in sugared cereal. When Calvin Collier became chairman in 1976, this proposal was rejected. However, in 1977, the debate flourished once more. Renewed interest in children's advertising, especially in regard to pre-sweetened, ready-to-eat cereals, was sparked by the FTC's unexpected reaction to the ACT and CSPI petitions.

---

[5]*Ibid.,* p. 131.

[6]Culkin, "Selling to Children," p. 7.

[7]Gilbert Molander, "Marketing Ready-to-Eat Breakfast Cereals at the Kellogg Company," p. 135.

[8]Part 5—TV Advertising of Food to Children. Hearings before the Senate Select Committee on Nutrition and Human Needs, 93rd Cong., 1st Sess., 1973, p. 258, as quoted by Molander.

1977–78. In April of 1977, ACT and CSPI presented their petitions to the FTC. As mentioned earlier, these proposals called for a ban on the advertisement of sugary, in-between-meal (snack) foods to children. Arguments were presented, however, against *all* foods with a high sugar content, including some cereals, and also against the practice of advertising to children *in general.* Shortly after the publication of these two petitions, in November 1977, Kellogg ran a newspaper advertisement countering the implication that pre-sweetened cereals are not nutritious, or are possibly harmful for young children. A series of "Facts" for which it claimed empirical support included:

1. Ready-sweetened cereals are highly nutritious foods.
2. Ready-to-eat cereals do not increase tooth decay in children.
3. Ready-to-eat cereal eaters skip breakfast less than non-ready-to-eat cereal eaters.
4. There is no more sugar in a one-ounce serving of a ready-sweetened cereal than in an apple or banana or in a serving of orange juice.
5. The sugars in cereals and the sugars in fruit are chemically very similar.
6. Ready-to-eat cereals provide only 2 percent of the total consumption of cane and beet sugars in the U.S.
7. On the average, when children eat ready-sweetened cereals as a part of breakfast, the nutritional content of that breakfast is greater than when they eat a non-ready-to-eat cereal breakfast.
8. Most ready-to-eat cereals are consumed with milk.
9. On the average when children eat ready-sweetened cereals as part of breakfast, consumption of fat and cholesterol is less than when they eat a non-ready-to-eat cereal breakfast.
10. The per capita sugar consumption in the U.S. has remained practically unchanged for the last 50 years.[9]

Three months later, in February of 1978, the FTC staff issued the aforementioned report, proposing an all-encompassing ban on children's advertising. This extensive 350-page document included concerns not only about the effects of advertising on children, but also about the nutritional value of the product advertised. This report described the preparation of commercials directed to children and the selling techniques they employ. The following procedures were detailed:

1. Magical promises that a product will build muscles or improve athletic performance.
2. The chase or tug of war sequence in which one character tries to take a product away from another.

[9]Molander, "Marketing Ready-to-Eat Breakfast Cereals at the Kellogg Company," Appendix 11–1.

3. The use of magic, singing, and dancing.
4. The use of super heroes to entice children.
5. The voice of authority.
6. The voices of children agreeing with the announcer.
7. Depictions of children outperforming adults.
8. Animation.
9. Peer group acceptance appeals.
10. Selling by characters who also appear in programming.

The report attacked 18 commercials in particular. Half of these were for pre-sweetened, ready-to-eat cereals. The following is a list of those cereals:

1. Count Chocula and Frankenberry cereals
2. Lucky Charms cereal
3. Cookie Crisp cereal
4. Crazy Cow cereal
5. Post Pebbles (Fruity and Cocoa)
6. Cocoa Puffs
7. Corny Snaps
8. Super Sugar Crisp
9. Honeycomb

This first staff report effectively argued for a complete ban on children's advertising. Three years later, in 1981, the FTC staff issued a second staff report. The interim period consisted of hearings, exchanges of papers, interviewing of witnesses, and—when the process was completed—600,000 pages of records.

1981. On March 31, 1981, the FTC issued its (presumably) final staff report and recommendations concerning children's advertising. Their recommendation was "that the [Federal Trade] Commission terminate proceedings for the promulgation of a trade regulation rule on children's advertising." They called for a halt on any further attempt to ban children's advertising. The following excerpt from this second report illustrates the degree to which they revised their initial statements:

> The record developed during the rulemaking proceeding adequately supports the following conclusions regarding child-oriented television advertising and young children six years and under: (1) they place indiscriminate trust in televised advertising messages; (2) they do not understand the persuasive bias in television advertising; and (3) the techniques, focus and themes used in child-oriented television advertising enhance the appeal of the advertising message and the advertised product. Consequently, young children do not possess the cognitive ability to evaluate adequately child-oriented television advertising. Despite the fact that these conclusions can be drawn from the evidence, the record establishes that the only effective remedy would be a ban on all advertisements ori-

ented toward young children, and such a ban, as a practical matter, cannot be implemented. Because of this remedial impediment, there is no need to determine whether or not advertising oriented toward young children is deceptive.[10] Staff's recommendation for this portion of the case is that the proceeding be terminated.[11]

This statement was actually a reiteration of findings put forth in the initial report. Most of the original *claims* were still embraced. For "practical" reasons, however, they recommended that "the proceedings be terminated." The "practical matter" that prohibited the FTC from banning children's advertising was two-fold. First, dental research is sufficiently primitive that one cannot positively identify which foods are cariogenic, or cavity producing. There are too many unknown factors involved in cavity formation to place a ban on any particular product or set of products. Second, although children *under* six cannot understand the intent of a commercial message, children *over* six often can. To ban the advertising to one group would automatically affect the other older group. For these "practical" reasons, then, the FTC terminated all investigative proceedings associated with children's advertising.

TWO MAJOR ISSUES

Two issues have been present throughout the debate between the FTC and the cereal companies. The first concern is whether the product (for our purposes, cereal) has significant nutritional value. Even if a product ranks high on a nutritional scale, a second consideration remains: Is the practice of advertising to children inherently unfair?

1. The Adequacy of Nutrition. The ACT and CSPI petitions, along with the FTC staff reports, all attacked children's cereals on the basis of high sugar content. Quoting the Staff of the Senate Select Committee on Nutrition and Human Needs, the ACT petition states:

> [Sugar calories] increase requirements for certain vitamins, like thiamin, which are needed [for the body] to metabolize carbohydrates. They may increase the need for trace minerals, chromium as well. Thus, a greater burden is placed on the other components of the diet to contribute all the necessary "nutrient density" to compensate for the emptiness of sugar calories.[12]

---

[10]Consumers Union of the U.S., Inc., and Committee on Children's Television, C-9, p. 1–46. Quoted in *FTC Final Staff Report and Recommendation in the Matter of Children's Advertising*, 43 Fed. Reg. 17967, TRR No. 215–60, (1981), p. 3.

[11]*FTC Final Staff Report and Recommendation in the Matter of Children's Advertising*, 43 Fed. Reg. 17967, TRR No. 215–60, (1981), p. 3.

[12]Select Committee on Nutrition and Human Needs, 93rd Cong., 2d Sess., *National Nutrition Policy Study, Report and Recommendation*, Vol. 9 (1974). Quoted in ACT petition to the FTC (1977), p. 4.

The initial 1978 staff report presented expert testimony from several fields on the nutritional value of ready-to-eat cereals. The following statement is from this report and illustrates its general conclusions:[13]

> Dr. Juan Navia, a nutritional biochemist who is senior scientist at the Institute of Dental Research, University of Alabama at Birmingham, has observed that:
>
> > Foods compete for space in the stomachs of mankind. Every time a person selects a sugar rich food, he does it at the expense of other foods, and these other foods are *always* better as a source of vitamins and minerals than the sugar that replaces them.[14]
>
> These other foods are "always better" because sugar contributes calories to the human diet, but is not otherwise nutritious.[15] This is the point of the phrase, "empty calories." The energy content of a calorie of sugar is, by definition, exactly the same as the energy content of a calorie of any other food.
>
> While children assuredly need calories, they have no need to get them in a form devoid of other nutrients. Ivalee McCord, Chairman of the Child Development and Family Relations Section of the American Economics Association has put the matter as follows:
>
> > "At a time when a body is growing at a more rapid rate and body structures are developing, the need for quality food is crucial. There is no room in the diet for 'empty calories'—those represented by most sugar-coated and snack foods. At this time children need balanced diets providing the nutrients needed for growth."[16]
>
> The Life Sciences Research Office (LSRO) of the Federation of American Societies for Experimental Biology has warned, in a report to the Food and Drug Administration, that at the present level of sugar consumption:
>
> > "It is likely that some individuals may eat enough to exclude adequate amounts of other foods that furnish required nutrients."[17]
>
> That warning has to be read in conjunction with the theory that sugar consumption may be proportionately highest and rising fastest among children. As Dr. Jean Mayer has observed:

[13]FTC, "Staff Report on Television Advertising to Children," *op. cit.* The following ten footnotes are quoted in this staff report.

[14]*Hearings on Nutrition Education, Part 3, TV Advertising of Food to Children,* Sen. Select Comm. on Nutrition, 93rd Cong., 1st Sess., (Mar. 5, 1973).

[15]U.S. Dept. Agr., *Nutritional Value of Foods, Home and Garden Bull.* No. 72 at 24 (April 1977).

[16]Letter to ACT, Feb. 23, 1972. To similar effect, *see* Arlen, *The Science of Nutrition* 253 (2d ed. 1977).

[17]The *LSRO Report (Dextrose)* and the *LSRO Report (Sucrose)* were commissioned by the Food and Drug Administration and submitted within the past two years by the Life Sciences Research Office (LSRO) of the Federation of American Societies for Experimental Biology. The full titles are *Evaluation of the Health Aspects of Sucrose as a Food Ingredient* (1976) and *Evaluation of the Health Aspects of Corn Sugar (Dextrose), Corn Syrup and Invert Sugar as Food Ingredients* (1976).

". . . particularly when you consider that a large part of the population eats relatively small amounts of sugar, it means we have a lot of children where sugar becomes a gigantic proportion [of the diet]."[18]

With a few fortified exceptions (*e.g.*, Hostess Twinkies), it is not claimed that the sugared snack foods and candies promoted to children on television have any nutritional value apart from calories. But claims are made that pre-sweetened cereals are "highly nutritious."[19] These claims are a matter of dispute. On the one hand, the manufacturers point out that most, if not all, of these cereals have been fortified by adding vitamins and minerals. This was not always the case; this fortification was added, for the most part, starting in the early 1970s, following congressional hearings on which it was pointed out that the nutritional value of the unfortified cereals was essentially nil.[20] The manufacturers, having added this fortification, now contend that some children are reluctant to eat breakfast at all, and that the sugar in these cereals is a necessary attraction in order to get them to swallow the now-added vitamins and minerals.[21]

In contrast to the manufacturers' position, Mayer has argued that "in spite of their being enriched with some vitamins and iron, the total effect [of these cereals] is one of inadequate nutrition (deficient, in particular, in trace minerals . . .)."[22] Dr. Mayer added to this assessment that:

> Cereals, some of which are extremely highly processed so that their *intrinsic nutrient content is very low,* particularly when combined with sugar, which is the prototype of "empty calories," are *not a complete food even if fortified with eight or 10 vitamins.*[23]

How many nutrients should cereal contain? Is vitamin fortification sufficient? Is it necessary that a cereal be a complete food? Is the nutritional content of pre-sweetened, ready-to-eat cereals great enough that children should be induced to eat them? This report took both the cereal manufacturers' and the nutritionists' testimonies into consideration when examining the nutritional value of pre-sweetened, ready-to-eat cereals.

---

[18]*Hearings on Nutrition Education, Part 3, TV Advertising of Food to Children.*

[19]This phrase was used by the president of the Kellogg Company in threatening to sue the American Dental Association for defamation of these products. See *The Washington Post*, December 2, 1971.

[20]*Hearings on Dry Cereal Before Consumers Subcommittee, Senate Commerce Committee*, 91st Cong., 2nd Sess. (1970); Robert Choate, "The Sugar Coated Children's Hour," *The Nation* (Jan. 31, 1972), p. 146.

[21]Kellogg's data, however, show that fewer children (5%) than adults (9%) skip breakfast, and that fewer consumers of *non*sugared cereals (5%) than of sugared cereals (7%) skip breakfast. See Kellogg, *Breakfast and Nutrition* (undated pamphlet) and the presentation of Dr. Gary Costley, Kellogg's Director of Nutrition, before the Commission on November 22, 1977.

[22]*Hearings on Nutrition Education, Part 3, TV Advertising of Food to Children.*

[23]*Ibid.*, emphasis added.

2. *Fairness of Advertising.* There are still many questions unanswered about children's television advertising. For example, there are questions about the *effect* of television advertising on children; about the ability of children to *process cognitively* the advertising information; about the ability of children to *discriminate* between the content of the program and the commercial; and about the ability of children to *resist* persuasive appeals even if they understand them to be commercial in character. While research in this area is relatively recent and still somewhat sparse, a 1977 National Science Foundation (NSF) study, *Research on the Effects of Television Advertising on Children,* came to two major conclusions on these questions. The first conclusion was that television commercials *do* affect children:

> Children have been shown to acquire specific product information presented in food commercials. There is also preliminary evidence indicating that information about the nutritional content and value of food products can be effectively communicated to children both within commercials and in brief (5 seconds) slide presentations. Studies have also demonstrated shifts in children's beliefs about advertised foods following their exposure to specific commercial messages. These may include incorrect as well as correct beliefs about promoted food products.

The second conclusion of the NSF study is that specific advertising practices—such as wording—affect the child's ability to understand and remember the message. Some have argued that these problems of comprehension are at the center of the problem:

> The important question . . . is not so much whether children are influenced by commercials, as whether whatever influence there is occurs because of failure to comprehend the commercial appeal. For example, there is little evidence that children comprehend typical commercial disclaimers much before the age of 7. . . .
> However, the relationship between comprehension of intent to persuade and resistance to persuasive appeals remains uncertain.[24]

John Culkin, writing in *The Hastings Center Report,* concentrates on the unfairness of manipulating children as a means of selling to their parents. Culkin quotes a 1978 advertisement that appeared in *Broadcasting* magazine soliciting advertising for a Boston television station. The ad was entitled "Kid Power is Coming to Boston." It read as follows:

> If you're selling, Charlie's mom is buying. But you've got to sell Charlie first.
> His allowance is only 50¢ a week but his buying power is an American

---

[24]Donald F. Roberts and Christine M. Bachen, "Mass Communication Effects," *Annual Review of Psychology* **32** (1981), section on Effects on Children and Adolescents, pp. 336, 338.

phenomenon. He's not only tight with his Mom, but he has a way with his Dad, his Grandma and Aunt Harriet, too.

When Charlie sees something he likes, he usually gets it.[25]

Culkin questions the morality of an industry that would spend half a billion dollars a year on TV advertising directed at children in order to sell to their parents. "Quite apart from the question of the real value of the advertised product, what is the propriety of the sponsor contesting the parent for control of the child? . . . Parents have enough difficulty in helping their children make wise choices without skewing the process by 500 million dollars worth of counter-persuasion."[26]

There is empirical evidence that children influence their parents' purchases. A study done by the Harvard Business School found that "5 to 7 year-olds successfully influenced parental purchases of cereals (88% of the time), snack foods (52%), candy (40%), and soft drinks (38%)." A survey of almost 600 mothers found that 75% of the women chose products and brands requested by their children.[27] However, there is still no evidence directly linking food commercials to the actual nutritional status of children.

Culkin points out that in fairness to the cereal industry, the broadcasters, and the advertising agencies, it must be acknowledged that parents and schools also have a responsibility to prevent the abuse of television by children, as well as the abuse of children by television. Culkin maintains that "even the best of all possible programming does not justify the four hours a day spent by the average American in front of the TV set. In our less than perfect world, the uncomfortable fact is that we have to reform ourselves as well as the networks."[28]

The cereal industry and its advertising agencies contend that claims of unfair and deceptive practices are unwarranted and that the cereal industry is being singled out for criticism on an issue that involves numerous products, especially candy and soft drinks. In particular, opponents of federal regulation argue:

1. that advertising to children is not unfair or deceptive;
2. that sugar in foods has been directly linked to dental caries, but not to many alleged health problems;
3. that the conflict between parents and children is an inevitable part of growing up and would not disappear if Frosted Flakes and Milkyway bars were banned from TV.[29]

[25]Culkin, "Selling to Children," p. 7.

[26]*Ibid.*, pp. 8–9.

[27]As quoted from Linda McJ. Micheli, "Kellogg Company Sugar, Children, and T.V. Advertising" (Boston, Mass.: Harvard Business School, 1979), p. 4.

[28]Culkin, "Selling to Children," p. 9.

[29]See Micheli, "Kellogg Company," p. 6. Craig Shulstad of General Mills helped formulate the wording here, which modifies Micheli's wording.

Opponents of proposed constraints on advertising also contend that First Amendment rights are at stake. Peter McSpadden, president of a large advertising agency, sees the primary issue as censorship: "The question is, do we have a right to market a product to a particular group—in this case, children—and does another group have the right to say, 'no, you can't'?"[30] Members of Congress also have taken seriously the censorship issue, with its implied threat to liberty. In 1978 the Senate Appropriations Committee threatened to cut off all FTC funding if the Commission continued its inquiry into these issues. The majority report of the Senate Committee took the position that "if the question of how many cavities for how much freedom is to be considered seriously at all, then it should be done with full Constitutional process and not as a matter of regulatory rulings."[31]

KELLOGG'S RESPONSE TO THE ISSUE OF CHILDREN'S ADVERTISING

Kellogg is the nation's largest manufacturer of ready-to-eat cereals, with more than 40% of U.S. sales and over $1.7 billion in 1978 annual sales (38.9% in 1982, with over $3.2 billion in sales). General Foods and General Mills, the next largest producers, have a *combined* total sales figure equal to Kellogg's (37.07% in 1982). The Kellogg Company has been active over the years in attempting to refute the charges leveled at its cereals in the areas of nutrition and advertising.

The Nutritional Value of Kellogg Cereals. As early as 1971, the Kellogg Company formally published an ambitious corporate nutrition policy; however, it cautioned as part of the policy itself that "Consumer acceptability of our products in flavor, texture and appearance is essential if they are to make any nutritional contribution." In early 1973 the Kellogg Company, along with General Mills, testified before the Senate Select Committee on Nutrition and Human Needs. Dr. Gary Costley, Kellogg's Director of Nutrition, argued that (1) "only a small part of a child's sugar intake comes from sweetened breakfast cereals"; (2) that "a normal serving of most canned fruits contained far more sugar" than a serving of cereal; (3) that pre-sweetened cereals do not cause a child to become "hooked" on sugar; and (4) that "research studies show no correlation between new dental caries and the amount of pre-sweetened cereal consumed."[32]

---

[30]*Ibid.*, p. 7.

[31]*Ibid.*, p. 6.

[32]Molander, "Marketing Ready-to-Eat Breakfast Cereals at the Kellogg Company," p. 136.

In October, 1981, the Consumer Service Department at Kellogg printed and distributed a pamphlet entitled "Cereal Fortification," which followed their 1980 monograph, *Ready-to-Eat Cereals and Nutrition*.[33] The pamphlet provided a detailed analysis or "nutrient profile" of their "Corn Flakes" and "Sugar Frosted Flakes." The pamphlet's purpose was to prove that Kellogg cereals, as presently fortified and when used with milk, easily provide the daily nutrient intake recommended by nutritionists.

In 1971, Kellogg's nutritional staff and marketing department worked in conjunction on two projects. First, in the process of marketing, Kellogg strove to retain as much as they could of the look, taste, and "mouthfeel" of the original cereal, while continuing to refortify it. Second, the nutritional and advertising staffs carefully examined their advertising to ensure that all nutritional claims were substantiated. In conjunction with these efforts, Kellogg also initiated a "Stick Up for Breakfast" educational program. This included television spots urging children to eat a balanced breakfast. By 1972, Kellogg and all the major cereal companies had introduced 100 percent natural cereals into their product lines.[34]

Kellogg's Advertising Practices. The Kellogg Company has worked tirelessly to refute charges that their advertising makes false nutritional claims. Kellogg issued a pamphlet on "Advertising" in late 1979. In this pamphlet the company argued as follows:

> Kellogg's has been recognized an unprecedented seven times by *Family Health Magazine* for excellence in nutritional advertising. . . .
>
> For years we have placed great emphasis on creating honest and tasteful advertising for youngsters with messages that convey the inherent nutritional value of our products. We present these messages in a way that is not only informative and interesting, but also appropriate for a child's level of understanding.
>
> Our advertising serves not only as a product selling tool, it also stresses the importance of starting the day with a nutritious breakfast. Since 1973 Kellogg cereal advertisements for both children and adults have shown cereal and milk being eaten as a part of a complete breakfast. Our advertising improves a child's awareness of the need for a complete, nutritious breakfast.

The Consumer Service Department at Kellogg has not directed the same level of effort at charges that their advertising practices are an *unfair* means of influencing children. The views of Seymour Banks,

[33]The pamphlet argued that in 1955, Kellogg's "Special K" was introduced to provide higher levels of essential nutrients and in 1966 "Product 19" had been introduced for the same reason.

[34]Molander, "Marketing Ready-to-Eat Breakfast Cereals at the Kellogg Company," p. 132.

vice-president of the advertising agency that handles the Kellogg account, have been widely quoted:

> Even if a child is deceived by an ad at age four, what harm is done? He will grow out of it. He is in the process of learning to make his own decisions. . . . Even if, as many psychologists claim, a child perceives children in TV advertising as friends, not actors selling them something, what's the harm? All a parent has to say is, "Shut up or I'll belt you."[35]

Kellogg believes that the products in question are nutritious and that children would be worse off if they were not available and not advertised. William E. LaMothe, president of Kellogg at the time of the proposed FTC ban on advertising, commented:

> We try to construct our commercials so that they can be entertaining, and have a message. We're convinced that if we could get every youngster in the country to eat a ready-to-eat cereal—the nutritional information we have says they would have a better diet than the mix of things they have now with high cholesterol and high fat, or no breakfast at all. We are almost evangelistic in our thrust to try to convince youngsters to be interested in breakfast.[36]

Kellogg's overall campaign has thus been to show that both charges of nutritional adequacy and advertising fairness can be met.

[35]Micheli, "Kellogg Company," p. 7. It deserves notice that Banks is not an officer of the Kellogg Company.

[36]Molander, "Marketing Ready-to-Eat Breakfast Cereals at the Kellogg Company," p. 138.

Listerine Antiseptic, Colds, and Sore Throats

"Listerine will not help prevent colds or sore throats or lessen their severity."[1] From September 4, 1978 through February 1, 1980, all advertisements for Listerine carried this disclaimer. The advertising that carried the disclaimer cost $10.2 million, an amount equal to the sum the manufacturer—Warner-Lambert of Morris Plains, New Jersey—had spent between 1962 and 1972 proclaiming the effectiveness of Listerine in fighting colds and sore throats.

The Federal Trade Commission had ordered the disclaimer statement in 1975 as part of an action (initiated in 1972) against Warner-Lambert for failure to maintain "truth in advertising." According to the original order, the disclaimer was to have read "Contrary to prior advertising, Listerine will not help prevent colds or sore throats or lessen their severity." Warner-Lambert declared the order unfounded and without legal authority or precedent and appealed the ruling in the Federal courts. In 1977 the United States Court of Appeals for the District of Columbia circuit upheld the FTC's position but also ordered the phrase *"Contrary to prior advertising . . ."* deleted, on the grounds that it was not necessary to the purpose of the disclaimer and that there was no need "to humiliate the advertiser."[2] In April 1978 the Supreme Court refused to hear a further appeal and the lower court ruling went into effect.

Listerine antiseptic, which has been marketed since 1879, is the leading mouthwash in U.S. sales. Approximately $275 million is spent annually on mouthwash. Listerine's share of that market varies from about 40% to 50%. Listerine is also the only brand of mouthwash that

---

[1]"FTC Tells Listerine to Take it all Back," *Consumer Reports* **41** (March 1976), p. 152.

[2]U.S. Court of Appeals for the District of Columbia Circuit, Argued March 25, 1977. Judgment entered August 2, 1977: *Warner-Lambert Co. v. Federal Trade Commission*, No. 76-1138 (August 2, 1977), p. 26.

This case was prepared by Martha W. Elliott, and revised by Tom L. Beauchamp and Cathleen Kaveny. **Not to be duplicated without permission of the authors and publisher.**

has consistently kept its "medicine bottle" shape and has continually focused its advertisements on the product's effectiveness as a remedy for colds and sore throats.[3]

From 1938 to 1972 Listerine labels proclaimed:

LISTERINE
Antiseptic
Kills Germs
By Millions
On Contact
For Bad Breath, Colds and
Resultant Sore Throats

For Colds and Resultant Sore Throats—Gargle with Listerine Antiseptic Full Strength at the First Sign of Your Cold.[4]

In print advertisements, Listerine's effectiveness as a cold fighter was a constant theme:

FIGHT BACK—The colds-catching season is here again! Nothing can cold-proof you . . . but Listerine Antiseptic gives you a chance to fight back!

Fight back with Listerine Antiseptic. Gargle twice a day—starting now—before you get a cold. You may find the colds you do get will be milder, less severe. That's why more people use Listerine during the colds-catching season than any other oral antiseptic. Why don't you?

Colds-catching season is here again! Nothing can cold-proof you— but Listerine Antiseptic gives you a fighting chance! For fewer colds, milder colds, try this:
Get plenty of rest.
Watch your diet.
Gargle twice a day with full-strength Listerine.[5]

Television commercials also used the fight-back-against-colds-and-sore-throat message. Two such advertisements are the following:

[1] In a commercial entitled "Rubber Stamp-Boy," a woman and young boy (obviously mother and son) are shown. The words "Cold Proof" appear on the boy's forehead. The following announcement covers the action that takes place: "Wouldn't it be great if you could make him cold-proof? Well, you can't. Nothing can do that (boy sneezes). But there is something you can do that may help. Have him gargle with Listerine An-

[3]Robert Young, "The FTC and Listerine," *Harvard Business School Case Services,* Harvard Business School, 1978, p. 3.

[4]FTC, *In the Matter of Warner-Lambert, Federal Trade Commission Decisions,* Vol. 86, July 1, 1975 to December 31, 1975 (Washington, D.C.: Government Printing Office), p. 1399.

[5]*Ibid.,* p. 1400.

tiseptic. Listerine can't promise to keep him cold-free, but it may help fight off colds. During the cold-catching season, have him gargle twice a day with full-strength Listerine. Watch his diet, see he gets plenty of sleep, and there's a good chance he'll have fewer colds, milder colds this year (the words "Fewer Colds, Milder Colds" are superimposed on the picture). It's a fact that more families use Listerine during these cold-catching months than any other oral antiseptic. So be sure your family gargles regularly with Listerine Antiseptic. We can't promise to keep your family cold-free, but Listerine may help you fight off colds" (the words "Fight Colds" are shown with a bottle of Listerine).

[2] In a commercial entitled "Boxer," a boy wearing boxing gloves is shown as the announcer says, "Can a 12 year old boy . . . wage a one-boy fight against the common cold? Well, he can give it a good try if right behind him there's a mother armed with Listerine Antiseptic (Mother appears). We can't promise that Listerine will keep him cold-free, no product can do that. But Listerine may help him fight off colds (the words "Fight Colds" are superimposed on the picture). If you have him gargle twice a day with full-strength Listerine, if you watch his diet and see that he gets plenty of sleep, there's a good chance that he'll have fewer colds, milder colds this year (the words "Fewer Colds, Milder Colds" are superimposed on the picture while the boy gargles). Many mothers see that their families gargle regularly with Listerine. In fact, during the cold-catching season, more people use Listerine than any other oral antiseptic. We can't promise to keep your family cold-free, but Listerine may help you fight off colds." (The words "Fight Colds" are superimposed on the picture.)[6]

The Federal Trade Commission evaluated these and several other advertisements and concluded that they deceptively portrayed Listerine as a cure for colds and sore throats. The FTC complaint and Warner-Lambert's response are summarized in the initial decision by Alvin L. Berman, the FTC Administrative Law Judge:

> The Commission's complaint charges respondent Warner-Lambert Company ("Warner-Lambert") with having engaged in unfair methods of competition and unfair and deceptive acts and practices in violation of Section 5 of the Federal Trade Commission Act by virtue of various statements and representations made in connection with, and to induce the sale of, its "Listerine" mouthwash preparation. More specifically, it is charged that, through various advertisements, including product packaging and labels, respondent has represented that the use of Listerine will cure colds and sore throats, will prevent colds and sore throats and will cause colds and sore throats to be less severe than they otherwise would be; that these representations are false, misleading and deceptive. . . .
> Another allegation of the complaint is that respondent misrepresented that the most recent tests conducted by or for it, or available to it, prove that children who use Listerine have fewer or milder colds and miss fewer days of school than children who do not use Listerine. Still another allegation is that respondent has misrepresented that the ability of Lis-

[6]*Ibid.,* p. 1410.

terine to kill germs is of medical significance in the prevention, cure or treatment of colds and sore throats.

Respondent, by its answer, admitted that it has represented that the use of Listerine as directed, in conjunction with a regimen of proper rest and diet, will cause fewer colds and will help reduce the severity of colds. It denied representing that the use of Listerine would cure or would totally prevent colds or sore throats. It admitted that Listerine would not cure colds or totally prevent colds or sore throats, but averred that the use of Listerine as directed, in conjunction with a regimen of proper diet and rest, had been demonstrated to result in fewer colds, milder colds and milder symptoms thereof and less severe colds and sore throats.

Respondent admitted that the severity of a cold is judged or measured by its accompanying symptoms, and that the representation that the use of Listerine would make colds less severe constituted a representation that such use would relieve or lessen the severity of cold symptoms to a significant degree. It denied, however, that the use of Listerine as directed will not have a significant beneficial effect on cold symptoms. Respondent denied other material allegations of the complaint.[7]

In developing its case against Warner-Lambert, the FTC relied heavily on medical evidence that colds are caused by viruses (not by bacteria or "germs"), that there are no treatments that cure a cold or shorten its severity, and that "catching cold" is not related to diet, rest, or exposure to the elements. The FTC did allow that gargling could relieve the uncomfortable symptoms of a cold, but held that warm water was as effective as Listerine for this purpose. The FTC also found the claim "Listerine kills millions of germs on contact" to be essentially irrelevant, because "germs" do not cause colds.

A number of the studies relate to the alleged antibacterial properties of Listerine. Since a cold is an infection caused by virus particles inhaled into the nose which enter into and damage the cells there, the antibacterial properties of Listerine are, for all practical purposes irrelevant. Bacteria play no part in the common cold, and the ability of Listerine to kill millions of bacteria in the oral cavity is of no medical significance in the prevention, cure or treatment of colds or sore throats. Listerine does not reach the site of infection or manifestation of symptoms in medically significant concentration and the tests and writings relied upon by respondent do not tend to show otherwise.[8]

In its defense Warner-Lambert executives noted that the company position was that Listerine would help prevent colds and sore throats only when conjoined with proper rest and diet. They denied their advertisements claimed that Listerine alone would *prevent* colds and sore throats. The company also relied on expert witnesses and on two clinical studies of the frequency and severity of colds. The first study, the

[7]*Ibid.*, pp. 1405–1406.
[8]*Ibid.*, p. 1456.

Reddish test, was done between 1932 and 1942, using employees of Warner-Lambert as subjects; the second study was done between 1967 and 1971 at the St. Barnabas Elementary School. The first study supposedly showed that the group that gargled with Listerine did in fact have fewer colds and sore throats than the control group and that the colds they did have were of lesser severity and shorter duration. From the results of the second study, it was again concluded that Listerine users had milder colds than nonusers (although the data can be interpreted to suggest that they also had more colds than nonusers and that their colds lasted longer).[9]

The FTC faulted both studies for their poor experimental design. It further alleged that the method of selection in the first test and the fact that neither study was blind indicated that the experiments were biased from the start. The FTC criticisms of the two supporting studies are summarized as follows:

1. The St. Barnabas Test

Students in an elementary school and a high school were randomly selected to participate in this study which spanned four years (the high school was dropped at the end of the third year). During the first two years, the participating students were assigned either to the treatment group, which gargled with Listerine twice a day, or to a control group which used no mouthwash at all. During the last two years the control group gargled with water colored to resemble Listerine's amber hue. Since it did not have Listerine's taste or odor, the ALJ concluded that this amber-colored water was not a true placebo, and that the absence of a true placebo biased the test results in favor of the tested agent, Listerine. . . . In order to determine whether the product has efficacy, the bias of the placebo effect should be removed. This bias can be neutralized by "blinding" the participants, *i.e.,* dispensing to the control group a placebo which simulates in taste, smell and appearance the product being tested. This practice of blinding the control group through the use of a placebo is a generally-accepted procedure today. Use of an adequate placebo becomes even more important where the evaluation of symptoms involves subjective judgments. The record demonstrates that a cold is a self-limiting infection, and evaluation of cold symptoms tends to be quite subjective.

We are not requiring in this case that the placebo duplicate the taste, smell, texture, color, etc. of the tested product. There may well be degrees of simulation short of duplication which would neutralize the placebo effect.[10] However, the use of caramel-colored water was patently inadequate.

[9]Young, "The FTC and Listerine," pp. 7–8.

[10]Dr. Vernon Knight, a witness for respondent, identified an alternative that may have proved adequate. A new study would have to be of the "double blind" type. This might be arranged by completely avoiding use of the word "Listerine." Listerine colored another color or conceivably flavored slightly differently as well could be compared with a colored, flavored, 25% alcohol solution. A third group could be given a non-alcoholic, non-germicidal solution of a different color and flavor.

Respondent urges that the absence of a true placebo can be counter-balanced by factors which tend to reduce the impact of the placebo effect, such as conducting the study over a long period of time, permitting the use of concomitant medication, and maintaining the "blindness" of the examining physician—precautions which respondent claims were taken in the St. Barnabas study. Perhaps in some drug studies other factors could compensate for the absence of a placebo but so many uncertainties permeate the St. Barnabas test that we cannot place any reliance in it. For example, it is unclear whether the examiner was properly blinded. We note that blinding the examiner is not merely a device for counter-balancing the absence of a proper placebo; it is essential that a properly administered test avoid bias on the part of the investigator. Whatever bias he may consciously or subconsciously possess can be neutralized by preventing him from knowing which subjects used the purported medication and which received no medication. In this sense, the examiner is "blinded.". . .

The ALJ concluded that the examiner, Dr. Benjamin W. Nitzberg, was not properly "blinded" because the test protocol required that the children gargle at 9:00 a.m., and he began examining them at 10 a.m. Although Dr. Nitzberg denied that he knew which children were in the test group or that he smelled Listerine on the student's breath except on rare occasions (*i.e.,* three or four children in six months), the ALJ concluded that Dr. Nitzberg must have detected the odor of Listerine on the students' breath because other witnesses for respondent testified, on the basis of their own experiences with Listerine, that Listerine can be smelled on the breath for 1½ to 2 hours after gargling.

The record offers support for the ALJ's concern. It establishes that Dr. Nitzberg knew that the test was being conducted for Warner-Lambert, that it involved Listerine and that the data would be used to determine the effect on colds of gargling with Listerine daily. Thus, if he knew which children used Listerine, he might have biased the results in favor of Listerine. The students gargled at 9:00 a.m.; Dr. Nitzberg arrived at 10:00 a.m. and left within an hour during the first two years of the study and within one and one-half hours during the last two years. Therefore, many students were examined one to two hours after gargling. Two physicians who testified for respondent stated that, on the basis of their own experience with Listerine, it can be detected on the breath for 1½ to 2 hours after gargling. . . .

Three additional infirmities heighten our concern about the study's probative value. Students were instructed to report to the medical examiner, usually Dr. Nitzberg, at the first sign of a cold. The medical examiner would evaluate and record the overall severity of the cold plus the severity of fourteen cold-related symptoms (only eight during the first two years of the study). The student returned to the examiner each day for the duration of the cold episode, and the physician examined and questioned the student about each symptom, recording the severity of the symptoms on the same sheet that he used the previous day (a rating scale of 0–4 was used during the first two years and 0–7 for the last two). Dr. Nitzberg allotted himself only 1½ to 2 minutes to examine and question each child. This procedure detracts from the probative value of the test in three respects. First, by using the same score sheet day after day Dr. Nitzberg would know how he evaluated a child's symptoms the previous day. As the ALJ found, Dr. Nitzberg's knowledge of what he had done previously would tend to bias his scores, and therefore he would not make an independent judgment each day. Second, given the number of symptoms which Dr. Nitzberg had to evaluate and the fine gradations he had to make in his evaluation, we question whether he spent an adequate amount of time on each subject. In addition to asking each child for historical data on every item on the report form, he would "examine the upper respiratory tract, the eyes, the ears, the nose and the throat, the sinuses by palpitation and the neck for cervical adenopathy." During the last two years of the study the examiner checked for six additional symptoms. On Mondays he often had to fill in the form for Saturday and Sunday. Third, even if Dr. Nitzberg had been properly blinded the scores he recorded could have been biased to the extent the scores were based upon the non-blinded child's subjective evaluation.

All of the foregoing defects have the cumulative effect of rendering the St. Barnabas study unreliable for evaluating the efficacy of Listerine. In view of this conclusion, we find it unnecessary to consider the parties' disagreement over the meaning of the results.

2. The Reddish Cold Tests

During the winters of 1932 to 1942 respondent conducted tests, mainly using its own employees, to determine whether Listerine has the ability to fight colds. These tests, which respondent claimed established Listerine's efficacy against colds and sore throats, have such grave deficiencies in design and execution that their results are meaningless. Of foremost concern, no placebo was used. (During some winters control groups gargled with a saline solution or tap water. These liquids cannot qualify as adequate placebos.) Moreover, employees were allowed to choose which group they preferred, thereby further biasing the results because those who thought that gargling was an effective method for fighting a cold would most likely join the test group. In addition, the ALJ found that the investigators themselves had predetermined beliefs that Listerine was good for colds. Finally, the investigators were not provided with a uniform definition of a "cold." Common colds last no longer than 10 days, yet illnesses lasting up to 69 days were counted as "colds" in the Reddish study. Even respondent's own expert, Dr. Knight, said that "present opinion would hold that satisfactory evidence for efficacy is no longer provided by these early studies."[11]

Expert witnesses introduced by Warner-Lambert relied heavily on these two studies to support the Listerine claims and to refute FTC charges. Warner-Lambert executives felt victimized by the regulatory system, since the Administrative Law Judge who settled the dispute between the FTC and the company was himself located at the FTC. The executives believed that the judge had cavalierly dismissed their scientific studies, in addition to data indicating customer satisfaction with Listerine and a substantial repurchase rate for the product. They also

[11]FTC, *In the Matter of Warner-Lambert.*

maintained that the decision reached by this judge was without precedent.

The FTC, however, had found the studies so faulty that the additional testimony in favor of Listerine was of little positive significance. Consequently it held that Warner-Lambert had failed to support the Listerine advertising claims. In December, 1975, the FTC concluded its case against Warner-Lambert and ordered the company to cease and desist from:

> Representing, directly or by implication, that any such product will cure colds or sore throats;
>
> Representing, directly or by implication, that any such product will prevent colds or sore throats;
>
> Representing, directly or by implication, that users of any such product will have fewer colds than nonusers;
>
> Representing, directly or by implication, that any such product is a treatment for, or will lessen the severity of, colds or sore throats;
>
> Representing that any such product will have any significant beneficial effect on the symptoms of sore throats or any beneficial effect on symptoms of colds;
>
> Representing that the ability of any such product to kill germs is of medical significance in the treatment of colds or sore throats or the symptoms of colds or sore throats.[12]

At the same time that the FTC issued its "cease and desist" order, it also issued the "corrective advertising" order, holding that "mere cessation" of the "false" advertising would not erase the beliefs that people had developed about the effectiveness of Listerine against colds.[13] The Commission held that the corrective advertising was necessary because "Consumer beliefs tend to continue once they are created," and "Future representation of Listerine as a germ killer, without corrective advertising, would automatically constitute, or remind the public of cold claims even in the absence of reference to colds":[14]

> Listerine has been on the market since 1879. Throughout its history, the product has been represented as being, *inter alia,* beneficial in certain respects for colds, colds symptoms and sore throats. Listerine has been advertised directly to the consuming public as a cold remedy since 1921. Since prior to 1938, Listerine labeling has included claims regarding colds and sore throats. . . .
>
> The record shows that over the past ten years, respondent has spent large sums of money in all major media for advertising Listerine as a remedy for the prevention and cure of colds and sore throats and as an ameliorative for cold symptoms. The vast majority of these expenditures

[12]*Ibid.,* pp. 1513–1514.
[13]"FTC Tells Listerine to Take it all Back," p. 152.
[14]Young, "The FTC and Listerine," p. 10.

were spent on network and spot television, covering all parts of the day and evening but particularly on prime time network television. Spot television commercials covered practically all the major media centers in the United States. Listerine "colds" print advertising was disseminated in major magazines and newspapers throughout the country.

Advertising acts both in creating a belief in consumers and in reinforcing a belief once it has been created. It has a large role in creating and shaping beliefs with respect to a new product. Its role with an older, established product such as Listerine is more to reinforce established beliefs and act as a reminder. It serves to keep people from changing their attitudes. It still influences some new beliefs. There are always new people coming into the market, *e.g.*, people who were not users who grow up and form households.

Advertising plays a relatively more important role for packaged goods, such as a mouthwash, than for items such as automobiles. Listerine having been advertised as a cold preventative, cure and symptom ameliorative for so many years, it is clear that it has acted both to create and reinforce beliefs in consumers corresponding with respondent's representations concerning that product. It is not plausible that respondent would have spent the millions of dollars that it has over such a long period of time to create and reinforce beliefs about Listerine's use for colds unless it were convinced that the advertisements were effective.[15]

Ironically, Warner-Lambert's own market research gave some support to the thesis that people think that Listerine is effective against colds and sore throats (and therefore lent support to the thesis positing a need for corrective advertising in addition to cessation of misleading claims). Between 1964 and 1971 the percentage recall of Listerine advertising claims showed that between 65 and 75% of the subjects tested held Listerine to be effective in killing germs and between 67 and 80% thought it effective for colds and sore throats.[16] Another poll conducted for Warner-Lambert showed that "nearly two-thirds of the shoppers polled thought Listerine was a help for colds but that fewer than one-fifth thought other mouthwashes were good cold antidotes."[17] The J. Walter Thompson Company, Warner-Lambert's advertising agency, reported that the major distinctive phrases remembered were "effective for colds and sore throats" and "effective for killing germs":[18]

Although recall of Listerine's "colds" advertising is at all times very high, such advertising is recalled to an even greater degree during the winter months' "cold season" when Listerine "colds" advertising is disseminated. This indicates that the advertising is especially effective during the

[15]FTC, *In the Matter of Warner-Lambert*, pp. 1468–1469.
[16]Young, "The FTC and Listerine," p. 11.
[17]"Back on the Warpath Against Deceptive Ads," *Business Week* (April 19, 1976), p. 151.
[18]FTC, *In the Matter of Warner-Lambert*, pp. 1472–1473.

months in which it is disseminated. At the same time, it is important to recognize that the "colds" theme is highly recalled as recent advertising even during the 6-month period when there is no such advertising. This is most significant in considering the propriety of requiring corrective advertising, particularly in view of the fact that the subjects are not being asked to recall the major themes of recent advertising, not of advertising, 3, 4, 5 or 6 months ago. It shows the lasting impression of the non-current advertising.[19]

What do consumers now think about Listerine? In October 1981 the FTC released the results of a mail survey which found that even at the end of the "corrective advertising" campaign about 39% of the Listerine users surveyed reported that they used the mouthwash to relieve or prevent a cold or sore throat: "While 22 percent of Listerine users associated the corrective message with Listerine advertising, . . . 42 percent still believed colds and sore throat effectiveness is a principal Listerine advertising theme."[20]

Warner-Lambert faced the possibility of federally mandated modifications of Listerine again in 1982. The "Oral Cavity Advisory Panel," composed of experts commissioned by the FDA but operating independently of it, released an exhaustive report on the safety and efficacy of the active ingredients in oral health care products placed on the market before 1962. Their report found that the active ingredients in Listerine were not *conclusively proven* to be germicidal and therefore should not be advertised as such. If the FDA were ultimately to accept these findings, Warner-Lambert might not be allowed to represent Listerine as anything more than a simple mouthwash. Without its germicidal capacity, its status would be the same as that of its competitor, Scope, and similar to Warner-Lambert's other mouthwash, Listermint.

Warner-Lambert contends that Listerine does indeed possess germicidal properties, and therefore is not simply a medicinally flavored version of the allegedly more pleasant-tasting Listermint. They are confident that their research will be conclusive enough to convince the FDA that Listerine kills germs. Moreover, the company holds that the FTC's present regulatory posture would not alter advertisng of the product in any event.

[19]*Ibid.*, p. 1473.
[20]UPI, "Study Says Ads by Listerine had Limited Support," *The Washington Post*, October 28, 1981.

Procter and Gamble's Rely Tampons

On September 22, 1980, Procter and Gamble voluntarily withdrew their Rely tampons from sale. The events surrounding that unusual corporate action were widely reported by the media under headlines about TSS or Toxic-shock syndrome. TSS was unknown by the medical profession until 1978. It was not until May 1980 that the Center for Disease Control (CDC), a division of the U.S. Public Health Service charged with monitoring the incidence of disease in the United States, alerted physicians to the problem. They reported a disease characterized by a sudden onset of high fever, usually over 104 degrees, vomiting and diarrhea, a rapid drop in blood pressure (usually below 90 systolic in adults), and a sunburn-like rash that later peels off in scales with an acute phase of 4–5 days. About 10% of reported cases were fatal. The disease appears to occur most in women under age 30 during their menstrual periods, although early studies of the disease dealt with cases of TSS in young girls and boys. The CDC supported research on the growing number of reported cases, and in June 1980, announced the preliminary findings of a study linking tampon use to toxic shock syndrome.[1]

Rely tampons became publicly identified with toxic shock syndrome when the CDC released a follow-up report on TSS on September 19, 1980. The report indicated that 71% of the women in the study (totalling 52) had been users of Rely.[2] The research also indicated that cases of TSS occurred with tampons produced by all five of the major U.S. tampon manufacturers.

---

[1]U.S. Public Health Service, "Toxic Shock Syndrome," *Morbidity and Mortality Weekly Report* (June 26, 1980). Note: The CDC first learned of a threat from TSS in January 1980.

[2]U.S. Public Health Service, "Follow Up on Toxic Shock Syndrome," *Morbidity and Mortality Weekly Report* **29 (37)** (September 19, 1980), pp. 443–444.

This case was prepared by Louisa W. Peat O'Neil and Tom L. Beauchamp. **Not to be duplicated without permission of the authors and publisher.**

Procter and Gamble had developed the Rely tampon to serve as their entry into the financially secure arena of feminine hygiene products. Introduced to the marketplace in 1974, Rely had garnered about 25% of the tampon market by September 1980.[3] Rely's design was innovative in the "superabsorbent" category, consisting in part of superabsorbent cellulose and polyurethane. It was test marketed in 1974 in Wayne, Indiana, and in 1975 in Rochester, New York.[4] Consumers resisted the new product due to its use of polyurethane as an absorbent material. Women who were interviewed reported fears of cancer and other health risks. The Center for Health Services at the University of Tennessee concluded that polyurethane was not carcinogenic, and thus, that these fears were unfounded. Aware of consumer concerns, however, Procter and Gamble reformulated Rely. The revised tampon consisted of polyester foam and superabsorbent cellulose sponges encased in a polyester sack.[5] The Food and Drug Administration (FDA) had known for several years about unconfirmed claims of certain injuries related to such tampons, including Rely, before the toxic shock syndrome studies were made public. Although difficulty with tampon removal and vaginal ulcerations and lacerations were the usual reports giving rise to consumer and physician complaints, two pages of the FDA's Device Experience Network computer printout were devoted to citations about other problems related to Rely.[6]

The FDA's regulatory role was unclear when the TSS problem arose because no research had demonstrated that tampons caused TSS. On the other hand, the FDA had a Congressional mandate to test all medical drugs and devices prior to marketing to the public. Prior to 1974–76, tampons were regulated under the drug section of the FDA, although they were not technically classified as drugs. In a reorganization process begun in 1974, tampons and other feminine hygiene products were reclassified as medical devices. Because tampons had a "history of safe use," they were placed in Class II, which bases safety on past performance rather than on specific pre-market testing,[7] as required for Class III medical devices. In Class II devices, small changes are permitted without review or testing by the FDA. Therefore, critics

[3]Carol J. Loomis, "P & G Up Against the Wall," *Fortune* **103** (4) (February 23, 1981), p. 53. Some sources gave Rely only a 20% market share.

[4]From a series on Rely by the *Chicago Tribune,* called to the case writers' attention by Tampax.

[5]Nancy Friedman, "The Truth about Tampons," *New West* **5** (21) (October 20, 1980), pp. 35–36.

[6]*Ibid.,* pp. 38, 40.

[7]More precisely, Class II devices are those devices for which safety and efficacy can be guaranteed by performance standards. As an "old" device, tampons are assigned to Class II, as devices were classified after the Medical Device Amendments of 1976.

have argued, by spacing minor changes over time, manufacturers have been able to change tampons without regulatory challenge.[8] That there *have* been such changes is denied by Tampax, and no doubt by others.[9]

When presented with the findings of the CDC study, Procter and Gamble executives were faced with a crisis. They could continue to market Rely tampons despite the publicity linking it to TSS; they could wait until the FDA took action attempting to restrict sale of the product; or they could voluntarily withdraw the product. At first, when scientific research indicated that the material in the tampons did not encourage bacterial growth, Edward G. Harness, Chairman of the Board and Chief Executive of Procter and Gamble, said he was "determined to fight for the brand, to keep an important brand from being hurt by insufficient data in the hands of a bureaucracy."[10] At the time the FDA did not have enough data to order a legal recall. However, by September 18, 1980, Procter and Gamble stopped production of the Rely tampon, probably because of negative publicity and the new report previously mentioned from the Center for Disease Control that linked Rely statistically to TSS—a report Procter and Gamble's own physicians, microbiologists, and epidemiologists were unable to refute. "That was the turning point," Mr. Harness said. The company subsequently pledged their research expertise to the Center for Disease Control to investigate toxic shock syndrome and agreed to finance and direct a large educational program about the disease, as well as agreeing to issue a warning to women not to use Rely. Referring to the Rely case, Mr. Harness later made the following public announcement:

> Company management must consistently demonstrate a superior talent for keeping profit and growth objectives as first priorities. However, it also must have enough breadth to recognize that enlightened self-interest requires the company to fill any reasonable expectation placed upon it by the community and the various concerned publics. Keeping priorities straight and maintaining the sense of civic responsibility will achieve important secondary objectives of the firm. Profitability and growth go hand in hand with fair treatment of employees, of direct customers, of consumers, and of the community.[11]

[8]Charlotte Oram and Judith Beck, "Tampons: Looking Beyond Toxic Shock," *Science for the People* **13** (5) (Sept./Oct. 1981), p. 16.

[9]Tampax, Private correspondence from Executive Vice President Thomas J. Moore (June 1, 1982).

[10]Dean Rotbard and John A. Prestbo, "Killing a Product," *Wall Street Journal,* November 3, 1980, p. 21.

[11]Edward G. Harness, "Views on Corporate Reponsibility," *Corporate Ethics Digest* **1** (September–October 1980). This citation and other points in this paragraph are indebted to Elizabeth Gatewood and Archie B. Carroll, "Anatomy of a Corporate Social Response: The Procter & Gamble Rely Case," *Business Horizons* (September 1981).

Although there were strong objections inside Procter and Gamble to the methodology and scope of the CDC studies, the company clearly believed it could not risk its reputation on a product that had received so much adverse publicity. A prominent question in the deliberations of corporate executives had been whether a profit-making company could continue to market a product that had not been associated (even if a causal relationship was not confirmed) with the sudden death of many young women and the illness and the disfigurement of many others. Harness said the withdrawal was intended to remove Rely from the controversy "despite evidence that the withdrawal of Rely will not eliminate the occurrence of TSS even if Rely's use is completely discontinued."[12]

There are "medical problems" with the entire issue about causation of TSS. First, no pathological mechanism has been demonstrated that shows the causal relationship between tampons and TSS. (By contrast, the USDA supports the tobacco industry even though there is direct evidence showing the harmful effects of byproducts of tobacco smoke on the smoker and indirect evidence showing its effect on others.) Second, staph aurens (the implicated organism) is well known for changing patterns of presentation (e.g., neonatal staph epidemics in the 1950s–1960s) and severity. It may be that the TSS "epidemic" was secondary to the emergence of a strain or strains of staph aurens. This is supported by the emergence of other unusual staphylococcal disease at the same time (bacterial tracheitis).

FDA officials met with Procter and Gamble executives, with representatives of other tampon manufacturers, and with consumer groups to determine how women should be warned about the relationship of TSS and all tampons, lest the public think that removal of Rely ended the problem. On October 20, 1980, the FDA proposed a voluntary warning label for packages and shelves directed to the population at risk and to new younger users of tampon products. Most tampon manufacturers volunteered to place the warning label on the outside of packages. Tampax did not, and it has been reported that this company increased its advertising budget while printing only part of the FDA's advice—omitting the FDA recommendation that women could reduce or eliminate the risk of TSS by not using tampons at all. In its package inserts, Tampax did mention TSS, but asserted that TSS is a "very rare illness" and that "tampons do not cause TSS," because "it is caused by a type of bacteria present in some women." Tampax's strategy apparently was financially beneficial, for in the month following Rely's withdrawal, Tampax's share of the market grew from 43% to

[12]Richard Severo, "Sharp Decrease in U.S. Reported in Toxic Shock Syndrome Cases," *New York Times,* January 30, 1981, sec. D, p. 15.

56%.[13] Tampax Executive Vice President Thomas J. Moore explains the company's views as follows:

> Research has not demonstrated *any* causal connection between tampons and TSS. . . . Tampax omitted from its warning a statement that TSS could be almost entirely avoided by not using tampons because that statement could not be proved true. It is now known that TSS affects non-menstruating women and girls and also men.
>
> The implication that Tampax increased its sales by the use of misleading advertising cannot be supported. Its advertising was complete and correct. In the eleven weeks following the withdrawal of Rely, the total U.S. tampon market shrank by nearly 20%. It should not be surprising that Tampax's share of the market increased following the withdrawal of a competitor that had accounted for 20–25% of the market.[14]

It is to be remembered that all warning labels were *voluntary*, not required by federal regulations. The FDA had only a *proposed* rule to require warnings.

Procter and Gamble undertook a four-week advertising campaign announcing the association between TSS and Rely. The extensive media campaign, including TV and radio commercials as well as half-page newspaper ads in 1,200 papers, was unprecedented. Procter and Gamble also took a $75 million tax write-off on Rely in fiscal 1981 to account for both its unrecovered investment in Rely and costs associated with the growing number of legal cases arising out of damages or death allegedly caused by Rely.[15] These lawsuits against Procter and Gamble were filed quickly after the first public announcement of the link between tampons and TSS. Within a year, Rely was named as cause of death or disfigurement from TSS in about 200 cases.[16] Some plaintiffs also named the Department of Health and Human Services and Food and Drug Administration officials in their suits, claiming that federal negligence permitted Rely to be marketed.

Procter and Gamble's decision to remove the product from sale may not have enhanced their position in these product liability suits, but largely due to news stories, it demonstrably enhanced their already tarnished image in the eyes of the general public.

Although the company voluntarily removed Rely from the shelves, Procter and Gamble executives continued to believe that the evidence linking Rely to TSS is unconvincing. They have subsequently undertaken further research of their own. By July 1981, Procter and Gamble

[13]Pamela Sherrid, "Tampons After the Shock Wave," *Fortune* **104** (August 10, 1981), p. 116.

[14]Tampax, private correspondence from Executive Vice President Thomas J. Moore.

[15]Loomis, "P & G Up Against the Wall," p. 53.

[16]Dean Rotbart, "Rely Counterattack: P & G Is Going All-Out to Track Toxic Shock and Exonerate Itself," *Wall Street Journal*, June 26, 1981, p. 1.

began financing research projects into TSS at a cost of around $2 million.[17] This financial commitment will enable researchers to better understand the origins and effects of toxic shock syndrome. They are also candid, however, about hoping to clear consumer suspicion. Should the results of the research prove Rely does have a specific relationship with TSS, then the company will have paid for results that are at least satisfactory in its own eyes. It also would tend to justify the earlier decision to withdraw the product from the market, for that judgment will become more circumspect in comparison to the judgments of others in the industry. On the other hand, if the research does indicate that Rely is safe to use, Procter and Gamble could remarket the tampon or some other menstrual product. The Rely tampons were at first kept in storage at considerable expense, held for sale to a future generation, or disposed of at another tax write-off. They were all eventually disposed of, beginning in June 1981 (used as fuel in one of their plants).

Following the release of information linking toxic shock syndrome and all high-absorbency tampons in January 1981, consumer tampon buying patterns changed. Kimberly-Clark Corporation began replacing its superabsorbent brands with regular tampons late in 1980. As a company representative explained to the *Wall Street Journal*, "consumers no longer show a preference for the superabsorbent" product.[18] Tampax's president also noted that, "There isn't any question that many women have an objection to them."[19] Whether the changes in purchasing and use patterns have affected the incidence of TSS is a question still under considerable debate. The CDC noted that since withdrawal of Rely, TSS cases have dropped. But this could be attributed to changes in reporting patterns and the general decline in tampon use following the publicity surrounding TSS. Further, the media coverage also may have caused increased reporting by physicians and consumers during the time between the first CDC announcements in May–June 1980, and withdrawal of Rely in late September 1980. TSS cases were reported throughout 1981–82 and by late December 1981, CDC had 1,400 cases on file, almost all involving menstruating women who wore tampons.[20]

Debate continues in the research community on the causal or catalytic role, if any, of tampons in toxic shock syndrome. Both diaphragms and sea sponges have been implicated in cases of TSS, al-

[17]"Jury Still Out on Toxic Shock," *The Globe and Mail* (Toronto, Canada), July 6, 1981, p. 13.

[18]Dean Rotbart, "State of Alarm: Tampon Industry is in Throes of Change After Toxic Shock," *Wall Street Journal*, February 26, 1981, p. 1.

[19]*Ibid.*

[20]"Toxic Shock Linked to Diaphragms," *The Washington Post*, December 24, 1981, sec. A, p. 2.

though in numbers too small to be studied. The exact relationship of
Rely to TSS is also still unresolved. The association between Rely and
TSS is not understood beyond the fact that it is a high-absorbent tampon.[21] A study with a sample size larger than that used in the CDC research (52 women), or perhaps Procter and Gamble's own TSS research team, may provide more information. It may be that marketing
and purchasing patterns account for the increased statistical association
of Rely with TSS. It is clear, however, that removal of Rely from the
marketplace did not *eradicate* TSS, though there has been a marked
decrease in tampon use and in reported cases of TSS since September
1980.[22] The disease continues in the United States, and is being reported in Sweden, Canada, West Germany, and other countries where
Rely was never marketed.

At the same time it is clear that some juries are willing to judge Procter and Gamble liable for damages in the case of TSS-related deaths
among users of Rely. For example, on April 21, 1982, a federal court
jury in Cedar Rapids, Iowa awarded $300,000 to the widower of a
woman whose death was allegedly caused by the use of Rely. Procter
and Gamble's argument that the woman's death was caused by a uter-
ine infection caused by a contraceptive device failed to convince the
jury. Four hundred other suits were pending against Procter and Gamble when this case was decided.[23]

[21]Jerry Bishop, "New Study Links Toxic-Shock Syndrome to the Use of High-Absorbency Tampons," *Wall Street Journal,* February 19, 1981, sec. D, p. 16.

[22]Charles E. Irwin and Susan G. Millstein, "Emerging Patterns of Tampon Use in the
Adolescent Female: The Impact of Toxic Shock Syndrome," *American Journal of Public
Health* **72** (May 1982), pp. 464–67.

[23]"Tampon Maker Held Liable in Toxic Shock," *The Washington Post,* April 22, 1982,
p. 2.

Giant Food's Elimination
of Item Pricing

One of the areas hardest hit by the recent rapid inflation spiral has been the grocery chain industry. Faced with a sharp rise in the whole-sale price index since the 1960s and with mounting pressure from the United Food and Commercial Workers Union for salary increases, the grocery industry began in the late 1960s to explore the possibility of automating its checkout and stocking procedures. The idea of marking each item to be sold with a distinctive label, which would come to be known as the "Universal Product Code" (UPC), had been around since the 1940s. With the development of optical scanning devices and rela-tively low-cost computers to store and process the information, the idea was becoming increasingly feasible. A joint Ad Hoc Committee of the National Association of Food Chains, the grocery industry's trade as-sociation, and the Super Market Institute, the research organization of the industry, met with Distribution Codes, Inc. and representatives of food wholesaler and processor groups to develop the now familiar "ze-bra code" of ten black and white stripes.

By use of the UPC, groceries can be rung up by passing the bar code label over an optical scanner located at the check stand. There a laser beam "reads" the code through electronic impulses transmitted to the store's computer. The computer in turn looks up the item name and price and sends them to the check stand for electronic display and to its own data files for sales and inventory recordkeeping. For the shop-per, it produces an enhanced register tape that describes each item as well as giving the price.

The cost of printing the UPC on containers is small. The capital out-lay in installing a checkout system capable of utilizing the UPC is cor-respondingly attractive. A study made by the Ad Hoc Committee found that in a ten-register store with a projected monthly sales vol-ume of $700,000, the introduction of a UPC system was expected to

This case was prepared by Sarah Westrick and revised by Tom L. Beauchamp. **Not to be duplicated without permission of the authors and publisher.**

produce roughly a $10,000 cost savings, or approximately 1.42% of sales.[1] The elimination of placing a price sticker on each individual item is a significant by-product of the UPC. This factor alone accounts for 0.5% of sales, while the balance would result from increased checkout speed, checkout and marketing accuracy, and routinized restocking. In addition, the data collected by the computer promised major advances in inventory control and pricing; chief among these were reduction of storage time and breakage through direct transfer of merchandiser from supplier to shelf and exact turn-over time of shelf stock.

Attracted by this opportunity to hold down operating costs and increase productivity, Giant Food, Inc., a major Maryland-Washington, D.C.-Virginia area grocery chain, began to consider the possibility of installing such a system in a new store. In order to better assess possible problems involved with introducing such novel technology, Giant's consumer advisor, Esther Peterson, organized an advisory committee composed of local consumer group representatives and members of the consumer affairs offices of local governments. Among issues considered by the committee were possible health hazards from the lasers used to read the UPC, improvement of register tape and shelf label formats, employee training, threats to consumer privacy, and the question of discontinuing item pricing.

The committee's position on this last issue was that consumers had not been exposed to computerized checkout systems long enough for Giant to try experimenting with all aspects of it, and that the abolition of item pricing should be postponed until shoppers were thoroughly familiar with the new system. Concurrently, the United Food and Commercial Workers Union was negotiating a contract with Giant which specified that no employee would be laid off or downgraded if the new system fulfilled all its expected labor-saving functions. Giant, however, was not obligated to replace employees lost to normal attrition from computerized stores if positions became redundant.

Despite a strongly stated policy of consumerism, Giant management chose to override the recommendations of its own advisory group and test the whole system immediately, including the experimental elimination of item pricing.

Before the new computerized store was opened in Severna Park, Maryland in 1975, Giant undertook a series of press conferences and educational measures to familiarize the public with the new system. Booklets were distributed that explained computerized checkout and

---

[1]These and other figures given by the Ad Hoc Committee or quoted by Giant representatives, unless otherwise noted, are taken from: "Giant Food and the Universal Product Code," in Earl A. Molander, *Responsive Capitalism: Case Studies in Corporate Social Conduct* (New York: McGraw-Hill, 1980), pp. 100–112.

the UPC, and a demonstration scanner was set up where customers could use it. Radio and TV spots were also used. When the Severna Park store was stocked, unit and item prices (mandatory in Maryland since 1972) were clearly marked on shelf labels, but individual bottles and boxes were not priced.

On opening day shoppers faced a picket line set up by the Maryland Citizens' Consumer Council (MCCC), which distributed leaflets claiming that the removal of item prices was an experiment by Giant to eliminate consumer awareness and leave the shopper at the mercy of a computer. The MCCC was not composed simply of traditionalists opposed to the progress and efficiency introduced by modern technology. They had a number of concerns, all focused on the conditions of consumer ignorance introduced by the new system. For example, computers frequently make mistakes. In order to know at the checkout counter whether a computer was making a mistake, one would have to remember the price of every item (as listed on the shelves) in order to know whether the computer was accurate. The MCCC also argued that it would be much harder for shoppers to follow price increases under the new system. Many shoppers prefer to make comparisons at home by comparing old purchases with new ones. This could now be done only by the tedious and complex process of checking old print-out tapes with new ones. The net effect, consumer groups argued, would be a decreasing awareness of the prices of all grocery store items. A series of concerns of this sort led the MCCC to urge shoppers to voice their complaints directly to the Maryland Legislature, where they found a sympathetic ear. The result was a quick introduction of a bill requiring virtually all groceries to be item priced.

In response to this unexpected attack, the Ad Hoc Committee of the National Association of Food Chains formed a Public Policy Subcommittee (PPS) to discuss UPC issues. It included Joseph Danzansky, chairman of Giant Food, Inc., as well as a representative from the National Consumer League and a labor representative from the industry's Joint Labor-Management Committee. The Severna Park store had opened in January 1975; by March the PPS had commissioned a study of the impact of omitting item pricing on consumer awareness and had published a preliminary study of possible industry responses to negative reaction toward price removal.

In the Maryland Senate, hearings were already underway on a mandatory pricing bill. It was agreed, however, to postpone them until February 1976, when the PPS's study would be completed. Meanwhile, due to the proximity of the action to the nation's capital and its resident advocate groups, the issue caught fire with other consumer organizations and the press. By fall of 1975 a bill mandating item pricing had been introduced in the U.S. Senate.

Meanwhile Giant had been collecting comment cards from its Severna Park store in order to conduct its own assessment of consumer reaction. Opinions represented by the first two months of responses stayed essentially the same throughout the year: 86.5% of shoppers liked the system; 7.8% disliked it; and 5.7% were undecided. 24.7% of all those surveyed still wanted item pricing. In August 1975 Giant had opened a second computerized store in the neighboring town of Glen Burnie, Maryland. In accordance with a promise made after the opening of the Severna Park store to retain item pricing in all other stores until a policy could be made, the Glen Burnie store used the UPC system but retained individually priced items. There it was found, in comparison with the figures from Severna Park, that while 93% of the shoppers liked the system, 32% wanted to keep individual pricing.

Shortly after the opening of Severna Park, in a speech before the Super Market Institute, Mr. Danzansky said:

> There are those who maintain that [the food retailer] is but an extension of the chain of food production, processing and manufacturing. I am among those who believe that the food retailer's function is to serve as the purchasing agent for the customer. The customer is no longer in a position to assess market conditions. . . . It is up to us to be sure that we, on her behalf, purchase good products at the best prices and give her the information she needs to buy intelligently.[2]

In November, before the Subcommittee on the Consumer of the U.S. Senate Commerce Committee, Danzansky urged the Subcommittee to give an unfavorable report on the mandatory pricing bill, arguing that unfavorable reaction was the result of ignorance and fear of novelty. He stressed that Giant had not yet decided what policy to follow in regard to item pricing and stated that the ultimate decision should come from the shoppers. He added that "the government (by aborting Giant's experiment with item price removal) should not deprive the consumer of the right to make that decision."[3] A few weeks later he was echoed by Mrs. Peterson:

> There is no room for debate on whether or not consumers have the right to be informed at the point of purchase about the prices they are paying for items. This is a basic right. . . . I do not believe, however, that we have legislated nor can we effectively legislate the specific manner in which this is done.[4]

[2]Speech given to the Super Market Institute, Washington, D.C., February 28, 1976, p. 1.

[3]*Hearings before the Subcommittee on the Consumer, U.S. Senate Committee on Commerce, on S.997*, "Amending the Fair Packaging and Labeling Act," November 3, 1975, p. 8 of Joseph Danzansky's testimony.

[4]*Ibid.*, November 17, 1975, p. 1 of Esther Peterson's testimony.

In February 1976 they both testified against mandatory item pricing legislation before the Maryland House of Delegates. It was reported then that Giant's actual savings from use of the UPC without item pricing at the Severna Park store amounted to two percent of sales, 11% above the savings that had been anticipated.[5]

Six weeks later the Maryland House passed a mandatory pricemarking bill. Three days thereafter, the Ad Hoc Committee's Public Policy Subcommittee released its study of consumer price awareness in the absence of item pricing. This study had been performed in matching stores, with and without individually priced items. It showed that some shoppers in the stores that omitted the price from individual items did indeed experience significant loss of price awareness. In an accompanying policy statement the Subcommittee said:

> The Public Policy Subcommittee is recommending to the industry that scanner stores follow the same traditional approach to individual item-marking as is used in conventional supermarkets. . . .
>   The Subcommittee believes that creating and maintaining consumer price awareness, while lowering the cost of food, are worthy and complex goals. The concepts and techniques of attaining these goals are far from resolved.[6]

Giant later announced that it would act on the Subcommittee's recommendation; Giant introduced item pricing to the Severna Park store and retained it in all existing and new stores.

In response, the Maryland Senate allowed the mandatory pricing bill to die. The following fall, the United Food and Commercial Workers Union ceased lobbying for item pricing on Capitol Hill, and there too mandatory pricing legislation was dropped. During the 14 months of Giant's experiment at Severna Park, four states—Massachusetts, Rhode Island, Connecticut, and California—had witnessed the successful enactment of mandatory pricing bills, either on the state or local level. Of the 28 states with pending legislation, only two more—New York and Michigan—passed their bills. Local ordinances in Florida were subsequently passed that required individual items to be priced, but no legislation affecting Giant ever passed. Meanwhile the UPC was so universally adopted by the food processing industry that 95–98% of all items came to bear the bar code.

In 1978 Giant had 36 stores using the scanning system and a resulting large data base from which to assess the effectiveness of the UPC system. Giant found that in a store grossing $700,000 monthly, the savings brought about by computer-assisted checkout were $6,634, or

[5]*Hearings before the Maryland Senate, Economic Affairs Committee, on S. 100,* "Pricing of Consumer Commodities," February 2, 1978, p. 3 of Joseph Danzansky's testimony.

[6]Public Policy Subcommittee of the Ad Hoc Committee on the Universal Product Code, *Policy Statement on Item Pricing* (Washington, D.C., March 23, 1976), p. 2.

slightly less than one percent of sales. This was 50% less than the savings experienced at Severna Park when item pricing had been omitted.

Giant subsequently opened a new store in Clinton, Maryland in October 1980. In this store cases of merchandise were set out directly on the shelves, with top and sides removed. While not a so-called "warehouse" store, the number of brands and package sizes available were significantly reduced (up to 50% of the usual selection). To the consternation of the Consumer's Right to Information Committee (CRIC)—a group originally composed of national and local consumer groups and local labor—the individual cans and boxes were not priced and Giant announced plans to continue the practice in its next three stores, scheduled to be opened within a few weeks. After meeting with Giant officials, CRIC expressed deep concern over this renewed threat to consumer price awareness. Giant's answer implied that the new system, including improved shelf labels and lower prices, would help shoppers and would lower their food bills.

The Economic Affairs Committee of the Maryland Senate was not pleased by the news of Giant's efforts. Joseph Danzansky had promised at the time Giant had agreed to follow the PPS's recommendation on item pricing that he would consult with the Committee if Giant should ever reconsider removing item prices. Mr. Danzansky died in 1979, however, and the present Giant officials had failed to communicate their intentions to the Committee. Backed by the Consumer's Right to Information Committee, the senators expressed their displeasure by introducing a bill requiring price tags on all items sold in the state. Local 400 of the United Food and Commercial Workers declined to take a position on the bill, stating only that Giant had failed to show how discontinuation of item pricing would result in labor reductions significant enough to create job losses. The bill ultimately expired.

In April 1981 Giant announced that due to the successful operation of its "no-frills" stores, it was instituting substantially decreased "warehouse prices" on 1,500 to 2,000 items, about 17% of the stock, in *all* its stores. These price reductions would be made possible, Giant officials said, by dropping item pricing entirely—thus producing savings in the labor costs of marking each item individually. Giant did not plan to stop marking prices on all items immediately, but as new stock was placed on the shelves the program would gradually be expanded to include all merchandise. A study done by *Food World,* a publication doing market-share surveys of the grocery industry, showed that during the month of April 1981, Giant's sales increased about 14%, bringing its percentage of the Washington area grocery dollar to $.34 or 7% over Safeway, a national chain and Giant's closest competitor.[7]

[7]*Washington Post,* "Shelf Pricing May Help Giant Food Win Cost War," May 10, 1981, sec. L, p. 1.

While Giant's lowered prices actually resulted in a net loss during the second half of 1981, the demand for scanning systems increased 168% during an 18-month period ending in August 1981, according to *Business Week*. Nearly 4,000 of an estimated 33,000 supermarkets in the United States and Canada employed them by mid-1981.[8] Giant's example and consumer reaction have been watched closely in Washington, where interest has increased markedly among other stores in the Washington-Maryland-Virginia area. In early 1982 twenty of the 125 Safeway stores in the area had scanning systems, and the chain had an additional 48 stores with "intelligent" registers, which are less sophisticated than the computer-linked registers used by Giant. Safeway adopted a no-prices policy in all stores equipped with scanners and hoped to install some type of scanning system in most of its stores as quickly as possible. Giant's customer counts and total sales never decreased throughout the entire period, and in fact showed a steady increase.[9]

[8]*Business Week*, "Supermarket Scanners Get Smarter" (August 17, 1981), p. 88.
[9]According to Mr. Barry F. Scher, Director of Public Affairs for Giant. Private correspondence of April 1, 1982.

Henningsen v. Bloomfield Motors, Inc. and Chrysler Corporation

Claus H. Henningsen purchased a Plymouth automobile, manufactured by defendant Chrysler Corporation, from defendant Bloomfield Motors, Inc. His wife, plaintiff Helen Henningsen, was injured while driving it and instituted suit against both defendants to recover damages on account of her injuries. Her husband joined in the action seeking compensation for his consequential losses. The complaint was predicated upon breach of express and implied warranties and upon negligence. At the trial the negligence counts were dismissed by the court and the case was submitted to the jury for determination solely on the issues of implied warranty of merchantability.* Verdicts were returned against both defendants and in favor of the plaintiffs. Defendants appealed and plaintiffs cross-appealed from the dismissal of their negligence claim. . . .

The purchase order [for the automobile] was a printed form of one page. On the front it contained blanks to be filled in with a description of the automobile to be sold, the various accessories to be included, and the details of the financing. The particular car selected was described as a 1955 Plymouth, Plaza "6", Club Sedan. The type used in the printed parts of the form became smaller in size, different in style, and less readable toward the bottom where the line for the purchaser's signature was placed. The smallest type on the page appears in the two paragraphs, one of two and one-quarter lines and the second of one and one-half lines, on which great stress is laid by the defense in the case. These two paragraphs are the least legible and the most difficult to read in the instrument, but they are most important in the evaluation of the rights of the contesting parties. They do not attract atten-

*["Merchantability": The articles shall be of the kind described and be fit for the purpose for which they were sold. Fitness is impliedly warranted if an item is merchantable. Ed.]

Atlantic Reporter 161 A2d 69, pp. 73–75, 78–81, 83–87, 93–96, 102. This opinion was written by Justice John J. Francis. The case was edited and prepared by Tom L. Beauchamp. **Not to be duplicated without permission of the author and publisher.**

tion and there is nothing about the format which would draw the reader's eye to them. In fact, a studied and concentrated effort would have to be made to read them. De-emphasis seems the motive rather than emphasis. . . . The two paragraphs are:

"The front and back of this Order comprise the entire agreement affecting this purchase and no other agreement or understanding of any nature concerning same has been made or entered into, or will be recognized. I hereby certify that no credit has been extended to me for the purchase of this motor vehicle except as appears in writing on the face of this agreement.

"I have read the matter printed on the back hereof and agree to it as a part of this order the same as if it were printed above my signature. . . ."

The testimony of Claus Henningsen justifies the conclusion that he did not read the two fine print paragraphs referring to the back of the purchase contract. And it is uncontradicted that no one made any reference to them, or called them to his attention. With respect to the matter appearing on the back, it is likewise uncontradicted that he did not read it and that no one called it to his attention.

The reverse side of the contract contains 8½ inches of fine print. It is not as small, however, as the two critical paragraphs described above. The page is headed "Conditions" and contains ten separate paragraphs consisting of 65 lines in all. The paragraphs do not have headnotes or margin notes denoting their particular subject, as in the case of the "Owner Service Certificate" to be referred to later. In the seventh paragraph, about two-thirds of the way down the page, the warranty, which is the focal point of the case, is set forth. It is as follows:

"7. It is expressly agreed that there are no warranties, express or implied, *made* by either the dealer or the manufacturer on the motor vehicle, chassis, of parts furnished hereunder except as follows.

" 'The manufacturer warrants each new motor vehicle (including original equipment placed thereon by the manufacturer except tires), chassis or parts manufactured by it to be free from defects in material or workmanship under normal use and service. Its obligation under this warranty being limited to making good at its factory any part or parts thereof which shall, within ninety (90) days after delivery of such vehicle *to the original purchaser* or before such vehicle has been driven 4,000 miles, whichever event shall first occur, be returned to it with transportation charges prepaid and which its examination shall disclose to its satisfaction to have been thus defective; *this warranty being expressly in lieu of all other warranties expressed or implied, and all other obligations or liabilities on its part,* and it neither assumes nor authorizes any other person to assume for it any other liability in connection with the sale of its vehicles. . . .' " (Emphasis ours) . . .

The new Plymouth was turned over to the Henningsens on May 9, 1955. No proof was adduced by the dealer to show precisely what was done in the way of mechanical or road testing beyond testimony that the manufacturer's instructions were probably followed. Mr. Henningsen drove it from the dealer's place of business in Bloomfield to their home in Keansburg. On the trip nothing unusual appeared in the way in which it operated. Thereafter, it was used for short trips on paved streets about the town. It had no servicing and no mishaps of any kind before the event of May 19. That day, Mrs. Henningsen drove to Asbury Park. On the way down and in returning the car performed in normal fashion until the accident occurred. She was proceeding north on Route 36 in Highlands, New Jersey, at 20–22 miles per hour. The highway was paved and smooth, and contained two lanes for northbound travel. She was riding in the right-hand lane. Suddenly she heard a loud noise "from the bottom, by the hood." It "felt as if something cracked." The steering wheel spun in her hands; the car veered sharply to the right and crashed into a highway sign and a brick wall. No other vehicle was in any way involved. A bus operator driving in the left-hand lane testified that he observed plaintiffs' car approaching in normal fashion in the opposite direction; "all of a sudden [it] veered at 90 degrees . . . and right into this wall." As a result of the impact, the front of the car was so badly damaged that it was impossible to determine if any of the parts of the steering wheel mechanism or workmanship or assembly were defective or improper prior to the accident. The condition was such that the collision insurance carrier, after inspection, declared the vehicle a total loss. It had 468 miles on the speedometer at the time. . . .

The terms of the warranty are a sad commentary upon the automobile manufacturers' marketing practices. Warranties developed in the law in the interest of and to protect the ordinary consumer who cannot be expected to have the knowledge or capacity or even the opportunity to make adequate inspection of mechanical instrumentalities, like automobiles, and to decide for himself whether they are reasonably fit for the designed purpose. . . . But the ingenuity of the Automobile Manufacturers Association, by means of its standardized form, has metamorphosed the warranty into a device to limit the maker's liability. To call it an "equivocal" agreement, as the Minnesota Supreme Court did, is the least that can be said in criticism of it.

The manufacturer agrees to replace defective parts for 90 days after the sale or until the car has been driven 4,000 miles, whichever is first to occur, *if the part is sent to the factory, transportation charges prepaid, and if examination discloses to its satisfaction that the part is defective.* . . .

Chrysler points out that an implied warranty of merchantability is an incident of a contract of sale. It concedes, of course, the making of the

original sale to Bloomfield Motors, Inc., but maintains that this transaction marked the terminal point of its contractual connection with the
car. Then Chrysler urges that since it was not a party to the sale by the
dealer to Henningsen, there is no privity of contract* between it and
the plaintiffs, and the absence of this privity eliminates any such implied warranty.

There is no doubt that under early common-law concepts of contractual liability only those persons who were parties to the bargain could
sue for a breach of it. In more recent times a noticeable disposition has
appeared in a number of jurisdictions to break through the narrow
barrier of privity when dealing with sales of goods in order to give realistic recognition to a universally accepted fact. The fact is that the
dealer and the ordinary buyer do not, and are not expected to, buy
goods, whether they be foodstuffs or automobiles, exclusively for their
own consumption or use. Makers and manufacturers know this and
advertise and market their products on that assumption; witness, the
"family" car, the baby foods, etc. The limitations of privity in contracts
for the sale of goods developed their place in the law when marketing
conditions were simple, when maker and buyer frequently met face to
face on an equal bargaining plane and when many of the products
were relatively uncomplicated and conducive to inspection by a buyer
competent to evaluate their quality. With the advent of mass marketing, the manufacturer became remote from the purchaser, sales were
accomplished through intermediaries, and the demand for the product
was created by advertising media. In such an economy it became obvious that the consumer was the person being cultivated. Manifestly,
the connotation of "consumer" was broader than that of "buyer." He
signified such a person who, in the reasonable contemplation of the
parties to the sale, might be expected to use the product. Thus, where
the commodities sold are such that if defectively manufactured they
will be dangerous to life or limb, then society's interests can only be
protected by eliminating the requirement of privity between the maker
and his dealers and the reasonably expected ultimate consumer. In
that way the burden of losses consequent upon use of defective articles
is borne by those who are in a position to either control the danger or
make an equitable distribution of the losses when they do occur. . . .

Under modern conditions the ordinary layman, on responding to
the importuning of colorful advertising, has neither the opportunity
nor the capacity to inspect or to determine the fitness of an automobile
for use; he must rely on the manufacturer who has control of its con-

*["Privity of contract": A contractual relation actually existing between the parties. A
partaker having an interest is a privy. Ed.]

struction, and to some degree on the dealer who, to the limited extent called for by the manufacturer's instructions, inspects and services it before delivery. In such a marketing milieu his remedies and those of persons who properly claim through him should not depend "upon the intricacies of the law of sales. The obligation of the manufacturer should not be based alone on privity of contract. It should rest, as was once said, upon 'the demands of social justice.' " . . .

In a society such as ours, where the automobile is a common and necessary adjunct of daily life, and where its use is so fraught with danger to the driver, passengers, and the public, the manufacturer is under a special obligation in connection with the construction, promotion, and sale of his cars. Consequently, the courts must examine purchase agreements closely to see if consumer and public interests are treated fairly. . . .

What influence should these circumstances have on the restrictive effect of Chrysler's express warranty in the framework of the purchase contract? As we have said, warranties originated in the law to safeguard the buyer and not to limit the liability of the seller or manufacturer. It seems obvious in this instance that the motive was to avoid the warranty obligations which are normally incidental to such sales. The language gave little and withdrew much. In return for the delusive remedy of replacement of defective parts at the factory, the buyer is said to have accepted the exclusion of the maker's liability for personal injuries arising from the breach of the warranty, and to have agreed to the elimination of any other express or implied warranty. An instinctively felt sense of justice cries out against such a sharp bargain. But does the doctrine that a person is bound by his signed agreement, in the absence of fraud, stand in the way of any relief? . . .

The traditional contract is the result of free bargaining of parties who are brought together by the play of the market, and who meet each other on a footing of approximate economic equality. In such a society there is no danger that freedom of contract will be a threat to the social order as a whole. But in present-day commercial life the standardized mass contract has appeared. It is used primarily by enterprises with strong bargaining power and position. . . .

The warranty before us is a standardized form designed for mass use. It is imposed upon the automobile consumer. He takes it or leaves it, and he must take it to buy an automobile. No bargaining is engaged in with respect to it. In fact, the dealer through whom it comes to the buyer is without authority to alter it; his function is ministerial—simply to deliver it. The form warranty is not only standard with Chrysler but, as mentioned above, it is the uniform warranty of the Automobile Manufacturers Association. Members of the Association are: General

Motors, Inc., Ford, Chrysler, Studebaker-Packard, American Motors (Rambler), Willys Motors, Checker Motors Corp., and International Harvester Company.[1] Of these companies, the "Big Three" (General Motors, Ford, and Chrysler) represented 93.5% of the passenger-car production for 1958 and the independents 6.5%.[2] And for the same year the "Big Three" had 86.72% of the total passenger vehicle registrations. . . .

In the context of this warranty, only the abandonment of all sense of justice would permit us to hold that, as a matter of law, the phrase "its obligation under this warranty being limited to making good at its factory any part or parts thereof" signifies to an ordinary reasonable person that he is relinquishing any personal injury claim that might flow from the use of a defective automobile. Such claims are nowhere mentioned. . . .

In the matter of warranties on the sale of their products, the Automobile Manufacturers Association has enabled them to present a united front. From the standpoint of the purchaser, there can be no arms length negotiating on the subject. Because his capacity for bargaining is so grossly unequal, the inexorable conclusion which follows is that he is not permitted to bargain at all. He must take or leave the automobile on the warranty terms dictated by the maker. He cannot turn to a competitor for better security.

Public policy is a term not easily defined. Its significance varies as the habits and needs of a people may vary. It is not static and the field of application is an ever increasing one. A contract, or a particular provision therein, valid in one era may be wholly opposed to the public policy of another. Courts keep in mind the principle that the best interests of society demand that persons should not be unnecessarily restricted in their freedom to contract. But they do not hesitate to declare void as against public policy contractual provisions which clearly tend to the injury of the public in some way. . . .

In the framework of this case, illuminated as it is by the facts and the many decisions noted, we are of the opinion that Chrysler's attempted disclaimer of an implied warranty of the merchantability and of the obligations arising therefrom is so inimical to the public good as to compel an adjudication of its invalidity. . . .

The principles that have been expounded as to the obligation of the manufacturer apply with equal force to the separate express warranty of the dealer. This is so, irrespective of the absence of the relationship of principle and agent between these defendants, because the manu-

[1]*Automobile Facts and Figures* (Automobile Manufacturers Association, 1958), p. 69.

[2]Standard and Poor (Industrial Surveys, Autos, Basic Analysis, June 25, 1959), p. 4109.

facturer and the Association establish the warranty policy for the industry. The bargaining position of the dealer is inextricably bound by practice to that of the maker and the purchaser must take or leave the automobile, accompanied and encumbered as it is by the uniform warranty. . . .

Under all of the circumstances outlined above, the judgments in favor of the plaintiffs and against the defendants are affirmed.

chapter 3

The Environment

INTRODUCTION   Much discussion about the environmental responsibility of corporations has emerged in the past two decades. There is now a widespread consensus that environmental problems, whether caused by business or not, are of critical importance. However, no comparable consensus has emerged regarding the proper lines of responsibility for cleaning up and protecting the environment. The multiple possible sources of responsibility and the seriousness of the threat to the environment and ultimately to human and animal health are the subjects of this chapter.

Because environmental issues have only recently come to prominence, it is commonly presumed that contemporary environmental problems are novel and without lengthy historical precedent. In fact, environmental problems have a long history. In the eighteenth century in English courts of common law and equity, numerous cases were brought by individuals who sought to be compensated for the costs of pollution by various businesses. Indeed, as early as 1273, the burning of coal was legally prohibited in certain English jurisdictions on grounds of harm to the public health—precisely the issue in the Acid Rain case in this chapter. Of course, early cases are only precedent models, and it is fair to say that recent cases before courts involving industrial discharge, the use of asbestos, hazardous waste disposal, and the like are largely unprecedented. Millions of dollars are now at stake in the courts (in the effort to secure compensation for harms), and society is confronted with anticipated and sometimes tragic tradeoffs—including tradeoffs between the health of workers and the economic health of corporations. The Reserve Mining and Love Canal cases in this chapter are clear instances.

In one of the most famous law cases in the history of United States courts (*U.S.A.* v. *Allied Chemical*), Judge Robert R. Merhige of Richmond, Virginia stringently penalized the Allied Chemical Corporation in 1976 for the environmental pollution of a river. This case is somewhat one-sided and for this reason is not included among the cases in this chapter. Nonetheless, the case has become symbolic of the struggle between environmentalists and business interests, and so deserves at least brief mention.

In the case, Allied and five of its employees were indicted on 153 charges of conspiracy to defraud the Environmental Protection Agency and the Army Corps of Engineers in their efforts to enforce water pollution control laws. Allied denied all charges, saying the indictments displayed an "extreme reaction" by public officials. However, Allied pleaded *nolo contendere* (no contest to the charges). Judge Merhige fined Allied $13.2 million, but later reduced the fine to $5 million because Allied put $8 million into a fund set up to relieve suffering that resulted from its pollution. This fine is the largest ever imposed in an environmental case, but the indictments were also the most ever returned in a single environmental case. In his ruling he argues the utilitarian thesis that corporations will "think several times before anything such as this happens again." But he also argues what would be construed by many in the business community as an unacceptable non-utilitarian thesis: "I don't think that commercial products or the making of profits are as important as the God-given resources of our country." He then goes on to advance the striking thesis that we are all collectively responsible for what happened in this case because we tolerate too much environmental pollution in contemporary society. This important judicial ruling, as we might expect, has been severely criticized by representatives of the business community.

The quality of air, water, food, and health are of course at the center of all discussions about the environment, "the public interest," and the interests of businesses. Innumerable issues fall under this general description. For example, since 1960 the United States Congress has enacted over twenty-five major pieces of legislation dealing with the control of toxic substances alone. Legislative documents are vague, broadly worded pronouncements that direct federal agencies to act "in the public interest" or "to protect the public health." The agencies are chartered to regulate business by deciding which chemicals should be regulated and what the standards of discharge, dose level, and the like should be. Many value judgments must be made as to "reasonable" levels of discharge and "dangers" to human health. In addition to the cases in this chapter, the Reserve Mining and OSHA-Benzene cases in Chapter 5 involve paradigmatic examples of such judgments.

Environmental problems do not always involve the public interest in conflict with the interests of business. Sometimes environmental problems involve the interests of one business in conflict with another. Thus, a fishing industry may be crippled by the airborne or waterborne discharges of chemical industries or factories—as the Acid Rain case illustrates. Naturalists' interests in species or wilderness preservation may also conflict with the ambitions of business. All such conflicts call for balancing considerations that fairly take into account the different interests of disputing parties. They also call for difficult judgments about the extent to which business or government can be trusted in taking the most reasonable course of action. The Reserve Mining case reflects problems of both balancing interests and making discretionary judgments.

One hotly contested issue at the present time is whether businesses and other responsible parties have obligations to natural objects, or at least to certain forms of animal life. It has been argued that various forms of nonhuman life deserve the same general legal and moral protections afforded humans. For example, various forms of poisoning, slaughtering, and trapping animals without consideration for "humane methods" and without formal penalty have been denounced by animal protection leagues as barbaric. Others have argued that plant life too deserves protection—and not simply because it is in the interests of humans to protect it, but because endangered species and wilderness areas inherently deserve protection. This is not merely a debate over whose interests are to count, and how heavily they are to count (if at all); it is also a debate over the worth of nonhuman life. The Acid Rain, Optical Distortion, and Cosmetics Industry cases in this chapter all incorporate some dimension of this problem.

The Optical Distortion and Cosmetics Industry cases would be described in some contemporary literatures as "animal rights" cases. Animals, as well as creatures lower on the phylogenetic scale, are obviously more convenient to use for purposes of research and labor than are humans—not to mention their ready availability as a food source. Research involving the use of animals and various techniques of raising animals for food have gone largely unchallenged in the past, but critics recently have argued that the time has come to challenge conventional uses of animals. They argue that animal life deserves protection against various methods of research, production, and slaughter. What is the relevant difference, critics ask, distinguishing the life of a human infant from the life of an adult chimpanzee so that infants are protected in ways that chimpanzees are not? What justifies the food and research industries in treating animals in ways they would never treat humans? The challenge presented by these questions is to find some morally relevant property of human beings that will justify restricting the protections afforded by principles of the "sanctity of life" to *human* life. This issue appears in a chapter on the environment, because "animal life" is understood here (by definition) as a part of the living environment. The issues in the final three cases in this chapter are ones of the protection of the "environment" in this broad sense.

In addition to considerations of whose interests are to count, important problems have arisen as to where the burden of proof rests in environmental matters. Most major controversies about the environment involve considerable uncertainty about the extent to which a chemical discharge, storage procedure, and the like present a threat to humans or nonhuman life. Is the burden of proof on industry or on the regulatory agencies of government to prove that a product or practice is safe or harmful? If this determination can be made, who should be responsible for taking steps to remove the problem—especially when no one was aware until recently that a problem exists? How is possible future harm to the environment to be weighed and balanced against the economic harms of tighter regulation of business? These issues are especially prominent in the Reserve Mining, Love Canal, and Acid Rain cases.

Reserve Mining's Silver Bay Facility

Since 1950, the Reserve Mining Company has been a jointly owned subsidiary of Armco Steel Corporation and Republic Steel Corporation. Reserve Mining was formed in 1939, on behalf of four steel firms, for the purpose of mining and beneficiating (crushing to free magnetic particles) taconite (low-grade iron ore). It was called "Reserve" because the iron ore was then considered a long-term investment needing new technology to be processed efficiently. In an expensive and innovative move, the Reserve Mining Company decided in 1944 to locate its prospective beneficiating plant on Lake Superior, and so began to acquire the land in 1945. This great body of water was considered essential because large amounts of water are needed for the processing. The taconite must be crushed into fine granules, the metallic iron separated through magnetic forces and collected into "pellets," and the residue flushed back into the water.

After nine hearings in Duluth, St. Paul, and Silver Bay, the state of Minnesota issued the necessary environmental permits in 1947, and in 1948 the U.S. Army Corps of Engineers granted Reserve a permit to construct harbor facilities that called for depositing tailings (the residue waste product) in Lake Superior. The taconite was to be mined near Babbitt, Minnesota and then shipped by rail approximately 45 miles to the beneficiating plant on the northwest shore of Lake Superior. Both the tax laws in Minnesota and mining technology had improved dramatically, to the point that efficient mining and beneficiating were by then possible. Work began on the Lake Superior facility in 1951, and full operations commenced at the plant in 1955.

The town of Silver Bay was built especially for these mining operations. Soon thereafter 80 percent of the 3,000 inhabitants of Silver Bay were employed by Reserve, and the total taconite work force in the state grew to 9,000. So successful was the operation that between 1956–60 Reserve sought and received permission for substantially increased

This case was prepared by Tom L. Beauchamp. **Not to be duplicated without permission of the author and publisher.**

production and corresponding discharges into Lake Superior. A final modest increase in production level was achieved in 1965. This increase brought Reserve's annual production capacity to 10.7 million tons of pellets. To achieve this level of production, Reserve dumped 67,000 tons of waste material into Lake Superior each day. The state had approved such discharges under the assumption they would sink and remain forever at the bottom of the lake.[1]

The basic technology at the facility has been summarized as follows by Professor Presson S. Shane of the George Washington University School of Business:

> Taconite is a hard, gray rock in which are found particles of magnetite, a black oxide of iron which is magnetic and has the approximate oxygen content designated as Fe_3O_4. The deposits of taconite near Babbitt, Minnesota, are sufficiently near the surface to permit their being taken from open pits. The taconite is crushed to a nominal 4 inch size and hauled along the Reserve railroad line to Silver Bay at a rate of about 90,000 tons per day.
>
> At Silver Bay the crushing operation is continued in order to free the particles of iron oxide for recovery and molding into pellets. A series of crushers, rod mills, ball mills, and magnetic separators are operated in processing the water slurry of ore. Two million tons of water are taken from Lake Superior each day (and returned) in the processing. The low-iron tailings are discharged back into the lake in the direction of a trough about 500-feet deep a few miles offshore. The discharge stream comprises the tailings, and the finest fraction, about 1½ percent solids, forms a dense current which flows toward the bottom of the lake. The magnetically recovered particles are the concentrate which is compressed to a cake with 10 percent moisture. It is then mixed with bentonite, which is a cohesive agent, and rolled into green pellets about ⅜ inches in diameter. The pellets are hardened by heating to 2350°F and are then ready for loading into ore boats at Silver Bay for the trip to the blast furnaces in Cleveland, Youngstown, Ashland, etc.[2]

Environmental questions about Reserve's discharges were publicized in 1963, when U.S. Senator Gaylord Nelson of Wisconsin investigated the possibility of water pollution violations. Various forms of new environmental legislation were passed in the next few years, and by 1968 concerns were being expressed about Lake Superior by Senator Nelson, a "Taconite Study Group," and then Secretary of the Interior Stewart Udall. A "Save Lake Superior Association" was founded in 1969. In 1971–72 the Environmental Protection Agency, the U.S. Jus-

---

[1]Points of early history mentioned in this case rely on E. W. Davis, *Pioneering with Taconite* (St. Paul: Minnesota Historical Society, 1964). Points of later history often depend upon Robert V. Bartlett, *The Reserve Mining Controversy* (Bloomington: Indiana University Press, 1980), and on a telephone conversation with Professor Bartlett in April, 1982.

[2]Presson S. Shane, "Silver Bay: Reserve Mining Company" (1973). Reprinted by permission of Professor Shane.

tice Department, and the Minnesota Pollution Control Agency all charged Reserve with violations of the Federal Pollution Control Act. The argument was that plant discharges of mineral fibers into the air and the water can be hazardous to health and can endanger drinking water supplies. Similar fibers were known to cause asbestosis, mesothelioma, and various cancers. Concerns in the past had been dominantly about water pollution—including effects on fish life and the water supply—but as the issues entered the courts, the focus of the case quickly shifted to threats to human health.

In 1973 a United States District Court in Minnesota entered an order closing Reserve's Silver Bay facility on grounds that it was discharging dustlike asbestiform (asbestos-like) particles into both the air and the water at great threat to human health. Asbestos workers had been shown to be highly vulnerable to cancer when they inhaled the product. Some 200,000 persons drank the water from Lake Superior, and many more might potentially be affected by airborne fibers. Reserve appealed to the Eighth Circuit Court of Appeals, where Judge Myron H. Bright summarized the situation as follows in an extremely influential opinion delivered on June 4, 1974 (139 days had been spent in the courtroom, and over 100 witnesses and 1620 exhibits had been considered):

> Although there is no dispute that significant amounts of waste tailings are discharged into the water and dust is discharged into the air by Reserve, the parties vigorously contest the precise nature of the discharge, its biological effects, and, particularly with respect to the waters of Lake Superior, its ultimate destination. . . .
>
> The suggestion that particles of the cummingtonite-grunerite in Reserve's discharges are the equivalent of amosite asbestos raised an immediate health issue, since inhalation of amosite asbestos at occupational levels of exposure is a demonstrated health hazard resulting in asbestosis and various forms of cancer. However, the proof of a health hazard requires more than the mere fact of discharge; the discharge of an agent hazardous in one circumstance must be linked to some present or future likelihood of disease under the prevailing circumstances. An extraordinary amount of testimony was received on these issues. . . .
>
> The theory by which plaintiffs argue that the discharges present a substantial danger is founded largely upon epidemiological studies of asbestos workers occupationally exposed to and inhaling high levels of asbestos dust. A study by Dr. Selikoff of workers at a New Jersey asbestos manufacturing plant demonstrated that occupational exposure to amosite asbestos poses a hazard of increased incidence of asbestosis and various forms of cancer. Similar studies in other occupational contexts leave no doubt that asbestos, at sufficiently high dosages, is injurious to health. However, in order to draw the conclusion that environmental exposure to Reserve's discharges presents a health threat in the instant case, it must be shown either that the circumstances of exposure are at least comparable to those in occupational settings, or, alternatively, that the

occupational studies establish certain principles of asbestos-disease pathology which may be applied to predicting the occurrence of such disease in altered circumstances.

Initially, it must be observed that environmental exposure from Reserve's discharges into air and water is simply not comparable to that typical of occupational settings. The occupational studies involve direct exposure to and inhalation of asbestos dust in high concentrations and in confined spaces. This pattern of exposure cannot be equated with the discharge into the outside air of relatively low levels of asbestos fibers. . . .

. . . In order to make a prediction, based on the occupational studies, as to the likelihood of disease at lower levels of exposure, at least two key findings must be made. First, an attempt must be made to determine, with some precision, what that lower level of exposure is. Second, that lower level of exposure must be applied to the known pathology of asbestos-induced disease, i.e., it must be determined whether the level of exposure is safe or unsafe.

Unfortunately, the testimony of Dr. Arnold Brown indicates that neither of these key determinations can be made. Dr. Brown testified that, with respect to both air and water, the level of fibers is not readily susceptible of measurement. This results from the relatively imprecise state of counting techniques and the wide margins of error which necessarily result, and is reflected in the widely divergent sample counts received by the court. . . .

Even assuming that one could avoid imprecision and uncertainty in measuring the number of fibers at low levels, there remains vast uncertainty as to the medical consequences of low levels of exposure to asbestos fibers. . . .

. . . In commenting on the statement, "This suggests that there are levels of asbestos exposure that will not be associated with any detectable risk," Dr. Brown stated:

> As a generalization, yes, I agree to that. But I must reiterate my view that I do not know what that level is. . . .

A fair review of this impartial testimony by the court's own witnesses—to which we necessarily must give great weight at this interim stage of review—clearly suggests that the discharges by Reserve can be characterized only as presenting an unquantifiable risk, i.e., a health risk which either may be negligible or may be significant, but with any significance as yet based on unknowns. . . .[3]

The Court's reluctance to pronounce an actual health hazard—or even attempt to quantify it—was a victory for Reserve, although the court went on to suggest that better air control and the "termination of Reserve's discharges into Lake Superior" should take place as quickly as possible. Judge Bright, speaking for the Court, then granted Reserve a 70-day stay of Judge Lord's order on the condition that Reserve submit an adequate pollution-control plan. During this 70-day

[3]498 F.2d 1073 (1974).

period Reserve jostled still further with Judge Lord, who in August 1974, declared a new Reserve disposal plan environmentally inadequate. Reserve then asked the Eighth Circuit Court of Appeals for an extended stay, which was granted; but the judges who heard the application for a stay warned Reserve that they must continue work underway on development of alternate disposal sites.

Reserve quickly announced plans for an on-land disposal facility to be called "Mile Post 7." Reserve applied to the state of Minnesota to construct this new facility; however, the state was displeased with these plans, and negotiations were undertaken. On April 8, 1975, the Eighth Circuit Court of Appeals handed down its much anticipated "final" decision on the merits of Judge Lord's order and on Reserve's responsibilities. The key parts of this decision, which to many were surprising, read as follows:

> As will be evident from the discussion that follows, we adhere to our preliminary assessment that the evidence is insufficient to support the kind of demonstrable danger to the public health that would justify the immediate closing of Reserve's operations. We now address the basic question of whether the discharges pose any risk to public health and, if so, whether the risk is one which is legally cognizable. . . .
>
> Plaintiffs' hypothesis that Reserve's air emissions represent a significant threat to the public health touches numerous scientific disciplines, and an overall evaluation demands broad scientific understanding. We think it significant that Dr. Brown, an impartial witness whose court-appointed task was to address the health issue in its entirety, joined with plaintiffs' witnesses in viewing as reasonable the hypothesis that Reserve's discharges present a threat to public health. Although, as we noted in our stay opinion, Dr. Brown found the evidence insufficient to make a scientific probability statement as to whether adverse health consequences would in fact ensue, he expressed a public health concern over the continued long-term emission of fibers into the air. . . .
>
> The . . . discussion of the evidence demonstrates that the medical and scientific conclusions here in dispute clearly lie "on the frontiers of scientific knowledge.". . .
>
> As we have demonstrated, Reserve's air and water discharges pose a danger to the public health and justify judicial action of a preventive nature.
>
> In fashioning relief in a case such as this involving a possibility of future harm, a court should strike a proper balance between the benefits conferred and the hazards created by Reserve's facility.
>
> Reserve must be given a reasonable opportunity and a reasonable time to construct facilities to accomplish an abatement of its pollution of air and water and the health risk created thereby. In this way, hardship to employees and great economic loss incident to an immediate plant closing may be avoided. . . .
>
> We cannot ignore, however, the potential for harm in Reserve's discharges. This potential imparts a degree of urgency to this case that would otherwise be absent from an environmental suit in which ecological pollution alone were proved. Thus, any authorization of Reserve to

continue operations during conversion of its facilities to abate the pollution must be circumscribed by realistic time limitations. . . .[4]

In all essentials, Judge Bright and his colleagues on the Court of Appeals had reversed their earlier views, now holding that Reserve's water and air discharges *did* create a major public health threat and that the courts need not shy away from decisions in the face of scientific uncertainties. (The judges shrouded their apparent reversal in some legal technicalities.)[5]

For several years after this decision, various courts witnessed arguments to show whether, as the Court of Appeals put it, "the probability of harm is more likely than not." Neither side succeeded in providing definitive scientific evidence, and the focus of the controversy shifted to the problem of finding a satisfactory on-land disposal site. A major battle erupted over Mile Post 7. Reserve was given heart when Judge Lord was removed from the case by the Eighth Circuit, which cited Lord's bias against Reserve. Lord's replacement, however, quickly fined Reserve almost $1,000,000 for past violations, and the search for a proper on-land site continued in and out of the courtroom. The state preferred an alternative to Mile Post 7, known as Mile Post 20. Reserve complained bitterly about the costs that would be involved in constructing on this site, and disputed with the state as to whether financing would be possible. (Their separate cost estimates varied by $50–60 million.)

Every health issue mentioned above, and new ones as well, remained in dispute, and each side won several major victories in the courts. Reserve repeatedly threatened to close down permanently its Silver Bay facility in the face of costs imposed by courts and the state. Finally, a bargain was struck: On July 7, 1978, Reserve agreed both to build the new facility at Mile Post 7 and to satisfy stringent conditions the state insisted upon for approval of the permits. The total investment in the new facility was set at $370 million. The facility would by itself contain one of the largest and most expensive pollution control programs in the world. The company agreed to stop all discharges into Lake Superior by April 15, 1980. It faithfully carried out this promise and the new facility began operations in August 1980.

Several scientific studies of health hazards had been completed by July 1978, and subsequent studies were also eventually completed. These studies, several of which were sponsored by Reserve, have not

[4]*514 Federal Reporter*, 2d Series, 492 (1975).

[5]A useful analysis of this second decision is found in William A. Thomas, "Judicial Treatment of Scientific Uncertainty in the *Reserve Mining* Case," *Proceedings of the Fourth Symposium on Statistics and the Environment* (Washington, D.C.: American Statistical Association, 1977), pp. 1–13.

shown any significant increase in disease related to asbestos in the region or in workers at the plant. Studies have not even shown a build-up of asbestiform bodies in lung tissue (of sufficient size to be detected), or in the bloodstream, among persons drinking the water from Lake Superior. Reserve's work force has not shown a significant outbreak of asbestosis or any similarly caused disease. Reserve claims that it has yet to see even a single dust-related disease in one of its employees.[6] In mid-1982 still further studies had been undertaken. On the other hand, Reserve's case clearly rests on arguments showing a *lack* of clear-cut evidence. Just as government officials have never been able to show any increased incidence of disease as a result of the Silver Bay facility, so Reserve has no way of showing that there will not be latent and serious long-term effects in 15–20 years—as is commonly the case with asbestos-caused diseases.

[6]Bartlett, *The Reserve Mining Controversy*, p. 209.

Hooker Chemical and Love Canal

> Today the Love Canal area of Niagara Falls looks like a war zone. The 235 houses nearest the landfill are boarded up and empty, surrounded by an 8-foot-high cyclone fence that keeps tourists and looters away. Still other houses outside the fenced area are also boarded up and deserted, their owners having fled the unknown. Here and there throughout the neighborhood, newly erected green signs mark the pickup points for emergency evacuation in case there is a sudden release of toxins. An ambulance and a fire truck stand by in the area as workers struggle to seal off the flow of chemicals and render the area once again safe—if not exactly habitable.[1]

What is Love Canal? How did this desolation occur? Who, if anyone, is responsible?

Love Canal is named for William T. Love, a businessman and visionary who in the late nineteenth century attempted to create a model industrial city near Niagara Falls. Love proposed to build a canal that would figure in the generation and transmission of hydroelectric power from the falls to the city's industries. An economic recession that made financing difficult and the development of cheaper methods of transmitting electricity dampened Love's vision, and the partially dug canal in what is now the southeast corner of the city of Niagara Falls is the sole tangible legacy of the project.

However, industry was still drawn to the area, which provided easy access to transportation, cheap electricity, and abundant water for industrial processes. Several chemical companies were among those who took advantage of the natural resources. The Hooker Electrochemical Company, now Hooker Chemical and a major figure in the later events at Love Canal, built its first plant in the area in 1905. Presently a subsidiary of Occidental Petroleum, Hooker manufactures plastics, pesti-

[1]Thomas H. Maugh, II, "Toxic Waste Disposal a Gnawing Problem," *Science* **204** (May 1979), p. 820.

This case was prepared by Martha W. Elliott and Tom L. Beauchamp. **Not to be duplicated without the permission of the authors and publisher.**

cides, chlorine, caustic soda, fertilizers, and a variety of other chemical products. With over 3,000 employees, Hooker is still one of the largest employers and an economic force in the Niagara Falls area.[2]

In the early 1940s the abandoned section of Love Canal—for many years a summer swimming hole—became a dump for barrels of waste materials produced by the various chemical companies. Hooker received permission in 1942 to use the site for chemical dumping. It is estimated (though no accurate records were kept) that between the early dumping period and 1953, when this tract of land was sold, approximately 21,800 tons of many different kinds of chemical wastes—some extremely toxic—were put into the old canal. The chemicals were in drums, which were eventually covered with clay-like materials—a reasonable maneuver at the time, since the site was ideal for chemical dumping. It was in an undeveloped and largely unpopulated area and had highly impermeable clay walls that retained liquid chemical materials with virtually no penetration at all. Research indicated that the canal's walls permitted water penetration at the rate of ⅓ of an inch over a 25-year period.

In 1947 Hooker purchased the Love Canal site from Niagara Power and Development Company. In 1953 the dump was closed and covered with an impermeable clay top. The land encompassing and surrounding the dump was acquired by the Niagara Falls School Board. This acquisition was against the advice of Hooker, which had warned of the toxic wastes. However, the Board persisted and started condemnation proceedings to acquire land in the area. Subsequently an elementary school and a tract of houses were built adjacent to the site. Thousands of cubic yards of soil were removed from the top of the canal in the process. This series of developments set the stage for the desolate scene described in the opening quotation. Apparently, the construction damaged the integrity of the clay covering. Water from rains and heavy snows then seeped through the covering and entered the chemical-filled, clay-lined basin. Eventually the basin overflowed on the unfortunate residents, who were treated to the noxious smell and unwholesome sight of chemicals seeping into their basements and surfacing to the ground.

In April of 1978 evidence of toxic chemicals was found in the living area of several homes and the state health commissioner ordered an investigation. A number of health hazards came to light. Many of the adults examined showed incipient liver damage; young women in certain areas experienced three times the normal incidence of miscarriages; and the area had 3.5 times the normal incidence of birth de-

[2]John F. Steiner, "Love can be Dangerous to your Health," in George A. Steiner and John F. Steiner, *Casebook for Business, Government and Society,* 2nd ed. (New York: Random House, Business Division, 1980), pp. 108–109.

fects. Epilepsy, suicide, rectal bleeding, hyperactivity, and a variety of other ills were also reported.

Upon review of these findings, the health commissioner recommended that the elementary school be temporarily closed and that pregnant women and children under the age of two be temporarily evacuated. Shortly thereafter the Governor of New York announced that the state would purchase the 235 houses nearest the canal and would assist in the relocation of dispossessed families. President Carter declared Love Canal a disaster area, qualifying the affected families for federal assistance.[3] However, families in the adjacent ring of houses were not able to move—although they firmly believed that their health was endangered. Early studies tended to confirm this view, but in mid-July, 1982, EPA released a study that concluded there was "no evidence that Love Canal has contributed to environmental contamination" in the outer ring of 400 homes. However, this report was on "health hazards" and did not address symptoms of stress that have been noted: For example, the divorce rate among remaining families increased as wives and children fled, while husbands tried to hold onto their investments: their houses and jobs.[4]

Since the investigation first began more than 100 different chemicals, some of them mutagens, teratogens, or carcinogens, have been identified. A number of unanswered questions are still being probed. One question has to do with the long range effects of chemical exposure. Cancer, for instance, often doesn't develop for 20 to 25 years after exposure to the cancer-producing agent. Chromosomal damage may appear only in subsequent generations. Other unanswered questions involve determining how to clean up the "mess" and who should be held responsible for it.

Hooker Chemical Company figures in both of these questions. In 1977 the city of Niagara Falls employed an engineering consulting firm to study Love Canal and make recommendations. Hooker supplied technical assistance, information, and personnel. The cost of a second study was shared equally by Hooker, the city, and the school board, which had originally purchased the land from Hooker. Hooker also offered to pay one-third of the estimated $850,000 cost of clean-up.[5]

In 1980 Hooker was faced with over $2 billion in lawsuits stemming from its activities at Love Canal and other locations. Thirteen-hundred

[3]Maugh, "Toxic Waste Disposal."

[4]Constance Holden, "Love Canal Residents Under Stress," *Science* **208** (June 13, 1980), pp. 1242–1244. "Some Love Canal Areas Safe, A New EPA Study Concludes." *The Washington Post*, July 15, 1982. Sec. A, pp. 1, 9 (Byline: Sandra Sugawara). See also Beverly Paigen below on the earlier data.

[5]Steiner, "Love can be Dangerous," p. 112.

private suits had been filed against Hooker by mid-1982. The additional complaints and suits stemmed from past and current activities in other states as well as from additional sites in New York. In addition, in 1976 suits of more than $100 million were filed by Virginia employees of Life Sciences who had been exposed to Kepone, a highly toxic chemical known to cause trembling and sterility in humans. Hooker was named in the suit as a supplier of some of the raw materials used in the Virginia manufacturing process. (This suit was ultimately settled out of court.) In 1977 Hooker was ordered to pay $176,000 for discharging HCCPD, a chemical used in the manufacture of Kepone and Mirex, which causes cancer in laboratory animals, into White Lake. In 1979 Michigan officials sued Hooker for a $200 million cleanup due to air, water, and land pollution around its White Lake plant. Hooker in 1978 acknowledged that it had buried an estimated 3,700 tons of trichlorophenol waste—which includes some quantities of the potent chemical dioxin—at various sites aound Niagara Falls from 1942–1972.[6]

At the same time that Hooker was defending itself in Virginia and Michigan, the state of California was investigating the company and ultimately brought suit on charges that Hooker's Occidental Chemical Plant at Lathrop, California had for years violated state law by dumping toxic pesticides, thereby polluting nearby ground water. While Hooker officials denied the charges, a series of memos written by Robert Edson, Occidental's environmental engineer at Lathrop, suggests the company knew of the hazard as early as 1975 but chose to ignore it until pressured by the state investigation. In April 1975 Edson wrote, "Our laboratory records indicate that we are slowly contaminating all wells in our area, and two of our own wells are contaminated to the point of being toxic to animals or humans. . . ." A year later he wrote, "To date, we have been discharging waste water . . . containing about five tons of pesticide per year to the ground. . . . I believe we have fooled around long enough and already over-pressed our luck." Another year later, Edson reiterated his charges and added that "if anyone should complain, we could be the party named in an action by the Water Quality Control Board. . . . Do we correct the situation before we have a problem or do we hold off until action is taken against us?"[7]

Other complaints stemmed from the same general area as Love Canal. In 1976 the New York Department of Environmental Conser-

[6]Michael H. Brown, "Love Canal, U.S.A.," *New York Times Magazine* (January 21, 1979), p. 23, passim; and Gary Whitney, "Hooker Chemical and Plastics" (HBS Case Services, Harvard Business School, 1979), p. 3.

[7]"The Hooker Memos," in Robert J. Baum, ed., *Ethical Problems in Engineering*, 2nd ed. (Troy, N.Y.: Center for the Study of the Human Dimensions of Science and Technology, Rensselaer Polytechnic Institute, 1980), Vol. 2: Cases, p. 38; and "An Occidental Unit Knowingly Polluted California Water, House Panel Charges," *The Wall Street Journal*, June 20, 1979, p. 14.

vation banned consumption of seven species of fish taken from Lake Ontario claiming that they were contaminated with chemicals, including Mirex. It was alleged that Mirex had been discharged from the Hooker Niagara Falls plant. A Hooker-sponsored study of Lake Ontario fish disputed this allegation of Mirex contamination. While this study has not been accepted by the state, the ban has, for the most part, been lifted.

Hooker's Hyde Park chemical waste dump, located in the Niagara Falls area, has also been a source of continuing concern and dispute to residents and government officials. In 1972 the manager of a plant adjacent to the dump complained to Hooker about "an extremely dangerous condition affecting our plant and employees . . . our midnight shift workers has [sic] complained of coughing and sore throats from the obnoxious and corrosive permeating fumes from the disposal site."[8] Apparently the "dangerous condition" was not adequately rectified, and in 1979 Hooker's Hyde Park landfill became the subject of a nearly $26 million suit filed by the town of Niagara. New York State filed a suit for more than $200 million for alleged damages at the Hyde Park site. A remedial program agreement, signed by the state, entailed an estimated $16 million in proposed work at this site.

In 1980 Hooker was also faced with four additional suits for $124.5 million in remedial work by the Environmental Protection Agency. Barbara Blum, EPA Deputy Administrator, explains the EPA concern and strategy as follows:

> To help protect against toxic by-products, EPA has launched a major regulatory and enforcement drive, including suits using EPA's "imminent hazard" or "emergency" provisions to force the cleanup of the most dangerous hazardous waste problems. I anticipate that 50 such cases will be filed before the end of 1980.
> The most widely recognized symbol of the hazardous waste crisis is Love Canal in Niagara Falls, where an entire neighborhood has been abandoned. There are, however, hundreds of other graphic examples scattered across the country.
> The issue of how to deal with our legacy of dangerous waste disposal sites and to prevent the development of new "Love Canals" may be the most difficult environmental challenge of the 1980's. EPA has launched four interrelated efforts to bring this problem under control.[9]

Two of these efforts are relevant to the actions against Hooker: (1) litigation under "imminent hazard" provisions of existing EPA laws and (2) the creation of programs, financed by government and industry, to clean up hazardous waste sites. The "imminent hazard" litigation is described as follows:

[8]Whitney, "Hooker Chemical and Plastics."
[9]Barbara Blum, "Hazardous Waste Action," *EPA Journal* (June 1980), p. 2.

> Primarily emphasizing injunctive relief, this program seeks to halt dangerous disposal practices and to force privately-funded clean-up. This approach gets results, of course, only where a responsible party can be identified and has adequate financial resources to carry some or all of the clean-up costs.[10]

Blum goes on to describe the specific statutes the EPA is acting under and the EPA's collaboration with the Justice Department in enforcing the statutes:

> Sections of the Resource Conservation and Recovery Act, Safe Drinking Water Act, Toxic Substances Control Act, Clean Water Act, and Clean Air Act all authorize EPA to ask the court for injunctive relief in situations which pose threats to public health or the environment. Section 309 of the Clean Water Act levies a penalty of up to $10,000 a day for unpermitted discharges to navigable waters (a leaking dump can be considered a discharge). The 1899 "Refuse Act" provides additional penalties for unauthorized discharges or dumping. Available common law remedies include the common law of nuisance and trespass, restitution, and "strict liability" for damages caused by those who engaged in ultra-hazardous activities. We are aggressively using each of these legal tools to address the hazardous waste disposal problem.
>
> The Agency—working with the Department of Justice—has launched a top-priority effort to pursue imminent hazard cases. . . .
>
> People are frightened by Love Canal and by the emergence of threatening hazardous waste sites in their local communities. They are demanding action—and they are getting it.[11]

The EPA currently estimates that only 10% of all hazardous wastes are disposed of in strict compliance with federal regulations. According to Thomas H. Maugh, II, writing in 1979 in *Science* magazine, "nearly 50 percent is disposed of by lagooning in unlined surface impoundments, 30 percent in nonsecure landfills, and about 10 percent by dumping into sewers, spreading on roads, injection into deep wells, and incineration under uncontrolled conditions."[12] Maugh goes on to argue that "legal dumpsites gone awry" are actually a lesser problem than the growing problem of illegally dumped wastes in unsecured dumpsites, often in the middle of cities.[13] In October 1981 the EPA announced that "there are at least 29 toxic waste disposal sites around the country as dangerous or more so than Love Canal. . . ."[14] This is partly

---

[10]*Ibid.*

[11]*Ibid.*, p. 8.

[12]Maugh, "Toxic Waste Disposal," pp. 819, 821.

[13]*Ibid.*, p. 110.

[14]Joanne Omong, "EPA Names 115 Toxic Waste Dump Sites for Cleanup," *The Washington Post*, October 24, 1981, p. 4.

because some clean-up has already been done at Love Canal and many of the endangered people have moved away.

Hooker Chemical believes that its role and defense have been misunderstood. While the company neither denies using the canal as a chemical dump nor denies that the dump has created a serious problem, officials of the company contend that (1) the company's efforts to prevent first the public and then the private development of the canal area are generally unrecognized; (2) the company has been an industry leader in safety; (3) Hooker is being unfairly blamed and singled out for waste disposal practices that were then almost universal throughout the chemical industry; and (4) a certain level of risk is an inevitable hazard in an industrial society.

Hooker has marshaled data to support its contentions. In the first place, Hooker believes that its efforts to warn the School Board and City against interfering with the waste disposal area are unappreciated. When the Niagara Falls School Board expressed an interest in selling a portion of the Love Canal tract to a developer, Hooker representatives argued against the plan in a public meeting and later reiterated to the Board its warnings of possible hazards. When the school board persisted in its plans and began to obtain adjacent parcels of land through condemnation proceedings, Hooker, in the deed to the School Board, again referred to the past use of the property and stipulated that all future risks and liabilities be passed to the School Board. One part of the deed stipulated:

> Prior to the delivery of this instrument of conveyance, the grantee herein has been advised by the grantor that the premises above described have been filled, in whole or in part, to the present grade level thereof with waste products resulting from the manufacturing of chemicals by the grantor at its plant in the City of Niagara Falls, New York, and the grantee assumes all risk and liability incident to the use thereof. It is, therefore, understood and agreed that, as a part of the consideration for this conveyance and as a condition thereof, no claim, suit, action or demand of any nature whatsoever shall ever be made by the grantee, its successors or assigns, against the grantor, its successors or assigns, for injury to a person or persons, including death resulting therefrom, or loss of or damage to property caused by, in connection with or by reason of the presence of said industrial wastes.[15]

When the school board later sold part of the land to a private developer who planned to build houses, Hooker officials protested the sale both verbally and in writing. Executives believe that the company is being unjustly blamed for the improvidence of others. Hooker also claims that it has no legal responsibility for the problem at Love Canal

[15]Steiner, "Love can be Dangerous," p. 110.

and that it has more than met its social and moral obligations in time and money spent on the clean-up effort. Through its experiences at Love Canal, Hooker environmental health and safety specialists have developed knowledge and skills that have enabled the company to take a leadership role in problems of underground pollution.

Hooker officials also argue that their past practices more than met then acceptable industry standards for waste disposal. During the period from 1942 to 1953 when Hooker was filling Love Canal with barrels of chemical wastes, the long-term environmental and personal hazards of these industrial "left-overs" were not adequately recognized either by the industries involved or by the health and regulatory professions. Putting the chemical wastes into a clay canal was actually an improvement on common methods of disposal in unlined and unsecured landfills.

The company's defense of its behavior in the Love Canal situation parallels in some respects the reaction of certain Love Canal residents. They directed the major thrust of their antagonism not toward Hooker Chemical, but toward the New York State Health Department, which had failed to provide open access to the results of state-conducted health studies and left unexplained delays in admitting that a health problem existed. The Health Department attempted to discourage, and even actively harrassed independent researchers whose reports indicated more widespread risks to the health of the community than the Department was willing to admit—or prepared to pay to rectify. Given these considerations, it was the Health Department, not Hooker Chemical, who did not meet its obligations to the community in the eyes of many residents.[16]

Hooker supports the common industry position that society will have to learn to accept a certain level of risk in order to enjoy the products of industrial society. Environmental hazards are just one more form of industrial "trade-offs." They cite such persons as Margery W. Shaw, an independent scientist who reviewed a chromosomal study of Love Canal residents. She points out that the level of acceptable risk is a general societal problem merely instanced in this case.

> In our democratic society, perhaps we will decide that 500,000 deaths per year is an acceptable price for toxic chemicals in our environment, just as we have decided that 50,000 traffic deaths per year is an acceptable price for automobile travel. On the other hand, we may say that 5,000 deaths per year is an unacceptable price for toxic chemicals.[17]

[16]Beverly Paigen, "Controversy at Love Canal," *Hastings Center Report* **12** (June 1982), pp. 29–37.

[17]Margery W. Shaw, "Love Canal Chromosome Study," *Science* **209** (August 15, 1980), p. 752.

Over the years Hooker has been among the most heavily criticized corporations for its environmental policies. Ralph Nader attacked Hooker as a "callous corporation" leaving toxic "cesspools." An ABC News documentary was highly critical of the company, concentrating on the increased incidence of disease at Love Canal. On the other hand, Hooker has picked up a number of defenders in recent years. In a July 27, 1981 editorial in *Fortune* magazine, the corporation was defended for having explicitly conformed to government standards of waste disposal, for resisting the construction at the canal, and for being the victim of exaggerated and irresponsible reports about the incidence of disease in the region.[18] An April 1981 editorial in *Discover* magazine laid the blame on the Niagara Falls board of education for Love Canal, but argued that Hooker did act irresponsibly in waste dumpage at a number of other sites.[19] The 1982 study released by the EPA had the effect of blunting some federal efforts and some law suits.

[18]*Fortune* (July 27, 1981), pp. 30–31.
[19]*Discover* **2** (4) (April 1981), p. 8.

Optical Distortion, Inc.

Late in the fall of 1974, Mr. Daniel Garrison, president and chief executive officer of Optical Distortion, Inc. (ODI), had asked Mr. Ronald Olson, marketing vice-president of ODI, to develop a marketing plan for ODI's new (and only) product—a contact lens for chickens. While contact lenses served the purpose of improving human eyesight, the purpose of the lens developed by ODI was partially to blind the chickens.

Mr. Garrison explained:

> Like so many other great discoveries, our product concept was discovered quite by accident. In 1962 a chicken farmer in Arizona had a flock of chickens that developed a severe cataract problem. When he became aware of the problem, he separated the afflicted birds from the rest of the flock and subsequently observed that the afflicted birds seemed to eat less and were much easier to handle. So dramatic was the difference that a poultry medical detailman visiting the farm, rather than being asked for a cure, was asked if there was any way to similarly afflict the rest of the flock. It has not proved possible chemically or genetically to duplicate the reduced vision of the chickens resulting from the cataracts, but a chicken wearing the ODI lenses has its vision reduced enough to obtain the good behavior the Arizona farmer observed. This behavior has important economic implications for the chicken farmer.

By late 1974, the ODI lens had been tested on a number of farms in California and Oregon with satisfactory results, and Mr. Garrison was convinced that "the time has come to stop worrying about the product and get this show off the ground." While his timetable was "tentative," he hoped that the ODI lens could be introduced in at least one region during the spring of 1975 and that national distribution would be achieved by the end of 1977 (at the latest). As he explained:

From Darral G. Clarke, as found in *Problems in Marketing*, eds. S. Starr, N. Davis, C. Loveloch, B. Shapiro (New York: McGraw-Hill, Inc., 1977), pp. 538–44. **Not to be duplicated without permission of the author and publisher.**

Our patent and license protection [see below] should hold off competition for at least three years, but—if we have the success I believe we will—I would expect the large agricultural supply firms to find a way around our patent by the late 1970's. By 1980, I would expect the big boys to have come in, and competition to be fierce. If we are to gain the fruits of our development work, we will have to be strong enough to fight them on their own terms. To do this, we will have to be a multi-product multi-market company which can provide effective service anywhere in the country.

COMPANY BACKGROUND

The ODI lens had been invented in 1965 by Robert D. Garrison (Daniel Garrison's father), working with Mr. Ronald Olson, the owner of a large chicken farm in Oregon. Mr. Robert Garrison had conceptualized and designed the original product and had then worked with Olson to test and refine the lenses on Olson's chicken farm. In 1966, their efforts attracted the attention of Mr. James Arnold, a local businessman, who invested approximately $5,000 in the venture. By late 1966, the three men had formed a corporation to exploit Garrison's invention.

Further testing of the lens in Olson's chicken farm during 1967 had, however, identified several technical difficulties with the product. In particular, the early prototypes did not always remain in the chicken's eyes after insertion, and frequently caused severe irritation by the later months of the chicken's 12-month laying life. Both problems had been quite serious because, as Daniel Garrison explained, "No farmer is going to spend time looking into the eyes of his chickens to make sure the lenses are still there and the eyes are not bloodshot."

By 1968, ODI had solved the retention problem by modifying the size of the lens and was issued a United States patent on the lens in December 1969. ODI found that the irritation problem could be essentially eliminated by making the lenses of a soft plastic called a *hydrophilic polymer*. The patents for hydrophilic polymer, the same material used by Bausch and Lomb to produce soft contact lenses for human use, were controlled by New World Plastics of Baltimore, Maryland. The New World Plastics' hydrophilic polymer could not be injection-molded, however, and manufacturing costs using alternative production processes were far too high for the chicken market. Since New World Plastics' hydrophilic polymer was the only such material known at the time, ODI had reached an impasse, and the company became dormant.

In 1973, Robert Garrison asked his son Daniel Garrison, a second-year student at the Harvard Business School, to contact New World Plastics and see if any progress had been made in the hydrophilic polymer. Daniel Garrison found that the hydrophilic polymer could now be injection-molded and became enthusiastic about the potential of the product. With the approval of the owners, Daniel Garrison obtained a long-term license from New World Plastics for the exclusive use of hydrophilic polymer for nonhuman applications.

Under the terms of the license, New World agreed not to produce the polymer for other firms seeking nonhuman markets and not to carry out development work on related polymers for such firms. ODI, in turn, agreed to pay New World Plastics $50,000 ($25,000 per year for the first 2 years) and to purchase its lenses exclusively from New World. New World would manufacture the lenses and sell them to ODI at a price of $0.032 per pair (in bulk), regardless of quantity. ODI was to supply New World with injection molds (at a cost of $12,000 each). Each injection mold had an annual capacity of 7.2 million pairs and an expected life of 15 million pairs.

During the negotiations with New World Plastics, Daniel Garrison purchased 25 percent of the stock of ODI from the previous owners and was elected president and chief executive officer of the firm. Having completed the license agreement with New World, he was able to raise $200,000 in the venture capital markets. About this time, Mr. Ronald Olson became vice-president–marketing, and the two men began devoting a substantial portion of their time to ODI. As of late 1974, Daniel Garrison and Olson were the only reasonably full-time employees of the firm, although Robert Garrison and James Arnold remained active as stockholders and board members.

THE POULTRY INDUSTRY

Poultry and egg production had its beginnings in the family barnyard. As late as 1900, it was not unusual for a family to have its own chickens or to buy eggs fresh from a small local farmer, even in urban areas. In 1921, the largest commercial egg farm in the United States was in Petaluma, California, and boasted a flock of about 2,000 hens. The hens were not housed, but ran loose in a large pasture with small roosting and laying houses nearby. The eggs were picked up twice daily and loaded into a horse-drawn wagon.

In an effort to increase the efficiency of egg production, some California farmers began confining the birds in large henhouses during the 1930s and 1940s. In other parts of the United States, eggs were still being collected from haystacks until the 1940s when henhouses became common in other areas of the country. Continuing their innovation, California poultrymen began to increase the utilization of henhouse space by further confining the birds in groups of three or four within multitiered wire cages of 18×12 inch size. By the 1950s, these innovations had spread widely throughout the United States and had led to considerable concentration in the poultry industry.

In 1974, the largest commercial flock of laying hens in the United States was 2.5 million birds, and 80 percent of the 440 million laying hens in the United States were housed on 3 percent of the known chicken farms. . . .

CANNIBALISM AMONG CHICKENS

Like many other fowl, chickens were social birds and chicken societies had a definite social structure. A self-selected ranking of chickens began when chickens were about 8 to 10 weeks of age and resulted in a complete peck order by the time the birds reached sexual maturity. According to Mark O. North, a poultry consultant, "This order is the result of the birds being able to identify other birds in the group, and through fighting and pecking, establish a hierarchical type of social organization."

Mr. North believed that the recognition of the comb on the head of the chicken was a means of preserving the peck order, as was the position of the head. Dominant-type chickens carried their heads high, while submissive birds maintained a low head level. If a submissive bird raised her head too high, she was immediately pecked by one or more of her superiors until the head was lowered. Pecking could increase until the birds became cannibalistic. Submissive birds were also pecked if they entered the "territory" of a cage claimed by a more dominant bird. Thus cannibalism was a greater problem when more birds were confined in cages. Cannibalism also varied with the breed of the chicken, and, unfortunately, the more productive strains tended to be more cannibalistic. According to Daniel Garrison, a major United States breeder had developed an extremely productive chicken, but "you had to put a sack over her head to keep her from killing her penmates."

Besides the obvious loss to the farmer when a bird was killed by her penmates, submissive birds got less time at the feeding trough and thus produced fewer eggs than the more dominant birds. Also, once the peck order was established, replacing a dead bird seriously disturbed the peck order.

Debeaking had been the major means of combating cannibalism for nearly 50 years. The debeaking process did not interfere with the formation of the peck order but reduced the efficiency of the beak as a weapon. The debeaking operation was simple in concept: Through the use of a hot knife and an anvil, the upper and lower mandibles of the chicken's beak were cut off at different lengths. The beak was then pressed against the hot knife to cauterize the wound and prevent excess bleeding. In the debeaking operation, the chickens were subjected to considerable trauma which resulted in a temporary weight loss and the retardation of egg production for at least a week; at this age, the loss was only one egg. If the beak were cut too short, the chicken would often enter a permanent regression; if left too long, the beak would grow back and become a deadly weapon again. The establishment of the peck order among debeaked chickens took a longer time and involved greater social stress than it did among chickens with their full beaks since clear victories were rare.

Experience had shown that debeaking reduced mortality due to cannibalism from as high as 25 percent for flocks of birds with full beaks to about 9 percent for debeaked flocks.

Debeaking was usually done during the first few weeks after the 20-week-old hens were purchased. The farmer's own employees or a service company could be hired to provide the debeaking crews, depending on the size of the farm. The cost of the debeaking operation was almost entirely labor. An experienced crew of three men, each earning about $2.50 per hour, could debeak approximately 220 birds per hour.

THE ODI LENS

Daniel Garrison felt that the ODI contact lens was the first product to actually confront the cause of cannibalization rather than just minimize its effects. A bird wearing the ODI lens had its depth of perception reduced to about 12 inches and its visual acuity greatly reduced through an induced case of astigmatism. Thus, the ability of one bird to recognize the comb of another was seriously impaired, and in order to feed, the chickens had to walk around with their heads lowered. Thus the main visual cues for the peck order were removed, no peck order emerged, and cannibalism was reduced significantly.

The ODI lens was much like the soft contact lenses worn by humans except that it was slightly larger, had a red tint, and had a distortion built into the crown. When asked why the lenses were colored, Daniel Garrison responded:

> It may sound like rubbish to many people but chickens, like humans, respond psychologically to the color of their environment. We have found that changing the color of the birds' environment will affect the birds in many different ways such as altering their appetites or rate of sexual maturity, as well as affecting their cannibalistic tendencies. When birds are placed in a red colored environment, deaths due to cannibalism are reduced. This red color, together with the distortion of the lenses, affects the chicken's ability to act out her aggressions. Our tests have shown that

flock mortality is reduced to an average of 4.5% when contact lenses are used instead of debeaking.

The lens was larger than the eye opening so that, when in place, the rim of the eye opening and the outer eyelid acted as retainers keeping the lens in place. The inner eyelid, or nicitating membrane, a semi-transparent membrane that flicked back and forth across the eyeball keeping it moist and clean, was under the lens and thus could perform its natural function.

Daniel Garrison estimated that a trained crew of three men, similar to the debeaking crews, could install the lenses in about 225 chickens per hour. The insertion of the lenses did not result in great trauma to the birds as debeaking did. The chickens were up and about within a few hours, and neither weight loss nor reduction in egg production were noticeable.

Daniel Garrison doubted that the lenses could be reused.

> The lenses are harder to take out than they are to put in, and a further problem in reusing them is the fact that the melting point of the hydrophilic polymer is very close to the sterilization temperature. You could end up with a mass of hydrophilic polymer rather than a pot full of contact lenses very easily.

Besides reducing chicken mortality due to cannibalism and egg production loss due to trauma, the ODI lens had the potential of reducing a farmer's feed cost. A debeaked chicken could only eat if the feed in her trough was at least ⅜ inch keep (the difference in length between the upper and lower mandibles of her remaining beak). Presumably, therefore, a farmer using ODI lenses instead of debeaking his chickens would be able to reduce the depth of the feed in his troughs by approximately ⅜ inch or more. Mr. Gil Jaeger, a University of Maine poultry extension specialist, had conducted a study which suggested that food disappearance per 100 birds per day was reduced from 24.46 pounds when the feed in the trough was 2 inches deep to 23.68 pounds when the feed in the trough was only 1 inch deep. In other words, a farmer with a 20,000-bird flock could save 156 pounds of feed per day if he could reduce the depth of feed in his trough from 2 inches to 1 inch. At $158 per ton for chicken feed, this would represent considerable annual savings, especially for large flocks. According to Mr. Garrison, ODI lenses would permit a farmer to reduce the depth of feed in his troughs by at least ⅜ inch (probably to a depth of 1 inch) and would result in further savings because "a bird with a full beak *and* the ODI lenses can't see well enough to be fussy so she doesn't bill much at all [billing throws feed out of the trough], and she doesn't drool in her food as debeaked birds do."

The Cosmetics Industry and the Draize Test

In a survey conducted in the United Kingdom, the vast majority of respondents objected to cosmetic testing on animals.[1] More recently, *Glamour* magazine asked its readers whether we should do cosmetic tests on animals and 84% said no.[2] However, in a 1977 BBC television program on animal experimentation, the following question was put to a number of shoppers: Would you use a shampoo if it had not been safety-tested on animals? All answered that they would not. The difference in the responses to the two surveys illustrates the complex nature of the problem.

Some argue that society does not need cosmetics but offer few constructive suggestions as to how a $10 billion dollar industry should be prevented from innovation in Western "free" market economies. Others argue that the products should not be tested on animals since humanity has no right to subject animals to pain and suffering for the sake of frivolous vanity products. However, many consumer organizations consider that cosmetics should be even more closely regulated and subjected to more intensive animal tests.[3]

Faced with the continuing threat of litigation as a result of adverse reactions, the cosmetics industry is unlikely to retreat from animal testing. It is known that tests do not necessarily protect consumers from all risk, but they reduce the extent of risk and also provide some protection for a company in the event of a large claim for damages.

Nevertheless, in a case against Beacon Castile, in which a woman ac-

[1]National Opinion Polls, *Report to Annual General Meeting of Royal Society for the Prevention of Cruelty to Animals* (June 28, 1974).

[2]*Glamour* (December 1981).

[3]R. Nader, on the regulation of the safety of cosmetics, in *The Legislation of Product Safety: Consumer Health and Product Hazards—Cosmetics and Drugs, Pesticides, Food Additives,* vol. 2, eds. S. S. Epstein and R. D. Grundy (Boston, Mass.: The MIT Press, 1974), pp. 73–141.

cidentally splashed concentrated shampoo in her eye, the verdict went against the FDA and in favor of the company.[4] The judge's ruling was based primarily on the contention that the concentrated shampoo would be unlikely to enter the eye under normal conditions. However, he also noted that "the rabbit studies, standing alone, do not warrant condemnation of this product." This indicated that this court, at least, was not impressed by the applicability of the rabbit data.

HISTORICAL BACKGROUND
ON EYE TESTING

The Draize eye test is a standard testing procedure for eye irritation. It is named after the principal author of a paper that outlined the main element of the test, together with a numerical scoring system to provide an idea of the irritancy of the tested substance.[5] Such irritancy testing primarily involves cosmetics, toiletries, agricultural chemicals, occupational and environmental hazards, and certain therapeutics, especially ophthalmological formulations. The development of the test followed the passage of the Federal Food, Drug, and Cosmetic Act of 1938 that required, *inter alia,* that cosmetics be free of poisonous or deleterious substances to the user.

In 1933, a woman suffered ulceration of both corneas as a result of having her eyelashes dyed with a coal-tar product called "Lash-lure." She was left blind and disfigured and the American Medical Association (AMA) documented seventeen similar cases, some resulting in death. "Lash-lure" remained on the market for five more years because the federal government did not have the authority to seize the product under the 1906 Food and Drug Act because the "Lash-lure" manufacturer made no medical claims.[6] However, the 1938 Act did not prevent accidents resulting in eye damage. In a 1952 hearing in Congress, a case was presented of an anti-dandruff shampoo containing a new polyoxyethylene compound that caused semi-permanent injuries.[7] A recent study of 35,490 people, covering a three-month period, turned up 589 adverse reactions that were confirmed by dermatologists as most likely to have been caused by cosmetics. Of the 589 reactions, 3% were classified as severe, 11% as moderate, and 86% as mild.[8] It is thus clear

[4]U.S. District Court of the Northern District of Ohio, Eastern Division, No. C71–53, January 7, 1974, pp. 164–166.

[5]J. H. Draize, G. Woodard, and H. O. Calvery, on methods for the study of irritation and toxicity of substances applied topically to the skin and mucous membranes, in *Journal of Pharmacology and Experimental Therapy* **82** (1944), pp. 377–390.

[6]R. D. Lamb, *American Chamber of Horrors* (New York: Farrar & Reinhart, 1936).

[7]T. Stabile, *Cosmetics: Trick or Treat* (New York: Houston Books, 1966).

[8]M. Morrison, "Cosmetics: Some Statistics on Safety," *FDA Consumer* (March 1976), pp. 15–17.

that there is a need to determine whether or not a new cosmetic product is likely to cause eye irritancy before it is released on the market. The question, therefore, concerns the method of determining a product's potential hazard, rather than whether or not testing is required.

Eye irritation usually has one or more of the following characteristics—ulceration or opacity of the cornea, iris inflammation, and conjunctival inflammation. The Draize test utilizes this fact and scores the extent of the injury to each part of the eye. The various scores are then combined to give a total, which is used to indicate the irritancy potential of the test substance.

The Draize test has undergone several modifications since 1944 and was adapted for use in enforcing the Hazardous Substances Labeling Act. In the modified version, 0.1 ml is instilled into the conjunctival sac of one eye of each of six rabbits, the other eye serving as a control. The lids are held together for one second and the animal is then released. The eyes are examined at 24, 48, and 72 hours.[9] The scoring system is heavily weighted towards corneal damage (80 out of 110) because corneal damage leads quickly to impairment of vision.

The Interagency Regulatory Liaison Group issued draft guidelines for acute eye irritation tests a few years ago.[10] They selected the albino rabbit as the preferred test animal and recommended the use of a single, large-volume dose (0.1 ml) despite the advantages (obtaining a dose-response effect) of using a range of volumes.[11] They also recommended that, in most cases, anesthetics should not be used. However, if the test substance were likely to cause extreme pain, the use of a local anesthetic (proparacaine 0.5% or butacaine 2%) was recommended for humane reasons.[12] The eyes should not be washed. Observations should be made 1, 24, 72, and 168 hours after treatment. The cut-off point for a non-irritant is set very low (i.e., minimal reaction) in order to provide a large margin of safety in extrapolating the human response.

[9]F. N. Marzulli and M. E. Simon, on eye irritation from topically applied drugs and cosmetics: preclinical studies, in *American Journal of Optometry, Archives of the American Academy of Optometry* **48** (1971), pp. 61–78.

[10]Interagency Regulatory Liaison Group, Testing Standards and Guidelines Workgroup, *Draft IRLG Guidelines for Selected Acute Toxicity Test* (Washington, D.C.: IRLG, 1979).

[11]J. F. Griffith, G. A. Nixon, R. D. Bruce, P. J. Reer, and E. A. Bannan, on dose-response studies with chemical irritants in the albino rabbit eye as a basis for selecting optimum testing conditions for predicting hazard to the human eye, in *Toxicology and Applied Pharmacology* **55** (1980), pp. 501–513.

[12]A. G. Ulsamer, P. L. Wright, and R. E. Osterbert, "A Comparison of the Effects of Model Irritants on Anesthetized and Nonanesthetized Rabbit Eyes," *Toxicology and Applied Pharmacology* **41** (1977), pp. 191–192 (abstract).

COMPARATIVE STUDIES

The parts of the eye that are most affected by topically applied substances are the cornea, the bulbar and palpebral conjunctivae, and the iris. The corneas of laboratory mammals are very similar in construction[13] and variations are, for the most part, minor. (The mean thickness of the cornea does vary: In man it is 0.51 mm; in the rabbit, 0.37 mm; and in the cat, 0.62 mm. The composition of the corneas of man and other species differs in the quantity and kind of enzymes.)[14]

The rabbit has historically been the animal of choice for the Draize eye test, but this seems to have occurred more by accident than by design. The use of the rabbit eye for predicting human ophthalmic response has been challenged from time to time. It has been suggested that the greater thickness of the human cornea and other anatomical differences may contribute to the rabbit's greater susceptibility to alkali burns of the cornea.[15] However, the rabbit is less sensitive than man to some other substances.[16] Tears are produced in smaller quantities in the rabbit than in man, but the rabbit nictitating membrane may supplement the cleansing effect of tears.

Procter and Gamble produced an extensive critique of the Draize test in their comments on the draft IRLG Guidelines for Acute Toxicity Tests.[17] They expressed disappointment at the fact that federal agencies have been singularly unresponsive to widespread criticism of the Draize test and have made little or no effort to encourage innovation. They commented on the differences between the human and rabbit eye[18] and the fact that the rabbit's response to the test material is greatly exaggerated when compared to human responses.[19] Procter and Gamble suggest that, when the rabbit result is equivocal, organizations should have the option of using monkeys.

The monkey has been proposed as a more suitable model because it

[13]S. Duke-Elder, *System of Ophthalmology, Volume 1: The Eye in Evolution* (St. Louis, Mo.: C. V. Mosby Co., 1958), p. 452.

[14]R. Kuhlman, on species variation in the enzyme content of the corneal epithelium, in *Journal of Cell Composition Physiology* **53** (1959), pp. 313–326.

[15]C. P. Carpenter and H. F. Smyth, on chemical burns of the rabbit cornea, in *American Journal of Ophthalmology* **29** (1946), pp. 1363–1372.

[16]Marzulli and Simon, on eye irritation.

[17]Procter and Gamble Company, Comments on draft IRLG Guidelines for Acute Toxicity Tests (Washington, D.C.: IRLG, 1979).

[18]J. H. Beckley, "Comparative Eye Testing: Man versus Animal," *Toxicology and Applied Pharmacology* **7** (1965), pp. 93–101; and E. V. Buehler, "Testing to Predict Potential Ocular Hazards of Household Chemicals," *Toxicology Annual,* ed. C. L. Winek (New York: Marcel Dekker, 1974).

[19]R. O. Carter and J. F. Griffith, on experimental bases for the realistic assessment of safety of topical agents in *Toxicology and Applied Pharmacology* **7** (1965), pp. 60–73.

is phylogenetically closer to man,[20] but there are still species differences.[21] In addition, use of monkeys for eye irritancy testing is inappropriate, in part because of their diminishing availability. Also, the expense does not warrant the purported fine-tuning involved in the use of monkeys. The rat has also been suggested as an alternative model but has not been investigated in any depth. Studies at Avon indicate that it may be less sensitive than the rabbit.[22] If one must use an animal for eye irritancy testing, then the rabbit would appear to be as appropriate as any other species.

TECHNICAL

It has already been stressed that the Draize eye irritancy test cannot be *routinely* used to grade substances according to their potential irritancy for human beings but only as a "pass-fail" test. In 1971, Weil and Scala[23] reported the results of a survey of intra- and inter-laboratory variability of the Draize eye and skin test. Twenty-four laboratories cooperated on the eye irritancy testing, including the Food and Drug Directorate (Canada), Hazleton Laboratories (USA), Huntingdom Research Centre (UK), Avon Products (USA), Colgate-Palmolive (USA), General Foods (USA), and American Cyanamid (USA). Twelve chemicals were selected for ophthalmic irritancy testing and distributed as unknowns to the various companies for testing according to a standard reference procedure employing the original grading scale.[24] Three of the substances were recorded as nonirritants by all the laboratories but there was considerable variation in the results for the other nine. For example, cream peroxide was recorded as a nonirritant by certain laboratories but as an irritant by others.

As a result of this study, Weil and Scala[25] concluded that "the rabbit eye and skin procedures currently recommended by the federal agencies for use in the delineation of irritancy of materials should not be recommended as standard procedures in any new regulations. Without

[20]J. H. Beckley, T. J. Russell, and L. F. Rubin, on the use of rhesus monkey for predicting human responses to eye irritants, in *Toxicology and Applied Pharmacology* 15 (1969), pp. 1–9.

[21]W. R. Green, J. B. Sullivan, R. M. Hehir, L. G. Scharpf, and A. W. Dickinson, *A Systematic Comparison of Chemically Induced Eye Injury in the Albino Rabbit and Rhesus Monkey* (New York: The Soap and Detergent Association, 1978).

[22]G. Foster, 1980—personal communication.

[23]C. S. Weil and R. A. Scala, on the study of intra- and inter-laboratory variability in the results of rabbit eye and skin irritation test, in *Toxicology and Applied Pharmacology* 19 (1971), pp. 276–360.

[24]Draize, et al., on methods for the study of irritation and toxicity.

[25]Weil and Scala, on the study of intra- and inter-laboratory variability.

careful re-education these tests result in unreliable results." It is pertinent to note that Scala considers that the Draize test can be used to
grade irritants, but only by experienced and careful researchers.[26]

RECENT PROPOSALS
AND POLITICAL ACTIVITY

Development of the Coalition to Abolish the Draize Test. During the last decade, the humane movement has increasingly called into question the
testing of cosmetics on laboratory animals. With one or two minor exceptions, the campaigns that have been launched against such cosmetic
testing have been poorly planned and their effectiveness has been un-
dercut by inadequately researched position papers and a dissipation of
energy in different directions. All this changed with the development
of a coalition of over 400 humane societies aimed specifically at the use
of the Draize eye irritancy test by cosmetic companies. This coalition
was the brainchild of a New York English teacher, Henry Spira, and
the Draize test was selected as the target for the following reasons.
First, the test has been criticized in scientific literature as being inappropriate and, in routine use, the data produced are unreliable for
regulatory purposes.[27] Second, the Draize test can cause trauma to rabbit eyes that is readily visible and that produces a strong reaction
among the general public as well as scientists. As Henry Spira states,
"it is the type of test that people can identify with—people know what
it feels like to get a little bit of soap in their eyes."[28] Third, the test has
remained essentially unchanged for over thirty years despite the fact
that the prospects for humane modifications are good. Also, relatively
little research has been undertaken in a search for an *in vitro* alternative and even fewer results have been made available in the scientific
literature.

The cosmetics industry was selected as the target because it is vulnerable to the image problem raised by the use of the Draize eye test. The
picture of the sultry model advertising a new beauty product does not
juxtapose readily with an inflamed and swollen rabbit eye. It has been
argued that the selection of the cosmetics industry is unfair since their
products are, by and large, the least irritant. However, the Coalition
took the view that the cosmetics industry is not a discrete group, totally
separate from other manufacturing companies. In many instances, a
single company will make a range of products including household

[26]R. A. Scala, 1980—personal communication.

[27]Weil and Scala, on the study of intra- and inter-laboratory variability.

[28]L. Harriton, "Conversation with Henry Spira: Draize Test Activist," *Lab Animal* **10**
(1) (1981), pp. 16–22.

cleaners, toiletries, cosmetics, and drugs. From the Coalition's point of view, it is important that the activities of all the members be narrowly focused in order to create the maximum impact and ultimately persuade policy makers that it is worth their while to change their priorities on the Draize test. The campaign's success may be measured by the following actions taken after it started in March 1980.

Government Responses. The Consumer Product Safety Commission started, on May 8, 1980, a temporary (6-month) moratorium on all in-house Draize testing until the effects of using local anesthetics to reduce pain could be elucidated. They have now identified tetracaine (a double dose) as an effective local anesthetic. The Office of Pesticides and Toxic Substances of the Environmental Protection Agency established a similar moratorium on October 1, 1980. Furthermore, they proposed to "establish the search for alternative test methods to the Draize as a research priority for the coming year." The FDA committed funds in 1981 to study a new *in vitro* technique.[29] In Congress, Senator D. Durenberger (R-Minn) and Congressman A. Jacobs (D-Ind) introduced resolutions that it was the sense of Congress that funds should be allocated to the development of a non-animal alternative to the Draize. The National Toxicology Program has yet to make a serious commitment to look for an alternative.

Industry Actions. The Cosmetics, Toiletries and Fragrances Association (CTFA) established a special task force to review alternative test systems. They sponsored a closed workshop of scientists to investigate the potential for modifying the Draize test and to develop an alternative.

A major breakthrough in the controversy occurred on December 23, 1980 when Revlon announced that it was giving Rockefeller University a grant of $750,000 to fund a three-year research effort aimed at finding an alternative to the Draize test. Revlon executives commented that while it would be naive to deny that the campaign, including an effort focused specifically on Revlon, did not have any effect, the grant was part of an ongoing program to research and develop possible alternatives. According to Donald Davis, editor of *Drug and Cosmetic Industry,* Revlon's plight engendered a great deal of sympathy from other leaders in the industry but there was a distinct lack of volunteers to help take the heat off Revlon. Revlon also called upon other cosmetic companies, including Avon, Bristol-Myers, Gillette, Johnson and Johnson, Max Factor, and Procter and Gamble, to join them as full partners in supporting this research effort.

The other cosmetic companies were taken by surprise by Revlon's

---

[29]*Congressional Record* E2953, June 15, 1981.

action, but they moved rapidly. Early in 1981, the CTFA announced the formation of a special research fund or trust to support research into alternatives. Avon committed $750,000, Estee-Lauder $350,000, and Bristol-Myers $200,000. Chanel, Mary Kay, and Max Factor also contributed undisclosed amounts. These funds have now been passed on to The Johns Hopkins School of Hygiene and Public Health to establish a Center for Alternatives Research. In the meantime, a number of proposed modifications have been suggested that would answer some of the humane concerns.

Possible Modifications to the Draize Test. Since there is no satisfactory non-animal alternative currently available for eye irritancy testing, any modifications that can be incorporated now to make the test more "humane" would be welcomed by humane groups. Such modifications range from not doing the test at all to the use of smaller volumes or local anesthetics. These proposals include the following:

(i) *Do not test substances with physical properties known to produce severe irritation* such as alkalis (above pH 12) and acids (below pH 3).[30] (Adopted by the IRLG, 1981)

(ii) Screen out irritants using *in vitro* or less stressful tests. The *in vitro* eye preparations described above could be used to screen unknown substances and irritant substances either labeled as such or discarded. One could also utilize results from skin irritancy studies and human patch testing to avoid testing substances that produce trauma since the skin is likely to be less sensitive than the delicate tissues of the eye.[31]

(iii) When the test is conducted in the living animal, smaller volumes should be used. It has been argued that the use of 10 µl, rather than the standard 100 µl, would be a far more realistic test in terms of assessing possible human hazard.[32] The use of smaller volumes would produce less trauma and one could also do some superficial dose-response studies to ensure that a non-irritant has a sufficient margin of safety.

(iv) Where it is necessary to test substances that cause pain and irritation in the rabbit, then local anesthetics should be used. This is recommended by the IRLG[33] and also by Johnson.[34]

[30]Interagency Regulatory Liaison Group, *Recommended Guidelines for Acute Eye Irritation Testing* (Washington, D.C.: IRLG, 1981).

[31]*Ibid.*

[32]Griffith, et al., on dose-response studies; and A. Johnson, on the use of small dosage volume and corneal anesthesia for eye test in vivo, presented at CFTA Workshop on Ocular Safety Testing: In Vivo and In Vitro Approaches (Washington, D.C., October 6 and 7, 1980).

[33]Interagency Regulatory Liaison Group, *Recommended Guidelines*.

[34]Johnson, on the use of small dosage volume.

CONCLUSION

The results of the campaign indicate that the companies and government agencies affected could have made more effort to seek an alternative to the Draize test or to modify the procedure to make it more humane. However, until the public raised the stakes on the issue, there was little motivation for action. Revlon ended up spending $750,000 instead of the $170,000 suggested at the beginning by the Coalition, and all the companies had to deal with large numbers of consumer complaints.

Acid Rain and the Uses of Coal

Acid rain, created by burning coal and other fossil fuels, has been cited in some scientific studies as the leading cause of lake acidification and fish kills in the Northeastern United States and Southeastern Canada. It also may be adversely affecting forest ecosystems, farmlands, and groundwater. The coal industry and its power generating and industrial consumers therefore have been prime targets of this latest environmental concern.

The chemical process creating acid rain and its impact on the environment are not yet well understood. However, it is known that gaseous sulfur dioxide is released into the air when coal with a high sulfur content is burned (primarily in utility power plants and some industrial plants). The sulfur dioxide and nitrogen oxides from transportation vehicles and unregulated oil burner emissions combine with water vapor to produce sulfuric and nitric acids. Carried by prevailing winds, perhaps far from the emission source, these acids infiltrate precipitation and lower the pH levels. "Pure rain" is naturally somewhat acidic, with a pH level of 5.6. The degree of acidity increases exponentially as the pH level decreases. Rainfall with pH levels of 3 or 4 is now common in the Eastern United States and Canada, and is thus anywhere from ten to over a hundred times more acidic than a normal 5.6. Levels as low as 1.5—roughly the acidity of battery acid—have been reported in Wheeling, West Virginia.[1]

Ecological systems have natural alkaline properties that can neutralize moderately acidic rain, but continued precipitation of low pH levels is difficult to compensate for. Large fish kills often occur in the early

---

[1]Lois R. Ember, "Acid Pollutants: Hitchhikers Ride the Wind," *Chemical and Engineering News* (September 14, 1981), p. 29.

This case was prepared by Nancy Blanpied and Tom L. Beauchamp, and revised by Sarah Westrick and Cathleen Kaveny. **Not to be duplicated without permission of the authors and publisher.**

spring, because as environmentalist Anne LaBastille has graphically depicted,

> all winter, the pollutant load from storms accumulates in the snowpack as if in a great white sponge. When mild weather gives the sponge a "squeeze," acids concentrated on the surface of the snow are released with the first melt. . . . This acid shock . . . produces drastic changes in water chemistry that destroy fish life.[2]

Those areas in the Northeastern United States and Southeastern Canada that show particularly high levels of acidification are naturally low in alkaline buffers, which neutralize the acids.

As a by-product of acidification, toxic metals such as aluminum are leached from the earth's surface. The aluminum can be lethal to fish and other forms of life, and even fish that survive may become poisonous to predators who eat them—including, in some cases, humans.[3]

The significance of the problem of acid rain and its future ramifications are still being studied and debated. For example, in the Adirondack region, which receives some acid rain, residents have noticed a steady decrease in the number of fish and other forms of wildlife. A forest ranger and life-long resident of the area notes that "the snowshoe rabbit is down, the fox is way down, deer are down, way down, the bobcat is down, the raccoon is down. Even the porcupine is disappearing. . . . Frogs and crayfish are way down. The loon has disappeared. . . . You don't see fish jump anymore. There are no fish to jump, and even if there were, there'd be no insects to make them jump."[4] Some lakes have become crystal clear and devoid of life.

Another example of the concern over acid rain is found in Scandinavia, where scientists have been studying the effects of acid precipitation in response to alarming changes in their rivers and lakes. Folke Andersson, coordinator of Swedish acid rain research on soils, forests, and waters has found that " '75% of nitrogen needed by forests comes from the work of soil organisms.' Laboratory studies show that increased acidity kills these microorganisms. 'Over the long term we ought to see a decrease in forest productivity due to the decrease in organisms releasing nitrogen to the soil. We can't see this yet'."[5]

In the United States, many of those who wish to prevent acid rain—and its possibly devastating consequences—focus their attention on the coal mines of Ohio. Coal mining is a major industry in southern Ohio and the West Virginia panhandle, employing 15,000 miners. Ohio

[2]Anne LaBastille, "Acid Rain: How Great a Menace?," *National Geographic* **160** (November 1981), p. 672.

[3]Robert H. Boyle, "An American Tragedy," *Sports Illustrated* (September 21, 1981), p. 75.

[4]*Ibid.*, p. 74.

[5]Lois R. Ember, "Acid Pollutants," p. 24.

coal, which has a particularly high sulfur content, is used throughout the region and is thought by environmentalists to be one of the primary sources of the acid rain falling in the Northeastern United States and Southeastern Canada. However, existing environmental regulations controlling the use of high sulfur coal have already taken their toll upon the region's economy. The state of Michigan has cut back orders for Ohio coal, and some power plants in the area have switched to a low sulfur coal. Miners are concerned about their jobs, and unemployment statistics in the region are increasing.

However, the National Coal Association reports that because of greater use of low-sulfur coal and "scrubbers" in power plants, there is little more sulfur dioxide in the air now than there was in the late 1940s. Also, some regions such as the lower Mississippi Valley and the state of Colorado seem not to be affected by relevant prevailing winds, and yet both report highly acidic rain. Furthermore, fish sometimes thrive in lakes directly affected by acid rain. (Other factors such as seepage from surrounding soils, the lake-bed composition, and fertilizer reactions may be contributory causal sources.) Because of these many unknowns about acid rain, the *Wall Street Journal* cautioned as follows in mid-1980:

> At least five more years of study is required to identify correctly the causes and effects of acidic rainfall. Precipitous regulatory action by EPA could cost utilities and other industries billions of dollars. Until more is genuinely known about acid rain, these expenditures may end up only going down the drain.[6]

Despite such warnings, EPA proceeded with regulatory efforts (by targeting coal- and oil-fired power plants) until the Reagan Administration in effect ordered the *Wall Street Journal* advice to become official policy. Anne Gorsuch, the new EPA administrator, adopted precisely the *Journal's* position. In late 1981, however, critics of "lax" regulatory efforts were supported by a panel report of the National Research Council. It pointed out that nitrogen oxide levels have tripled in the last 25 years, and the panel placed the burden of responsibility for environmental deterioration on coal-burning industries. The "circumstantial evidence" of a causal connection between coal-burning and environmental damage, it argued, is "overwhelming." It recommended stringent control measures.[7]

"Scrubbers," which remove sulfur dioxide from coal, are generally regarded as the most effective control technology, though decreased reliance on fossil fuel may be the most promising policy. To modify other plants with scrubbers would be very costly, but it has proven ef-

---

[6]"Review and Outlook: Acid Rain," *Wall Street Journal,* June 30, 1980.

[7]Committee on the Atmosphere and the Biosphere, *Atmosphere-Biosphere Interactions* (Washington, D.C.: National Academy Press, 1981).

fective in Japan, where sulfur emissions have been reduced by 50%, while energy consumption increased 120%. A cheaper, though less efficient alternative is to "wash" coal prior to combustion. Many small industrial users of Ohio coal say that they would find it difficult to survive if they were forced to comply with more stringent regulations. They contend that the cost of additional emission control equipment or out-of-state coal would be prohibitive. A union president in Ohio goes to the nerve of the issue: "Everyone wants a beautiful environment, but how do you balance that with making a living?"[8]

Cost estimates vary, but whatever the method of calculation, the cost of effectively controlling sulfur dioxide emissions would be substantial:

> According to DOE's [Department of Energy's] Jim Bartis, an internal study estimates that to reduce emissions permanently 3% or 1 million tons per year in the utility sector alone would cost about $2 billion in 1981 dollars. Beyond that incremental reduction, the cost rises rapidly, he says. To reduce emissions a significant amount—5 million to 10 million tons per year—would cost $5 billion to $7 billion. . . .

> EPA [Environmental Protection Agency] estimated that a 10 to 30% reduction in sulfur dioxide emissions in the utility sector would cost $1 billion, and raise utility customer bills 2 to 3% per year on a national average. Customers in the Ohio River Valley, however, would be socked with rate hikes of 10 to 15% per year.[9]

It is also difficult to determine with precision who is responsible for the situation. Tracking the atmospheric routes of acid rain from sources to destinations is a complex problem that some believe also must be solved if emissions are to be controlled effectively. Sulfur dioxide over the Adirondacks may vary by only 10% through a given period, while rainfall acid concentration may change 100%.[10] A DOE report has cast doubt altogether on the major role of acid rain that once was assigned to "imported" coal-produced pollutants, focusing instead on local automobile and oil-burner emissions as the source.[11] (This report was filed approximately nine months *before* the report of the panel of the National Research Council mentioned earlier. The studies ran concurrently, however.)

Uncertainties in the source/receiver relationship have prompted industry to claim that costly control techniques may prove ineffective if enacted without more adequate data. Raymond Robinson, Canadian assistant minister of the environment, considers these demands for precise data on the source-receiver relationship a "dead herring" and

[8]Amos A. Kermisch and Richard G. Zimmerman, "Poison from the Skies?" *Cleveland Plain Dealer* (August 2–August 7, 1971), Introduction.

[9]Lois R. Ember, "Acid Pollutants," p. 31.

[10]*Wall Street Journal*, see note 6.

[11]Michael Woods, "Theory Blamed Midwest Utilities: Study Disputes Cause of Acid Rain," *Toledo Blade* (January 28, 1981).

has called for corrective measures as soon as possible.[12] On the other hand, the Canadian government has not closed perhaps the largest emitter of sulfur dioxide on the North American continent—the International Nickel copper smelter at Sudbury, Ontario. Even "goals" set for reducing these emissions have thus far not been met.[13]

Representatives of the coal industry generally contend that there are too few definite answers to warrant further emission regulations, and should they be instituted too quickly, there may be needless expenditures. The Electric Power Research Institute has therefore developed an extensive international research plan to look into the causes and effects of acid rain. The Tennessee Valley Authority, the U.S. Geological Survey, and the other government agencies mentioned above, are also pursuing further research.[14] Industry spokespersons believe that further research is all that can and should be done until the phenomenon of acid rain is better understood. For example, Al Courtney, the designated spokesperson for the nation's investor-owned electric utilities, offers the following as that industry's preferred policy:

> A careful examination of the available facts leads to four conclusions: first, the only adverse effect which has been documented is the acidification of certain local water bodies; second, the causes of this acidification are not clear; third, the contribution of power plant emissions to this problem is not known, and as a result, it is not known whether emission reductions would retard or reverse this acidification; and further, requiring substantial additional emission reductions by the electric utility industry would impose great economic burdens on the financially troubled nation and on the already weak economy without assurance of commensurate benefits to the public. . . . It is clear that many of the critical chemical, meteorological, ecological, and economic questions related to acid rain remain unanswered. . . . Pending the completion of the research program established by the Acid Precipitation Act of 1980, claims regarding irreversible ecological impact should be investigated, and mitigating measures, such as liming, should be instituted where appropriate. . . . In enacting the Acid Precipitation Act of 1980, Congress recognized this essential prerequisite and in response, instituted a program designed to explore the acid deposition phenomenon in a deliberate, methodical manner. We should permit this rational, problem-solving approach to produce the information which we so badly need.[15]

The "receivers" of acid rain, on the other hand, have asked for international cooperation and quick responses to what they believe is a worsening environmental situation. In 1982 several bills were pending

[12]*Ibid.*

[13]*Acid Rain Fact Sheet,* "Canada's Campaign for Economic/Energy Supremacy," prepared by the Coalition for Environmental-Energy Balance, Columbus, OH.

[14]"Acid Rain," *Energy Researcher* (June 1981)—A publication of the Electric Power Research Institute.

[15]Edison Electric Institute Information Service, Release of October 20, 1981, pp. 1–2.

in the United States Senate intended to amend the Clean Air Act in order to better handle the acid rain phenomenon. Various strategies had been proposed by these bills—such as placing a cap on sulfur dioxide and nitrogen oxide emissions and making fossil-fuel burning generating plants a primary regulatory target.[16]

However, even the basic facts about acid rain remain hotly disputed, and the legislative and regulatory situation is cloudy. A *Report by the Comptroller General of the United States* on "The Debate Over Acid Precipitation" sums up the situation as follows:[17]

> Summing up the evidence on the acid precipitation debate, even the most conciliatory representatives of the opposite sides arrive at different conclusions.
>
> Those most concerned with the additional costs and problems expected from further emissions controls argue from the point that there is no firm proof that reductions of emissions would result in lessening acid deposition. Therefore, they conclude, it is inappropriate to take any additional control actions at this time, because the controls would be certain to involve costs but would stand a risk of producing no benefits.
>
> On the other side, those most concerned with the present and anticipated damage due to acid precipitation start from the point that the oxide precursors of deposited acids, particularly SO2, come predominantly from man-made emissions. From this they conclude that reducing oxide emissions upwind from threatened areas is most likely to prevent or reduce damage, so they urge that at least moderate steps in this direction should be started promptly. They view as inequitable the present situation, in which they see all costs and risks being borne by the regions suffering damage, contending that the emitting regions should also take some share of risks and costs. . . .
>
> Milton J. Socolar
>
> Acting Comptroller General
> of the United States

A stalemate over the interpretation of data and over the proper role of regulatory bodies usually leads to legal battles, and extremely important cases are now beginning to appear in courts and agency hearing rooms. The state of Pennsylvania, for example, has filed with EPA a formal protest and proposed set of actions against the Cleveland Electric Illuminating Co., on grounds that its emissions are blanketing the entire western half of Pennsylvania. At the same time, Pennsylvania has asked the Sixth Circuit, U.S. Court of Appeals, to overturn standards governing current permitted emissions.[18]

[16]Cf., e.g., Senate Bills 1706, 1709.

[17]"The Debate over Acid Precipitation: Opposing Views; Status of Research," *Report by the Comptroller General of the United States* (Washington, D.C.: U.S. General Accounting Office, September 11, 1981), pp. 7–8.

[18]"Pa. Fights CEI Emission Break," *Crain's Cleveland Business* (September 14, 1981), p. 2.

chapter 4

The Society

INTRODUCTION   The idea that a corporation should be "socially responsible" and should live up to the demands of "social justice" is at
the center of many controversies in this volume. However, some hold
that the corporation has no obligations whatever to society. This view
does not mean either that the corporation should *not* take actions that
benefit others in society or that it is free to do *whatever* it determines to
be its best course. Rather, the view usually takes one of two (mutually
consistent) forms: Either it is held that the corporation is a legal fiction
and so not a moral or social agent, and therefore not responsible to
others, or it is held that the corporation's responsibility is chiefly to its
stockholders and others to whom it is directly obligated. One version
of this thesis is the widely proclaimed maxim that "the business of business is business"—meaning that the responsibilities of a business are
exclusively the demands of the business world of contracts, stockholders, profits, taxes, and the like. Anything outside that world is not the
business of business.

Naturally such a view is highly resistant to the encroachment of government and to the notion that a corporation has broad moral and social responsibilities. Some who take this point of view even maintain
that if business were to set social objectives for itself, it would be en-
croaching into the region of government, which is the social institution
properly equipped to protect the public interest. The business community has no parallel role, it is maintained, and it has neither the expertise, the motivation, nor the social charter to engage in such
activities.

On the other hand, the legal system does hold corporations responsible in a variety of ways. Corporations are chartered, and this charter
permits a corporation to do business only within certain limits. In the
Napalm-B case in this chapter, there is discussion about whether corporations are as responsible as governments for a war effort when the
corporations supply materials for the military forces. However this may
be, it is clear that many decisions made in a corporation emerge from
complicated interactions and procedures of decisionmaking, which

may well involve moral deliberation. Moreover, the welfare of the corporation and the welfare of society are intimately connected—indeed so intimately bound together that it would, under some conditions, be artificial to distinguish exclusive functions of government and business. For example, as the previous chapter on The Environment shows, corporate activities can cause various kinds of social harm. In this chapter, the Napalm-B case illustrates this problem, while the Lakewood Bank and Dow-Central Michigan cases discuss the connection between business and society when business stands to contribute to the public interest. These cases all turn on whether a corporation has social responsibilities, and if so, how to characterize those responsibilities. The Plasma International case focuses on the problem of the limits governing social responsibilities once a contractual relation has been established.

These issues inescapably lead to reflection on the proper objectives of the corporation, and indeed more generally on what constitutes just and worthy business practices. Many issues in the cases in this chapter lead to reflection on what is generally referred to as "social justice," a notion used to refer to the proper or fair distribution in society of social benefits and burdens. The principles of social justice relied upon in law and morality say a great deal about the terms of cooperation in any given society, often specifying what one person or group may expect from another and what is fair in any social transaction. Such requirements of social justice are present in virtually all of society's major and pervasive institutions, including branches of government, laws of property ownership, lending institutions, and systems of allocating benefits. For example, in many social and economic systems, government intervention beyond mere protection of individual rights is initiated specifically on grounds of social justice. Governments use progressive taxation scales, and in effect redistribute wealth in order to satisfy the "welfare needs" of citizens.

On the other hand, law and government are rarely adequate to decide controversial matters of social justice of the sort raised in this chapter. For example, the justice of the present situation in which roughly 20 percent of the wealth in the United States is owned by 5 percent of the population, while the poorest 20 percent of the population controls 5 percent of the wealth, is hardly decided by abstract principles of American law or morality. The Lakewood Bank case points directly to problems of businesses' responsibilities under such conditions of social imbalance. Such cases are often extremely difficult to resolve, because different *theories* of justice may be at work in discussion of a particular case. Disputants will appeal to different "principles" of justice—some based on human needs, others on considerations of equality, and still others based on merit, performance, or effort. Utilitarian goals of efficiency conflict with egalitarian views about equal distribution and libertarian conceptions of a free market. This complexity about the demands of "justice" will be found in several cases in this chapter.

Among the most widely agreed upon theses about social justice is that programs, services, and opportunities in society must as a matter of justice be open to or available to *all* qualified members of the society. To provide some with access while denying access to others who are equally or more qualified (and so entitled) is discriminatory and so unfair. Social justice is often invoked in order to resolve problems of social inequality such as those generally involved in "unfair practices" of hiring, promotion, and firing.

Government policies intended to insure fairness in employment, promotions, and admissions for women and minority groups have sometimes eventuated in target goals and timetables established for corporations. These objectives have seemed to many persons in business to be unfair, for these goals can work against the interest of the business and also can discriminate against those not favored by the goals. More talented applicants who are excluded would be hired or accepted on their merits were it not for the preferential advancement of others. Government policies requiring preferential treatment are thus said to create a situation of "reverse discrimination" because white males and others not favored by the programs are discriminatorily excluded from consideration by the company, even though they may be the most qualified applicants or employees. Such practices are said to violate basic principles of justice and equal opportunity.

This viewpoint has introduced sustained controversy, however, because many hold that these practices simply reverse the flow of past discrimination and do *not* "reverse discriminate" in the present at all. They hold a different account of what constitutes justice in a society characterized by a long history of discriminatory practices. In particular, they look to principles of "compensatory justice" that require that just compensation or reparation be provided for injured parties when an injustice has been committed. Since discrimination from the past continues in the present (or at least its effects continue), the thought is that compensation is justified and can be provided in the form of preferential programs for women, blacks, and others discriminated against.

In this chapter government policies and corporate initiatives aimed at preferential treatment on grounds of social justice are encountered in the McAleer–A.T.&T. and the Dutchland Power cases. A central issue in both is whether justice demands practices involving equal opportunity and merit alone, or also demands some form of preferential treatment.

In the American system of government, the free-market economy and representative democracy function as final "procedures" or systems through which judgments about social and economic justice are made. Yet agreement that democratic procedures are just will not of itself resolve all problems of justice; unjust results occur in the political process, and it must be determined how a "representative" or "official" ought to vote on any given issue. Thus the cases in this chapter might be approached best through the question: From a moral point of view, what would you do if you were running a business?

Dow Chemical Funding of Central Michigan

In 1977 the Association for Women Students and the Women's Health Information Project of Central Michigan University (CMU) planned and sponsored a project on campus called Women's Month. The planned activities were supported by funding from the University. CMU monies had been used in the past to bring a varied array of speakers to the University, including individuals representing many parts of the continuum of political opinion. Among the various activities for Women's Month was a speech given on October 10 by Jane Fonda, the well-known actress and then political activist. An admission fee of $1.00 for students and $1.50 for others was charged for the talk, and Ms. Fonda received a speaker's honorarium of $3,500. At Warriner Auditorium on the campus, she addressed a capacity audience of over 1,500 students in a two-hour talk, followed by a question-and-answer period. Since it had been publicized that she would speak on "Politics in Film," the audience was surprised when she sharply criticized both multinational corporations and conditions of economic freedom in America. She went on to argue that these large multinational enterprises have too much power over our lives.

Ms. Fonda cited the Dow Chemical Company as an example of this "new group of rulers, tyrants." The mention of Dow Chemical brought forth in response some hisses from the audience.

Just three days before Fonda's visit, a highly toxic liquid chlorine

This case was prepared by Barry Smith and Tom L. Beauchamp and revised by Cathleen Kaveny. Sources consulted include: the Dow Chemical Company (Mr. E. N. Brandt); "Dow Exec Loses Cool Over Fonda Speech," *Chemical and Engineering News*, November 7, 1977, p. 5; George Will, "The Incandescent Fonda," *The Washington Post*, November 3, 1977, p. A27; *Midland* (Michigan) *Daily News*, October 11, 1977; interviews with a student at CMU; and a longer presentation of the case by John F. Steiner, whose *Casebook for Business, Government, and Society*, 2nd ed. (New York: Random House, Business Division, 1980), pp. 27–36, provided the following quoted material: (1) Oct. 12 letter of Paul F. Oreffice which originally was published in *Central Michigan Life*, Oct. 18, 1977, p. 1; (2) Excerpts of letters addressed to Dow Chemical Company; and (3) Excerpt of editorial that originally appeared in *Central Michigan Life*, Oct. 31, 1977. **Not to be duplicated without permission of the authors and publisher.**

spill had occurred at a Dow plant in close proximity to the campus. Some students also believed that Dow was gradually "poisoning" the water in the region. Some students were therefore eager to discover Fonda's reasons for her own animosity toward Dow and drew her into a lengthy tangential discussion. Students and speaker alike directed a broad range of allegations against the chemical manufacturer. Their charges pertained largely to Dow's role as a chemical supplier in previous wars and its influence in the United States economic system. Ms. Fonda said that Dow and other powerful corporations had learned to "manipulate the tax laws to get away from paying their fair share." (Dow had paid $429.6 million in taxes the previous year.) She also argued that such giant corporations are making free enterprise virtually obsolete. Ms. Fonda had not been invited to speak on this topic, and virtually all of her comments about Dow were clearly prompted by student questions.

Ms. Fonda did not know at the time of her speech that the world headquarters of Dow is just 28 miles east of the campus in Midland, Michigan. It is a major factor in the economic welfare of the region, and Dow had contributed directly and generously to the University in several ways, including approximately $73,000 in cash grants the previous year. There were no stipulations regulating the use of company contributions to the University's general fund. Central Michigan was not the only institution to which Dow made donations; approximately 450 schools around the nation benefited from Dow contributions—totalling 1 million dollars in 1977.

Although best known to consumers through such innocuous products as Saran Wrap, Dow had long been closely scrutinized by environmentalists and government officials for its development of toxic chemicals—despite its good record for health and safety precautions in the workplace. Most of its products are basic chemical commodities such as pesticides, insecticides, epoxy—and of course the controversial napalm that was produced for the Air Force for use in bombing during the Vietnam War. (See the Napalm-B case elsewhere in this text for further details.)

Paul F. Oreffice, then president of Dow Chemical USA, was greatly disturbed by Fonda's speech, which he considered provocative and unfair to Dow's record. He was also confronted at this time with increasing public criticism of both big business and Dow's contracts with the Air Force. On October 12 he responded with the following letter to CMU's President, Dr. Harold Abel:

Dear Dr. Abel:

Yesterday's paper carried a front page story reporting that Jane Fonda was paid a fee of $3,500 to spread her venom against free enterprise to the student body at your university. Of course, it is your prerogative to have an avowed communist sympathizer like Jane Fonda, or anyone else speak at your university, and you can pay them whatever you please. I have absolutely no argument with that.

While inviting Ms. Fonda to your campus is your prerogative, I consider it our prerogative and obligation to make certain our funds are never again used to support people intent upon destruction of freedom. Therefore, effective immediately, support of any kind from the Dow Chemical Company to Central Michigan University has been stopped, and will not resume until we are convinced our dollars are not expended in supporting those who would destroy us.

In addition, resumption of any Dow aid to Central Michigan is contingent on balancing the scales of what your students hear. I am open to an invitation to give a speech to a group of students similar to the one Ms. Fonda addressed, for the same fee. This fee will be donated to a non-profit organization which supports the free enterprise system.

Though intended to be a private communication, word of this letter eventually spread. To dispel rumors and to demonstrate his firm convictions on this matter, Oreffice released the letter. It appeared on the front page of *Central Michigan Life,* the student newspaper, on October 18, and immediately generated public controversy. Over 3,000 letters poured into Dow, the great majority of which favored the Dow funding cut-off and approved of Dow's justifications for this action, which were based on the "need to sustain the free enterprise system." Nationally syndicated columnist George F. Will wrote a warm endorsement of Dow's reaction to the speech. In the column entitled "The Incandescent Fonda," he argued that universities should be free from the close control of donors but that "there should be some limits to intellectual frivolousness." Dow, he urged, was exercising an awareness of those limits. He offered as a general premise that "those who support universities have not only a right, but also a duty, to withdraw support from institutions that recognize no limits."

However, an editorial in the October 31 edition of *Central Michigan Life* defended the University and the student activities in question:

> Dow Chemical Co. U.S.A. has taken all its corporate support from CMU and gone home to sulk. Some people, it seems, just have not learned money cannot buy everything, esp. the rights to freedom of expression. . . . Decisions to bring speakers here should not be based upon whether the speaker will anger some University supporter such as Dow.

Also, Dr. Charles House, executive assistant to the president of CMU, pointed out that in all probability none of Dow Chemical's contribution was actually used to pay for Fonda's speech. The company's gifts were normally tied to specific purposes; and it is possible that there was no Dow money in the General Fund at the time of the speech. Even if there were, it would have been mixed with donations from other sources, and hence untraceable.

On November 4 there was a congenial meeting between President Oreffice and President Abel. Differences seemed to have receded, and it was announced that Oreffice would both speak at CMU and run a symposium on free enterprise. However, Abel did not promise to modify the school's policy for choosing speakers and Oreffice did not commit Dow to restoring funding. As it turned out, no Dow money was ever cut off (though a small threat of nonfunding later materialized at a Dow stockholder meeting). Jane Fonda had accepted an invitation for a return visit, but filming responsibilities allegedly prevented her from coming. The public debate continued for some while, even somewhat bitterly in press editorials, but eventually momentum was lost and the dispute vanished. In order to ensure "the ideological balance" that the entire affair had called into question, CMU instituted a Platform Series, and the administration retained a veto right over speakers invited to the campus.

Lakewood Bank & Trust

INTRODUCTION

In 1973 Mr. George Elliot, President and Chief Executive Officer of Lakewood Bank & Trust, faced a critical decision about the bank's development. The older neighborhood in which the bank was located was beginning to deteriorate rapidly, a situation that could have an adverse impact on deposit growth and loan activity and risk. Elliot debated whether or not the bank should make a financial commitment to the neighborhood in the form of admittedly risky residential and commercial rehabilitation and purchase loans. If such a commitment were made, he had to decide also on its form and extent.

HISTORY

Lakewood Bank & Trust was one of the largest state-chartered banks in the Dallas metropolitan area in 1973. It ranked tenth among all city banks in total deposits ($63.4 million). Total ownership was held by some 400 individual stockholders. The bank was opened in 1942 near its present location some three miles east of Dallas' central business district. The East Dallas area at that time was stable and growing, providing substantial support for deposit growth and local lending opportunities. To the west of the bank were the older middle- to upper-income subdivisions of Munger Place and Junius Heights, with heavy concentrations of large prairie-style and smaller bungalow-style frame homes built in the first three decades of the twentieth century. Adjoining these subdivisions on the north was the Swiss Avenue district, a neighborhood of distinction, traditionally the residence of Dallas' elite. To the north and east of the bank was the newer Lakewood upper-

This case was prepared by Kerry D. Vandell and Sydney C. Reagan of the School of Business Administration, Southern Methodist University. It is designed to be used as a basis for class discussion rather than to illustrate either effective or ineffective handling of an administrative situation. Presented at a Case Workshop. Reprinted with permission of the authors. **Not to be duplicated without permission of the author and publisher.**

145

middle income subdivision. The Lakewood Country Club to the immediate east of the bank, opened in 1913, completed the area's prestigious image. The bank was located within Lakewood Shopping Center, which was designed to serve the surrounding affluent population.

Lakewood Bank prospered in the 1940s and 1950s, along with its neighborhood. However, in the 1960s several changes began taking place that threatened its position. The city in the 1950s rezoned most of the older East Dallas area to multifamily dwellings in the expectation that there would be considerable demand for close-in luxury-apartment living. This had the effect of reducing expectations of a single-family character for these neighborhoods. High rates of home-building on the suburban fringe and new expressways shifted upper-middle income housing demand away from the older, more established areas. The older prairie-style frame architecture was no longer in vogue, being replaced by the newer brick, ranch-style homes. Maintenance costs on the older structures were increasing. Finally, civil rights activity generated white flight through fears of racial transition to black or Mexican-American occupancy of the area. Large concentrations of black and Mexican-American households resided to the south of the East Dallas neighborhoods.

These factors created a generally perceived state of decline in the old East Dallas area by the early 1970s. Racial transition to largely Mexican-American occupancy was advancing from the southwest. Median incomes and property values in the area were dropping. Larger single-family homes were being partitioned into apartments and rooming houses. Physical conditions rapidly degenerated. By 1973, even property values in the more isolated Lakewood area were stabilizing or dropping, and considerable fears were expressed that decline there was imminent. To complement residential decline, Lakewood Shopping Center was being supplanted by the newer shopping malls in the suburbs; its design was considered outdated, accessibility was relatively difficult, and congestion was increasing. The older shops catering to an upper-middle income clientele were being replaced by thrift shops, liquor stores, record shops, bars, and other commercial establishments oriented more toward the incoming lower-income population.

BANK PROFILE

This change in conditions of the surrounding neighborhood had not as yet seriously affected the bank's profitability or growth by 1973. Profitability had consistently remained comparable to that of other banks of a similar size in Dallas. Deposits since 1960 had been rising at an average annual rate of 14.5 percent. The bank's growth in deposits was historically higher than average for the city of Dallas, although there were indications it might be falling below the average in the early

1970s. Elliot attributed this growth to aggressive loan and deposit development programs that actively sought loans and deposits beyond the bank's neighborhood. In the mid 1960s the bank began searching for additional lending opportunities in the real estate market. It had had some prior limited experience with financing the purchase of a few homes and commercial properties, largely as favors to regular customers, but no significant real estate investment effort had ever been made. A Real Estate Loan Department was established in 1967. In 1968 the bank expanded into construction financing in the profitable apartment and shopping center markets in Dallas. During the late 1960s and early 1970s the bank's real estate loan portfolio increased as a share of total assets, largely due to the higher yields available in real estate at that time.

CHANGES

Although the bank enjoyed continuing financial strength in the 1960s and early 1970s, Elliot observed certain changes in bank operating conditions that appeared to be related to the changes that were taking place in the surrounding neighborhood:

1. INABILITY TO GENERATE INSTALLMENT LOANS
   One type of loan that was very profitable but that Lakewood was increasingly unable to generate in large volumes was consumer installment loans. Elliot felt this lack of success was in part attributable to the bank's neighborhood, which was composed of mature households rather than young couples, many of whom did relatively little borrowing.

2. DECLINING DEPOSIT POTENTIAL
   The bank had for a number of years competed with four other banks in the area for deposits and lending opportunities. Elliot's aggressive development programs were successful at increasing the bank's size from fourth to first place in only a few years. In fact, one of the competing institutions moved out of the area entirely, relocating to a newer suburban market. Elliot regarded this as a victory of sorts but also as a warning of the declining potential of the area.

3. HEAVY FINANCIAL COMMITMENT TO NEW BUILDING
   In 1963 Elliot recommended, and the board of directors agreed to, the construction of a new $700,000 building that would replace the existing rented quarters. Although there was some talk of relocating, the decision was made with little debate to again locate in the same neighborhood in Lakewood Shopping Center, less than one block away from the old structure. Deterioration of the surrounding area had not advanced far enough at this time to arouse concern about the future of the bank in the East Dallas area. However, the decision of Elliot and the board to build in the same area meant to Elliot the bank had a substantial long-term financial stake in the community and was increasingly vulnerable to adverse change in the area. The

new structure was opened in 1965 and an addition was completed in 1971. It was the first new commercial construction in the area in 30 years.

4. DISPERSAL OF LOAN AND DEPOSIT SOURCES AND LOWERED LOCAL CREDITWORTHINESS
Most new lending and deposit sources were increasingly originating from outside the bank's area. Since Texas does not allow branch banking, the bank could not expand physically into surrounding areas. Elliot surmised that this geographical anchor would ultimately prevent the bank from penetrating more distant markets much more deeply than it already had through the development programs. In addition, those loan applications, both for commercial credit, installment credit, and construction and repair credit that did originate in the immediate area were increasingly of lower quality. Credit records of applicants were worse and loan security was generally less satisfactory.

The bank had established a goal in 1968 of $75 million in total resources by 1975. Elliot, with the support of long-term projections completed by the bank, by the early 1970s came to the conclusion that the growth trend the bank had enjoyed in the past could not continue, and this goal would not be met if current trends in migration, deterioration, and current bank attitudes and policies continued. At some point a decision would have to be made on a strategy designed to achieve this goal, with the most obvious strategies being a substantial redevelopment effort in the immediate area or relocation to a more profitable suburban location.

ARGUMENTS IN FAVOR
OF REDEVELOPMENT

Several factors provided support to a redevelopment strategy. First, several officers, including Elliot, and several board members, including Conway Walker, a former Dallas mayor and very active board member, lived in the East Dallas or Lakewood areas and had a substantial personal commitment to the area. Walker was a long time resident of the Swiss Avenue district that was being immediately threatened by change. Second, the bank already had some experience with community involvement. Elliot, as early as 1964, had emphasized community involvement by the bank, although more at the individual volunteeer service level than at the institutional financial support level. Several officers and other employees had been active in organizations such as the local Chamber of Commerce, the Boy Scouts, and local business and professional associations. The bank had also been active in supporting enlargement and modernization of the shopping center, street widening programs, and the attraction of new business.

The most active involvement by Lakewood Bank in the redevelopment of the area had come recently, since 1972, in the form of over $800,000 worth of home improvement and home purchase loans on Swiss Avenue. Elliot had decided that default risks on such loans would not be excessive in view of the unique character of the area and the limited scope of lending activity. He was strongly supported in his decision by Walker and several other board members. The project was given impetus in the summer of 1973 with the creation of the Swiss Avenue Historic District by the city of Dallas, an act that reestablished the future of the area as a prestigious single-family neighborhood and brought with it increased city services and development controls. The eleven loans made by Lakewood Bank on Swiss in 1972–73 acted as a catalyst for other lenders to return to the area. By late 1973 it was clear that Swiss Avenue would remain a stable upper and upper-middle income enclave.

Elliot enjoyed the success of the Swiss Avenue experience, and it encouraged him toward a redevelopment strategy. However, he realized several factors mitigated this success as a portent of future broader success in "revitalizing" East Dallas. First, the Swiss Avenue homes were large stately mansions—very unique and with a high degree of architectural quality. Such was not the case with all of East Dallas. Second, although some of the homes had been converted to rooming houses, the Swiss Avenue area had not declined to the extent that other neighborhoods, such as Munger Place and Junius Heights, had. Third, he had some doubt as to whether there would be sufficient demand for older homes in close-in deteriorated neighborhoods by middle and upper-middle income families to significantly impact the area.

ARGUMENTS OPPOSED
TO REDEVELOPMENT

There was also considerable skepticism from within and without the bank over expanding redevelopment lending activities in the East Dallas area. This skepticism originated from some lending officers and appraisers in the marketplace—individuals who should have expertise on market potential. None of them resided in the East Dallas-Lakewood area and thus were not influenced by personal commitments to the area. These individuals advanced several arguments against a further commitment, which Elliot seriously evaluated.

First, they said that physical and functional depreciation of the housing stock in older East Dallas (besides Swiss Avenue) was already far advanced and was irreversible. Any expectation of rising property values was pure speculation and not justified by appraisal practices. Only a limited number of younger households felt favorably toward older, deteriorated structures and even these households would move to the suburbs when their children reached school age, in view of the inferior reputation of Dallas public schools. There were few amenities in the area for such households. City services were minimal in most areas, and the crime rate was increasing. Racial transition to Mexican-American and some black occupancy was now past the "tipping point" and extended to within a few blocks of Lakewood Shopping Center, further reducing middle-income white demand. Finally, many of the structures were of questionable architectural quality anyway, especially in the Heights area, lacking the "uniqueness" necessary to revitalize an area.

A second point of skepticism related to the expansiveness of the area and the limited resources of the bank. To turn an area around, they reasoned, would require substantial resources. Property values were in the $10–16,000 range for most of the run-down homes in the area. To bring most structures up to code would require roughly equivalent expenditures. Thus a combined home purchase–home repair loan would require an average commitment (and in some cases more) by bank and borrower of $20–32,000 or more. If the purchase and repair of 30 percent of the 22,000 units in East Dallas were assumed to provide a suitable critical mass for revitalization, to be successful the bank would have to commit itself to almost $150 million worth of such loan activity, an amount obviously far beyond its capability, especially since it was a commercial bank and not primarily in the business of long-term residential mortgage lending. The danger of making fewer than a critical number of loans in the area was that the loan program would have little impact and result in substantial losses in view of the low property values and high per-loan loss exposure. Reducing the area for lending to allow intensive lending would mean the neighborhood would be subject to adverse external forces hastening decay. Committing too large a portion of the bank's assets to such lending would unwisely expose the bank to high risks without compensating returns.

Rather than increasing commitment to the local area, these individuals advocated further loan and deposit development on a metropolitan-wide basis and gradual withdrawal from the area along with eventual relocation in more stable surroundings after finding a replacement tenant for the bank building.

[Postscript and editor's note: The Lakewood Bank case is an actual case developed from a single Dallas bank. Many banks in the United States have encountered parallel circumstances. A most interesting case about the South Shore National Bank of Chicago, Illinois, was published in *Chicago* (February 1977). T.L.B.]

Dow Chemical Company and Napalm-B

"This Napalm is a good discriminate, strategic weapon, and we feel these folks ought to have it."[1]

Herbert Dow Doan, President
Dow Chemical Company

Napalm was developed exclusively for military purposes. It was pursued in World War I as a method for stopping tanks, but in fact had been used in roughly the same chemical form 1300 years ago, when it was known as "Greek fire." It was subsequently used for strategically important military purposes, including the siege of Constantinople (A.D. 674–678).[2] In more recent times, napalm attracted attention when used against human targets at Guadalcanal in 1942. Napalm had been improved by the work of a team of Harvard chemists, who subsequently noted napalm's effectiveness in "driving the enemy out of cover and underground defensive installations, and in burning out whole areas held by stubbornly resisting Japanese troops."[3] The American press and public enthusiastically cheered these strategic victories in driving the Japanese from their so-called "Pacific Island pillboxes."

Poisonous gases had been developed for strategic purposes in open-field situations and might have been applied to bunker situations, had they not been prohibited by the Geneva agreement. Napalm, a gel, was not interpreted by the U.S. government as prohibited under any agreement that it had accepted. Napalm also was thought to be especially appropriate for the war in the Pacific Islands: The Japanese soldier did not retreat in the face of overwhelming odds as did the Ger-

---

[1]Saul Friedman, "This Napalm Business," in Robert Heilbroner, et al., In the Name of Profit (Garden City, N.Y.: Doubleday & Co., Inc., 1972), p. 128.

[2]E. N. Brandt, The Dow Chemical Co. (Correspondence of March 15, 1982), relying on Michael Grant, Dawn of the Middle Ages (New York: McGraw-Hill, 1981), pp. 36–37.

[3]From Friedman, "This Napalm Business," p. 129.

This case was prepared by Martha W. Elliott and revised by Tom L. Beauchamp. **Not to be duplicated without permission of the authors and publisher.**

man, but rather "defended his foxhole, pillbox, or bunker to the death regardless of the odds against him."[4]

First used in flame throwers, napalm later was used in bombs as well. By the end of World War II, chemists at Eglin Air Force Base had produced napalm-B, an "improved" product that replaces soap with polystyrene as a jelling agent. Napalm-B

> produced just the right balance for killing—thin enough to spread over great distances, thick enough to adhere to anything it touched. With a mixture of two parts polystyrene and one part each of gasoline and benzene, a six pound bomb could splatter an area the size of a football field with sticky flame as hot as 2,000 degrees, capable of burning up to twenty minutes.[5]

Polystyrene, the "new improved" jelling agent was produced by the Dow Chemical Company, and in 1966 Dow began to manufacture napalm-B directly for the Air Force, as well as to supply polystyrene to the United Technology Center. United Technology was a subsidiary of United Aircraft, the other napalm manufacturer under contract to the government. In the first year of the contract, the Air Force ordered 150 million pounds of napalm-B from its two suppliers—more than three-quarters of the amount used throughout World War II. Within a year United Technology withdrew from the manufacture of napalm and left the field to Dow. Eventually the Dow production of napalm-B reached 50 million pounds a month.[6]

The press dramatized various uses of napalm in Vietnam, and in late 1966 the peace movement began a campaign against Dow.

> Challenging Dow Chemical, like resisting the draft or demonstrating at the Pentagon, essentially represented another way of expressing opposition to the American military presence in Indochina.
> Dow, more than any other corporation, became a major focus of the student movement. On many campuses, the issue of whether or not Dow should be allowed to recruit became one of the most important and divisive controversies. . . .[7]

Groups other than students also protested against Dow. In Washington, D.C. a group of priests, nuns, and draft resisters broke into company offices and poured blood over company files. Many of the company's sales offices and factories were picketed, and in 1969 Dow experienced a major confrontation, led by students and clergymen, at

[4]*Ibid.*, p. 133.
[5]*Ibid.*, p. 135.
[6]*Ibid.*, p. 136.
[7]David Vogel, *Citizen Challenges to Business Authority* (New York: Basic Books, 1978), pp. 43–44.

their annual stockholders meeting. A consumer boycott was organized against popular Dow household products (particularly Saran Wrap), and some physicians ceased prescribing Dow-produced drugs. In 1968 and again in 1969 the Medical Committee of Human Rights, an anti-war organization of medical personnel, tried unsuccessfully to force the company to propose an amendment to the company's charter of incorporation specifying that "napalm will not be sold to any buyer unless that buyer gives reasonable assurance that the substance will not be used on or against human beings." New York's Union Theological Seminary sold its 6,000 shares of Dow stock in protest against the continued manufacture of napalm. The total number of stockholders fell from 95,000 to 90,000.[8]

How did Dow react to the protests? Herbert (Ted) Dow Doan, president of Dow from 1962 to 1971 claimed that he knew nothing about Dow's involvement in the production of napalm until 1966:

> You don't run around and approve every order that any salesman makes or anything that's going on with the government. Our government affairs people went out and got this order because we make polystyrene, and it wasn't until the public furor came along that this thing got examined.[9]

The claim that the president and the chairman of Dow did not know that Dow was manufacturing napalm-B became part of an ongoing controversy, but the claim is not intrinsically implausible. The corporate structure at Dow had been deliberately decentralized. Dow had a specialized structure of leadership in which no one examined contracts except those directly responsible for them. No one person, therefore, had overall responsibility for napalm.[10] There was a separate government affairs department in Washington that lobbied for the company's interest and sought government contracts.[11] Scientists at Dow also tended to be isolated from the final uses of the products they developed. According to Dr. Turner Alfrey, Jr., a senior Dow chemist, "When we complete a process, it is taken from us by the production people, the finance people, the marketing people, and the sales people. We have nothing more to do with it."[12]

Dow claimed that at no time did napalm-B represent more than a fraction of Dow sales. In 1966 Dow claimed total sales of $1.3 billion and napalm-B sales of $6.5 million.[13]

[8]*Ibid.*, pp. 44–46.
[9]Friedman, "This Napalm Business," p. 136.
[10]*Ibid.*, p. 137.
[11]*Ibid.*, pp. 137–138.
[12]*Ibid.*, p. 138.
[13]*Ibid.*, p. 142.

Doan justified the production of napalm-B as in the national interest, much as it had been accepted as being in the national interest during World War II. Shortly after the protests began, Dow issued a statement that said:

> Our position on the manufacture of napalm is that we are a supplier of goods to the Defense Department and not a policy maker. We do not and should not try to decide military strategy or policy. Simple good citizenship requires that we supply the government and our military with those goods which they feel they need whenever we have the technology and capability and have been chosen by the government as the supplier.[14]

A view sympathetic to the Dow position was delivered in an opinion by Judge Edward A. Tamm in a court case resulting from the attempted introduction of the stockholders resolution by the Medical Committee for Human Rights:

> The management of Dow Chemical Company is repeatedly quoted in sources which include the company's own publications as proclaiming that the decision to continue manufacturing and marketing napalm was made not *because* of business considerations, but *in spite of* them; that management in essence decided to pursue a course of action which generated little profit for the shareholders and actively impaired the company's public relations and recruitment activities because management considered this action morally and politically desirable. The proper political and social role of modern corporations is, of course, a matter of philosophical argument. . . .[15]

However, a document illegally taken from Dow's Washington office in 1969 by a group of antiwar protestors revealed that in addition to the published sales Dow had a substantial share in

> . . . the $20 million plastic ammunition container business, the tons of aluminum and magnesium that go into military and space programs, and the quantity of chemicals and plastics that move through distributors and fabricators into government application. . . .[16]

Saul Friedman, a reporter for the *Detroit Free Press* and a long-standing, sharp critic of Dow, suggests that support of government policy was simply self-serving on the part of Dow:

[14]Friedman, "This Napalm Business," p. 137.

[15]*Medical Committee for Human Rights* v. *Securities and Exchange Commission, Federal Reporter* 432 F.2d 259 (1970), as reprinted in Tom L. Beauchamp and Norman E. Bowie, *Ethical Theory and Business*, 1st ed. (Englewood Cliffs, N.J.: Prentice-Hall, Inc., 1979), p. 385.

[16]Friedman, "This Napalm Business," p. 147.

Like other corporations with far-flung interests, Dow could not exist without the protection of the United States Government. Dow's interests and the Government's, therefore, tend to coincide. Dow executives, so conventional in their views, do not challenge basic Government policies, especially those that generate need for Dow's products. . . .[17]

The conflict over napalm also reached to personal friendships in the Dow corporate structure. James H. Laird, a minister with the American Friends Service Committee, sent pictures of child victims of napalm to Carl Gerstacker, his old friend and then Chairman of Dow. The accompanying letter read in part:

I think napalm is a morally outrageous weapon and its use is utterly unjustified. . . . Imagine how we would feel if these were our children. Could we be persuaded that any political objective justified visiting such indignity on human beings?[18]

Gerstacker was troubled by Laird's argument, but ultimately he came to an opposite conclusion about the morality of napalm-B based on obligations to American soldiers:

We have compelled young Americans, . . . many of whom are poor, to fight in Vietnam. Would Laird deprive them of the most effective weapons? Was it not right for America to give weapons to these underprivileged soldiers that were merely the equal of those of the enemy? . . .[19]

Doan and Gerstacker both held that the production of napalm-B was a justifiable industrial enterprise. They determined that Dow would continue to produce it. However, when the contract was up for renewal, Dow was outbid by American Electrical Company of Los Angeles, which was already manufacturing napalm containers. It has been alleged, but never confirmed, that Dow's losing bid was deliberate.[20]

Dow leadership has expressed bitterness over several aspects of the controversy. The first was that throughout the time of the protests, Dow's positive social contributions were ignored. Dow had a fifty-year history of conscientiously testing products before marketing them in order to minimize the possibility of harmful effects. The second was that specific, beneficial products, such as a vaccine for measles, were ignored. Another was that American Electric, which continued the production of napalm-B, never became a target of large-scale protests.

[17]*Ibid.*, p. 139.
[18]*Ibid.*, p. 144.
[19]*Ibid.*, p. 145.
[20]*Ibid.*, p. 151.

Two ironies followed the close of the Dow involvement with napalm-B. In 1971 Ted Dow Doan suddenly stepped down as president of Dow, giving up a salary of $249,000 a year and allowing the leadership of Dow to pass for the first time out of the Dow family.[21] In 1975 Milton Markowitz, editor of *Business and Society* newsletter, cited Dow's outstanding record of social responsiveness and included the company in his list of the nation's ten most socially responsible corporations.[22]

[21]*Ibid.*, p. 153.
[22]Cited by Vogel, *Citizen Challenges*, p. 150.

Plasma International

The Sunday headline in the Tampa, Florida, newspaper read:

Blood Sales Result in Exorbitant Profits for Local Firm

The story went on to relate how the Plasma International Company, headquartered in Tampa, Florida, purchased blood in underdeveloped countries for as little as 15 cents a pint and resold the blood to hospitals in the United States and South America. A recent disaster in Nicaragua produced scores of injured persons and the need for fresh blood. Plasma International had 10,000 pints of blood flown to Nicaragua from West Africa and charged the hospitals $25 per pint, netting the firm nearly a quarter of a million dollars.

As a result of the newspaper story, a group of irate citizens, led by prominent civic leaders, demanded that the City of Tampa and the State of Florida revoke Plasma International's licenses to practice business. Others protested to their congressmen to seek enactment of legislation designed to halt the sale of blood for profit. The spokesperson was reported as saying, "What kind of people are these—selling life and death? These men prey on the needs of dying people, buying blood from poor, ignorant Africans for 15 cents worth of beads and junk, and selling it to injured people for $25 a pint. Well, this company will soon find out that the people of our community won't stand for their kind around here."

"I just don't understand it. We run a business just like any other business; we pay taxes and we try to make an honest profit," said Sol Levin as he responded to reporters at the Tampa International Airport. He had just returned home from testifying before the House Subcommittee on Medical Standards. The recent publicity surrounding his firm's activities during the recent earthquakes had once again

This case was prepared by T. W. Zimmerer and P. L. Preston, Florida Atlantic University. From *Business and Society*, eds. Robert D. Hay, Edmund R. Gray, and James E. Gates (Cincinnati, Ohio: South-Western Publishing Co., 1976). Reprinted with permission of the publisher. **Not to be duplicated without permission of the authors and publisher.**

fanned the flames of public opinion. An election year was an unfortunate time for the publicity to occur. The politicians and the media were having a field day.

Levin was a successful stockbroker when he founded Plasma International Company three years ago. Recognizing the world's need for safe, uncontaminated, and reasonably priced whole blood and blood plasma, Levin and several of his colleagues pooled their resources and went into business. Initially, most of the blood and plasma they sold was purchased through store-front operations in the southeast United States. Most of the donors were, unfortunately, men and women who used the money obtained from the sale of their blood to purchase wine. While sales increased dramatically on the base of an innovative marketing approach, several cases of hepatitis were reported in recipients. The company wisely began a search for new sources.

Recognizing their own limitations in the medical-biological side of the business, they recruited a highly qualified team of medical consultants. The consulting team, after extensive testing and a worldwide search, recommended that the blood profiles and donor characteristics of several rural West African tribes made them ideal prospective donors. After extensive negotiations with the State Department and the government of the nation of Burami, the company was able to sign an agreement with several of the tribal chieftains.

As Levin reviewed these facts, and the many costs involved in the sale of a commodity as fragile as blood, he concluded that the publicity was grossly unfair. His thoughts were interrupted by the reporter's question: "Mr. Levin, is it necessary to sell a vitally needed medical supply, like blood, at such high prices especially to poor people in such a critical situation?" "Our prices are determined on the basis of a lot of costs that we incur that the public isn't even aware of," Levin responded. However, when reporters pressed him for details of these "relevant" costs, Levin refused any further comment. He noted that such information was proprietary in nature and not for public consumption.

McAleer v. A.T. & T.

Daniel McAleer was a $10,500 per year service representative who handled orders for telephone service in A.T. & T.'s Washington, D.C. Long Lines Division. In 1974 he asked for a promotion that he did not receive. Instead, a staff assistant named Sharon Hulvey received the promotion. She was qualified for the job, but she was not as qualified as McAleer, had less seniority, and had scored slightly lower on the company's employee evaluation scale. The job was given to Hulvey because of an affirmative action program at A.T. & T. McAleer claimed that he had been discriminated against on the basis of sex. He then brought a lawsuit against A.T. & T., asking for the promotion, differential back pay, and $100,000 damages (on grounds of lost opportunity for further promotion). Together with his employment union, he also made the claim that A.T. & T. had interfered with the ability of the union (Communications Workers of America) to represent its members and secure employment rights under the relevant collective bargaining agreement.

Some historical background is essential to understand how this situation arose.

This case was prepared by Barry Smith, Sara Finnerty Kelly, and Tom L. Beauchamp. Sources consulted include: *McAleer v. American Telephone and Telegraph Company*, 416 F. Supp. 435 (1976); Earl A. Molander, *Responsive Capitalism: Case Studies in Corporate Social Conduct* (New York: McGraw-Hill Book Co., 1980), pp. 56–70; Theodore Purcell, "Management Development: A Practical Ethical Method and a Case," unpublished; "A.T.&T. Denies Job Discrimination Charges, Claims Firm Is Equal Employment Leader," *Wall Street Journal* (Dec. 14, 1970), p. 6; "A.T.&T. Makes Reparation," *The Economist*, 246 (Jan. 27, 1973), p. 42; Byron Calame, "Liberating Ma Bell: Female Telephone Workers Hit Labor Pact, Say Men Still Get the Best Jobs, More Pay," *Wall Street Journal* (July 26, 1971), p. 22: "FCC Orders Hearing on Charge that A.T.&T. Discriminates in Hiring," *Wall Street Journal* (Jan. 22, 1971), p. 10; "Federal Agency Says A.T.&T. Job Bias Keeps Rates From Declining," *Wall Street Journal* (Dec. 2, 1971), p. 21; Richard M. Hodgetts, "A.T.&T. versus the Equal Employment Opportunity Commission," in his *The Business Enterprise: Social Challenge, Social Response* (Philadelphia: W. B. Saunders Company, 1977), pp. 176–82. **Not to be duplicated without the permission of the authors and publisher.**

HISTORICAL BACKGROUND

The U.S. Equal Employment Opportunity Commission (EEOC) had long been in pursuit of A.T. & T. on grounds of discrimination. In 1970, the EEOC claimed that the firm engaged in "pervasive, system-wide, and blatantly unlawful discrimination in employment against women, blacks, Spanish-surnamed Americans, and other minorities."[1] The EEOC argued that the employment practices of A.T. & T. violated several laws, including the Civil Rights Acts of 1964 and 1866, the Equal Pay Act of 1963, and the Fair Employment Practices Acts of numerous states and cities. In some hearings the EEOC maintained that A.T. & T. "suppressed" women workers and that for the past thirty years "women as a class have been excluded from every job classification except low paying clerical and telephone-operator jobs. . . ."[2] A.T. & T. denied all charges brought against it, claiming that its record demonstrated equality of treatment for minorities and women. It adduced supporting statistics about minorities in the work force, but these statistics were all vigorously challenged by the EEOC.

In the spring of 1972, the Department of Labor intervened and assumed jurisdiction in the matter. Negotiations reached a final agreement on December 28, 1972. An out-of-court settlement was proposed and a Consent Decree was entered in and accepted by a Philadelphia court (January 18, 1973). This agreement resulted in A.T. & T.'s paying $15 million in back wages to 13,000 women and 2,000 minority-group men and giving $23 million in raises to 36,000 employees who had presumably suffered because of previous policies. Despite all these events, A.T. & T. never admitted any wrongdoing.

Out of this settlement came an extensive, company-wide recruitment and promotion program ("affirmative action"). A.T. & T. set rigorous goals and intermediate targets in fifteen job categories to meet first-year objectives. The goals were determined by statistics regarding representative numbers of workers in the relevant labor market. Also, as part of the agreement, if during this campaign its progress were to fall short of deadlines, A.T. & T. would then have to depart from normal selection and promotion standards by more vigorously pursuing affirmative action goals.[3]

---

[1]U.S. Equal Employment Opportunity Commission, "Petition to Intervene," Federal Communications Commission Hearings on A.T. & T. Revised Tariff Schedule, 10 December 1970, p. 1.

[2]"Bias Charges in Hiring: A.T. & T. Fights Back," *U.S. News & World Report,* 14 August, 1972, p. 67.

[3]The stipulations of the agreement were met by the company before an established 1979 deadline.

At the same time, A.T. & T. had a union contract that established ability and merit as the primary qualifications for positions, but also required that seniority be given "full consideration." This contract stood in noticeable contrast to the Consent Decree, which called for "an affirmative action override" that would bypass union-contract promotion criteria if necessary to achieve the affirmative action goals. Therefore, the Decree required that under conditions of a target failure, a less qualified (but qualified!) person could take precedence over a more qualified person with greater seniority. This condition applied only to promotions, not to layoffs and rehiring—where seniority continued to prevail.

MCALEER AND THE COURTS

The McAleer case came before Judge Gerhard A. Gesell, who held on June 9, 1976 that McAleer was a "faultless employee" who became an "innocent victim" through an unfortunate but justifiable use of the affirmative action process. More specifically, Gesell ruled that McAleer was entitled to monetary compensation (as damages), but was not entitled to the promotion because the discrimination the Consent Decree had been designed to eliminate might be perpetuated if Hulvey were not given the promotion. The main lines of Gesell's ruling are as follows:

> After the filing of the Philadelphia complaint and AT&T's contemporaneous answer, and following an immediate hearing, the Court received from the parties and approved a Consent Decree and accompanying Memorandum of Agreement which had been entered into by the governmental plaintiffs and AT&T after protracted negotiation. This settlement was characterized by Judge Higginbotham as "the largest and most impressive civil rights settlement in the history of this nation.". . .
>
> Integral to the affirmative action program was a so-called "seniority override" or "affirmative action override" provision which in effect required AT&T to depart from the promotion criteria specified in the collective bargaining agreement that had in the past governed employee advancement. Prior to the Consent Decree, the contractual standard for promotion among nonmanagement employees called for the selection of the best qualified employee and for consideration of net credited service (seniority), so that when the qualifications of competing employees were substantially equal, net credited service was decisive. "Affirmative action override" requires AT&T to disregard this standard and choose from among basically qualified female or minority applicants if necessary to meet the goals and timetables of the Consent Decree and if other affirmative efforts fail to provide sufficient female or minority candidates for promotion who are the best qualified or most senior. . . .
>
> This entire process occurred without the participation of Communications Workers of America (CWA), the certified collective bargaining rep-

resentative of approximately 600,000 nonmanagement employees at
AT&T and the parent union with which plaintiff Local # 2350 is affili-
ated. Although it was consistently given notice in the Philadelphia case of
the efforts to reach a settlement, and although it was "begged . . . to ne-
gotiate and litigate" in that proceeding, 365 F.Supp. at 1110, CWA per-
sistently and repeatedly refused to become involved. . . .

Judge Higginbotham presently has before him and has taken under
advisement the question of modification of the Consent Decree because
it conflicts with the collective bargaining agreement. . . .

It is undisputed that plaintiff McAleer would have been promoted but
for his gender. This is a classic case of sex discrimination within the
meaning of the Act, 42 U.S.C. § 2000e-2(a)(2). That much is clear. What
is more difficult is the issue of defenses or justifications available to
AT&T and the question of appropriate relief under the circumstances
revealed by this record. McAleer seeks both promotion and damages.
The Court holds that he is entitled only to the latter.

General principles of law also support plaintiff McAleer's right to damages. It is true that AT&T was following the terms of the Consent Decree, and ordinarily one who acts pursuant to a judicial order or other
lawful process is protected from liability arising from the act. . . . But
such protection does not exist where the judicial order was necessitated
by the wrongful conduct of the party sought to be held liable. . . .

Here, the Consent Decree on which defendant relies was *necessary only
because of AT&T's prior sex discrimination.* Under these circumstances the
Decree provides *no defense against the claims of a faultless employee such as
McAleer.* . . . [Italics added]

Since McAleer had no responsibility for AT&T's past sex discrimination, it is AT&T rather than McAleer who should bear the principal burden of rectifying the company's previous failure to comply with the Civil
Rights Act of 1964. An affirmative award of some damages on a "rough
justice" basis is therefore required and will constitute an added cost
which the stockholders of AT&T must bear.

In the same year that Judge Gesell's decision was reached, the same
Judge (A. Leon) Higginbotham mentioned by Gesell rejected the new
union petition to eliminate the affirmative action override from the
Consent Decree—a petition that Gesell noted as pending. Higginbotham went out of his way to disagree with Gesell, saying Gesell's
findings wrongly decided the case. He found A.T. & T. to have im-
munity as an employer because of its history with and commitments to
a valid affirmative action plan. However, since he was hearing a union
case, Higginbotham's ruling did not directly overturn or otherwise affect Gesell's ruling. A.T. & T.'s lawyers—Mr. Robert Jeffrey, in particular—felt strongly that Judge Gesell's arguments were misguided and
that Judge Higginbotham did the best that he could at the time to set
matters right.

A.T. & T. and McAleer settled out of court for $14,000, $6,500 of
which went to legal fees for McAleer's attorney. Both McAleer and

Hulvey are currently employed by A.T. & T. A.T. & T.'s lawyer, Mr. Jeffrey, still believes that this case was an aberration and that subsequent *legal* developments have vindicated their point of view. From the *moral* point of view, Mr. Jeffrey believes that both Judge Gesell's rulings and the law being promulgated at the time in the White House deserve the most serious ethical scrutiny and criticism.[4]

[4]According to Mr. Jeffrey (of the legal staff in A.T. & T.'s Washington, D.C. office), in a phone conversation on March 10, 1982. Mr. Jeffrey handled the McAleer case for A.T. & T.

Dutchland Power and Light Co.

Following a particularly severe winter and as a result of the recent energy crisis, the Dutchland Power and Light Company of New City, Pennsylvania applied for and received a one-year grant from the federal government to provide home-based energy conservation educational services to its residential consumers. One component of the project involved advertising for and hiring ten educational specialists knowledgeable in the area of home management and energy requirements. The specialists would work with homemakers in their geographic area on ways of conserving energy in homes. Following a one-week orientation session, the specialists were to work through community agencies and groups to establish a series of home contacts; the primary activity of the specialists was to work with families, especially those of low income, in their homes, studying family patterns and suggesting ways to reduce energy usage.

One of the terms of the grant award was that the Dutchland Power and Light Company would follow an aggressive affirmative action program in seeking and hiring the educational specialists. Partially as a result of a governor's Upward Mobility program three years previous, the Company had hired a personnel officer with strong commitments to hiring and upgrading women and minorities. In the proposal for the federal grant the Company acknowledged the importance of hiring specialists from the geographic area they would be serving. Management felt that local people, familiar with the special characteristics of the neighborhoods and towns would be most knowledgeable about living patterns in the area and particular needs or attitudes of the local clientele.

The following advertisement was placed in local papers:

This case was prepared by Professors Barbara Brittingham and Dennis Callaghan of the University of Rhode Island, as a basis for class discussion rather than to illustrate either effective or ineffective handling of an administrative situation. Reprinted with permission of the authors. **Not to be duplicated without permission of the authors and publisher.**

We are seeking an educational specialist with knowledge in home management practices and energy utilization to work with families in the _____ area helping them to reduce energy consumption and lower their energy bills. Successful applicants should have a background in home management, experience working with homemakers in their own settings and be familiar with the community and its special needs. This job requires the use of a car. Time of employment: October 1, 1976 to September 30, 1977.

> Apply by August 30 to:
> Frederick Edwards, Personnel Officer
> Dutchland Power and Light Company
> 110 Madison Street
> New City, Pennsylvania

An equal opportunity/affirmative action employer.

Edwards received the applications and reviewed them. He and Georgia Winters, Training Coordinator, interviewed all of the applicants for the position. Each applicant was rated on the following characteristics:

1. Background in home management
2. Experience working with homemakers in their own settings
3. Familiarity with the community
4. Access to a car

The top three candidates for each geographic region were re-interviewed before the final selection. For all ten positions, the applicant pool was as follows:

17 white males
94 white females
6 minority males
21 minority females

Dutchland Power hired the following:

1 white male
7 white females
0 minority males
2 minority females

THE AFFIRMATIVE ACTION COMPLAINT

On October 15, 1976, Frederick Edwards was notified by Susan Shoppe, the State Affirmative Action Officer, that George Anderson, a white male, had filed a discrimination complaint against Dutchland

Power for their failure to hire him as an educational specialist. Mr. Anderson charged "reverse discrimination," stating that he believed that Dutchland Power had not hired him because he was a white male.

On October 20, Susan Shoppe, Frederick Edwards, and Georgia Winters met to discuss the Anderson complaint. Edwards and Winters assured Shoppe that although Dutchland Power actively recruited women and minorities for the position, they did not feel in any way that they discriminated against white males in the hiring. A review of the specifics in the case indicated that for the geographic area in question, Dutchland Power had hired Mrs. Phyllis League. Specific qualifications of Mrs. League and Mr. Anderson were as follows:

MRS. PHYLLIS LEAGUE

Three years of college education with specialization in home economics education with coursework in Home Management.

One year's experience as a cooperative extension agent with Larson County, working with homemakers in the area of food purchasing and meal planning and nutrition.

Had lived in the geographic area of the position for five years. Was active in school and community organizations.

Had access to a car.

MR. GEORGE ANDERSON

Four years of college education in the areas of small business administration and sociology. Bachelor of Arts degree.

Two years of managing a small grocery store.

Did not and had not lived in the geographic area in question.

Resided in a neighboring community. Had helped to coordinate a community action program for employment of women and minorities.

Had access to a car.

THE STATE'S POSITION

After spending an hour and a half with Edwards and Winters, Shoppe informed them she would return to her office and review the facts in the case. She informed them that, as is the customary practice of the State Affirmative Action office, she had co-filed Anderson's complaint with the regional office of the Equal Opportunities Commission. She informed them that they would receive a written copy of her findings and recommendations within three weeks.

On November 7, 1976, Edwards received the following letter from Shoppe.

Re: Complaint of discrimination filed by Mr. George Anderson

Dear Mr. Edwards:

I have reviewed the facts in the case of Mr. George Anderson who applied to Dutchland Power and Light Company for the position of educational specialist. Based on the material you submitted to me and the information I received from Mr. Anderson, I do not find probable cause that Mr. Anderson was treated in a discriminatory fashion by Dutchland Power. As I mentioned to you earlier, the complaint has been co-filed with the regional office of the Equal Employment Opportunities Commission. I will forward my findings to them and to Mr. Anderson. Though EEOC may choose to take action on Mr. Anderson's behalf, the State Affirmative Action Office has concluded its investigation of the complaint.

We thank you for your cooperation in this matter. The assurance of affirmative action and equal opportunity is the responsibility and opportunity of all citizens.

Sincerely,

Susan Shoppe
Senior Complaint Investigator

THE EEOC STEPS IN

On December 1, 1976, Frederick Edwards received communications from the regional EEOC office saying they wished to meet with him to discuss George Anderson's complaint. They explained that they had received Susan Shoppe's letter reporting her findings but wished to pursue the complaint to their own satisfaction. A meeting was arranged for December 15 with Edwards, Winters, Shoppe, and Georgette Manchester from EEOC.

After a meeting to review the facts and documents in the case, EEOC requested copies of the applications for all candidates for the ten positions. On January 15, 1977, Edwards received a communication from EEOC stating that they did not find probable cause for discrimination in the case of George Anderson, but that they were pursuing the matter on a class action basis on the behalf of a Mr. Jerome Phillips, a white male with a degree in Family Ecology and prior consumer work in the area of family budgeting with a social action agency. Mr. Phillips was an unsuccessful applicant in another regional area and had applied for a position for which a minority female had been hired. Mr. Phillips had not yet filed a complaint of discrimination, but EEOC explained that they would be in contact with him to ask him if he were interested in doing so. They asked to arrange a conciliation meeting with Dutchland Power to discuss future hiring practices, with particular emphasis on increasing the number of males for such positions.

In the conciliation meeting, on January 23, 1977, EEOC asked that Dutchland Power agree to the following terms:

1. Establish affirmative action goals of hiring 60 percent men for all further home-related positions (the 60 percent estimate was based on the percent of men in the workforce in the nearest standard metropolitan statistical area).
2. Pay Jerome Phillips $3,436 in back pay for not being hired as an educational specialist.
3. Offer Mr. Phillips a position at comparable pay to the educational specialists within Dutchland Power.

Manchester from EEOC explained that contact with Jerome Phillips indicated that, for personal reasons, he did not wish to file a complaint of discrimination, but that he would be interested in future employment with Dutchland Power.

After meeting with other management officials of the Power company, Edwards wrote to EEOC telling them that:

1. While they were interested in hiring without regard to sex stereotypes, they believed that the 60 percent figure for home-related positions was an unrealistic figure. Information obtained from other agencies indicated that of the workforce in the area who were qualified for home-related positions, approximately one-fourth were male. Edwards proposed that their affirmative action figure for positions in this area be set at 25% male.
2. Dutchland Power did not feel it had discriminated against Jerome Phillips for the position for which he had applied. They explained that at the time of the interview, Mr. Phillips had expressed doubts as to his own interest in the position. Edwards and Winters also felt that the personal skills in relating to homemakers were much higher on the part of the minority candidate who was hired. Dutchland Power did not therefore feel that it owed Phillips back pay.
3. Edwards also explained that Dutchland Power could not at this time offer Mr. Phillips a position with the company. He proposed however, that Mr. Phillips be notified of and interviewed for all future positions at the company for which he was interested.

In a subsequent communication, EEOC said that the Power Company response was interpreted as a failure on the part of the Company to agree to conciliation. They turned the case over to the Justice Department.

In two meetings, officials from the Justice Department met with Edwards and Winters of the Power Company and reviewed the facts in the case and the proposed conciliation agreement. Dutchland Power would not agree to the 60 percent goal that they felt was unrealistic; nor would they agree to paying Phillips back pay or offering him a position immediately.

An impasse had apparently been reached and the parties were preparing to go to court.

chapter 5

The Government

INTRODUCTION   Many industries have long been "self-regulated," that is, they have determined their responsibilities to society and to others free from government regulation. Sometimes there is no specific regulatory mechanism in the profession. More commonly, professional codes and governance procedures, together with established systems of incentives and punishments, serve to regulate the conduct of businesspersons. The strategy has been to institutionalize proper moral behavior as a part of professional practice; and when top management supports such codes, they often tend to be successful. However, enforcement of codes has proved lax in some cases and impossible to achieve in others. The government has therefore intervened and regulated circumstances that involve potentially serious offenses against competitors or society.

Government intervention and regulation of free trade arose in the United States and in most industrial nations in the late nineteenth century, when large corporations began to control the economy in ways that curtailed competition and led to inflated prices. This caused decreased wages and the cost of living increased dramatically. The social judgment at the time was that some corporations had gained too much control over the competitive free market, and indeed over workers and the economy. Through the years government regulatory bodies grew steadily in both size and power. Gradually railroads, food and drug companies, investment houses, advertising agencies, and most major industries were regulated by rules specific to the trade. Eventually other regulations were passed that covered all industry hiring practices, environmental controls, advertising, and the like.

As government power grew, the identical complaint of "too much power" that used to haunt industry came to haunt government. The original idea of regulation had been to free the free enterprise system, but now criticism was increasingly heard that regulation inhibits the free enterprise system; the system is shackled by other goals—such as nondiscriminatory hiring, a pollution-free environment, smut-free broadcasting, and the like. "The public interest" had become the rallying defense of those who favored a heavy element of government regulation; but regulation in the public interest spawned two major controversies: What precisely is the public interest (and how is the protection of a free market related to the public interest)? How can the public interest be protected without unduly harming the private interests at stake in free competition?

As social and political systems have become more complex, the problem of fair and adequate government regulation has compounded in difficulty and become mired in controversy—as the Laetrile, Tris Sleepwear, OSHA-Benzene, and Automobile Air Bags cases in this chapter clearly indicate. Skepticism has emerged from various quarters that business has any capacity to regulate itself, and from other quarters that government has anything like an adequate body of information and expertise to regulate business. (The OSHA-Benzene case presents some of the severe constraints presented by lack of information and expertise.) State and local governments have complained almost as much about federal intervention and ownership as has business, which tends to view federal, state, and local requirements as jointly overwhelming. The compromise has been to regulate most heavily where the problems seem most acute—for example, in the regulation of fetus-deforming drugs such as thalidomide and dangerous chemicals such as kepone that produce nervous disorders. The Tris Sleepwear case presents a clear example of the problem of vacillating regulatory efforts.

The result of government hesitancy and outright reversals of policy is a patchwork of inconsistent government regulations directed at particular problems, rather than comprehensive or systematic programs of regulation and enforcement. For some industries this has meant decreased regulation; for others it has indicated a need for a more systematic and perhaps a more comprehensive approach. Regulation has sometimes even been finalized in highly political contexts, where important questions of fairness persist beyond new legislation. A situation thus prevails where virtually no one is satisfied with the current government-business relationship—a situation obviously rife for the conflicts and uncertainties reflected in the cases in this chapter.

On the other hand, it would be dubious to claim, as some critics have, that the U.S. government has remained passively oblivious to problematic issues raised by its regulatory activities. Since the inception of government requirements, the regulatory structure has undergone repeated modification and refinement in light of both internal and external scrutiny, even though this process has not always reflected a recognition of special problems posed by government regulations to business. The precise and changing implications of the developing regulations are therefore difficult to distinguish, and it is only fair to bear in mind that regulation is an ongoing process often responsive to constructive criticism and legislative initiative.

Moreover, even in those domains of business activity that have been left free of government control, the initiatives of self-regulation discussed earlier have often proved no more satisfactory. Professional codes also can be uncertain and can present problems of a conflict of interest on the part of those who administer and enforce codes. Some moral dilemmas are compounded rather than eased by codes and their procedures. These problems in the domain of self-regulation are posed in this chapter in the Aurora-Baxter and ASME Boiler Code cases.

The specter of government regulation raises a number of important *ethical* issues that are reflected in the cases in this chapter. One question is whether the government can legitimately play a paternalistic role. Can business activities be regulated to protect business against itself? to protect customers against their own foolish decisions? to protect clients against their own ignorant choices? The government often makes judgments about "consumer waste" and "health foods" that are not nutritious, drugs that are inefficacious, and the like. Are the legitimate freedoms and rights of citizens and businesses unduly restricted by such judgments? These questions are poignantly raised in this chapter in the Laetrile case, which involves a decision by the Food and Drug Administration (FDA) to ban the manufacture and marketing of an apricot-derived product popular with some cancer victims but declared inefficacious by the FDA.

A second question is whether the government should support businesses that have sustained losses because of government intervention when the businesses were not guilty of moral or legal violations. Sometimes a business or an entire industry is threatened by government-imposed standards. Is the government acting unfairly by regulating and not indemnifying small, under-capitalized industries that could fold or sustain serious losses because of regulatory intervention? This question is unavoidable in the Tris Sleepwear case.

Finally, many questions have been raised about the use of cost/benefit judgments of efficiency as a way of establishing public policies. The basic idea behind cost/benefit judgments is to measure costs and benefits objectively, at the same time identifying uncertainties and possible tradeoffs, in order to present policymakers with relevant information on which to base a decision. Many believe that such information can be used to make clear what tradeoffs are being made and why one alternative is more efficient than another. Yet this rational ideal has proved difficult to achieve and in many cases we are faced with *moral* choices rather than *economic* choices. Considerations of justice, for example (as found in the cases in Chapter 4), might lead us to choose a less efficient but more just outcome. Moreover, it is often debatable what counts as a "cost," a "benefit," or a "valuable" outcome. Government regulatory activities often spark such debates—as the OSHA-Benzene and Air Bags cases dramatically illustrate.

Tris Sleepwear and Government Indemnification

In November 1978 President Jimmy Carter vetoed United States Senate Bill 1503, a bill that would have authorized government indemnification of businesses that had sustained losses as a result of the ban on the use of the chemical "Tris" in children's sleepwear. This veto was a severe disappointment for the beleaguered children's sleepwear manufacturing industry. The industry viewed the veto as one more example of the great difficulty of meeting various government standards.

The relevant history of the debate surrounding Tris dates from the 1967–1971 period. During these years, in response to a growing concern about burns to children—allegedly caused by flammable children's clothing—the federal government (in 1971) established strict flammability standards for children's sleepwear in sizes 0 to 6X. Meeting these standards was difficult, as most children's sleepwear manufacturers are small, undercapitalized, and without extensive research capabilities. In addition, it proved difficult to find flame-retardant chemicals that did not make the fabric stiff and unattractive. Representatives of the children's sleepwear industry (The American Apparel Manufacturers Association) had argued during congressional hearings that the government's proposed standards were technologically unimplementable and that the whole problem of flammable sleepwear had been exaggerated. The industry also explicitly noted that little was known about potential health hazards of the new flame-retardant chemicals that were available. The government did take note of these arguments, and when Secretary of Commerce Maurice Stans finally released the government standards (in July 1971), they were slightly more favorable to industry than previous proposed standards had been. On the other hand, the industry had unsuccessfully argued for amendments to the proposed standards for safe sleepwear. For example, an exemption was sought for sleepwear for infants under one year

---

This case was prepared by Martha W. Elliott and Tom L. Beauchamp. **Not to be duplicated without permission of the authors and publisher.**

of age, on grounds that they did not move enough to encounter significant burn risks. (Government flammability standards in some other countries included such an exemption.) Industry and government alike were concerned that it would prove difficult to comply with the new standard by the established dates (July 1972 and July 1973).

Most manufacturers nonetheless eventually settled on use of the flame retardant chemical (2, 3—dibromopropyl) phosphate—known commercially as "Tris," which had been around for 20 years but had never been used in apparel of any sort. The companies significantly altered their manufacturing operations and ordered large amounts of Tris-treated fabric in order to resume production of sleepwear. In 1974, similar but slightly less strict flammability standards were promulgated by the Consumer Product Safety Commission or CPSC (which had taken over responsibility from the Commerce Department) for sizes 7 to 14 as well.

In 1975 two new pieces of information brought both the strict government flammability standards and the use of Tris into question. A study published by CPSC suggested that previous estimates of the burn risks of untreated sleepwear had been grossly overestimated. An earlier study had estimated 200,000 burn injuries and 4,000 deaths annually due to flammable fabrics; the new data reduced the estimate to 3,000 burn injuries and 100 deaths.[1] Government officials were skeptical of this statistical accounting (by two chemists).

At about the same time (1976), the National Cancer Institute published evidence suggesting that Tris was a carcinogen. Michigan Chemical, the largest producer of Tris, then released laboratory evidence showing low toxicity levels, in effect indicating no substantial problem with Tris. However, this evidence was viewed with skepticism even in the apparel industry. The Environmental Defense Fund (EDF) then petitioned CPSC to compel cautionary labeling of Tris-treated sleepwear. The treated garments contained a volume of Tris as high as 10% of the fabric's weight, a small amount of which could be absorbed through the child's skin or ingested by sucking on the fabric. Washing the garment prior to sale would in theory reduce the surface Tris content without reducing the flame retardant properties, but this was never confirmed. Washing would also have increased the cost of the garments, according to manufacturers, and would have reduced customer appeal by making the garments look used. Government officials were skeptical of this industry argument.

After more testing, in April 1977, the CPSC banned the sale of *all* children's sleepwear containing Tris as a "Hazardous Substance" under

[1]Arlene Blum and Bruce N. Ames, "Flame Retardant Additives as Possible Cancer Hazards," *Science* **195** (January 7, 1977), p. 21.

THE GOVERNMENT

the Federal Hazardous Substances Act. No fabric (as distinct from apparel) manufacturer was still using Tris in its production facilities, but many had Tris-treated fabrics and Tris-finished fabric and garments, both in company inventory and in retail outlets. Because the Federal Hazardous Substances Act requires the automatic repurchase, replacement, or repair of banned items, the children's sleepwear industry faced a potential loss of between $50–200 million dollars.[2]

Industry comments on the ban ranged from concerns about the financial impact to skepticism about substitute flame-retardant chemicals. *Business Week* reported that small companies feared being put out of business altogether and even an industry "giant," the William Carter Company, was pessimistic. The year before the ban, Carter had sales of $97 million, of which $35 million were on Tris-treated products. The president of Carter, Leo J. Feuer, estimated that buying back goods already in customers' hands would cost several times the worth of the company. Fred B. Shippee, the Director of Technical Services for the American Apparel Manufacturers Association focused on the problem of substitutes for Tris: "There are alternative substances but they are more expensive and development is usually three years. Now we are being forced to use chemicals after only 11 months of development work in some cases. We are using substitutes that we're not sure won't later be found unsafe, and at higher prices that may prove unacceptable to the consumer."[3]

New studies also suggested that the risk of cancer might actually outweigh the risk of burns, and after the ban most manufacturers abandoned the use of Tris for sizes 7–14 sleepwear, because the more lax flammability standards allowed use of readily available substitutes. "Lax" here means "easier to meet," but the government standards for the protection of customers were uniform, and safety standards were not compromised. It was the *testing* that was primarily easier to satisfy. Many firms continued to use Tris for sizes 0–6X where stricter standards made substitutes more difficult.

Faced with the prospect of having to buy back millions of dollars worth of Tris-treated garments, while disposing of Tris-treated fabrics in stock, the struggling children's sleepwear industry sought congressional support to secure direct federal reimbursement for these losses. While pursuing court remedies, the manufacturers also went to Congress. In working for the passage of the indemnification bill, some sen-

[2]Subcommittee on Oversight and Investigation, Committee on Interstate and Foreign Commerce, House of Representatives, *Consumer Products Safety Commission's Regulation of Tris: The Need for an Effective Chronic Hazard Program* (Washington, D.C.: Government Printing Office, 1978); "A Flame-Retardant Ban Dishevels An Industry," *Business Week* (April 18, 1977), p. 46.

[3]"A Flame-Retardant Ban Dishevels An Industry," p. 46.

176

ators (largely from Southeastern states) stressed the disastrous economic impact the ban had had on the industry and on the small towns where most of the plants were located. The industry as a whole is a small one, with a total workforce of about 27,000 and a total annual output of about $500 million, and many plants have less than 100 employees.[4] Despite their comparatively small size, these plants are often the largest employers in the small communities in which they are located. The financial losses threatened by the ban on the Tris-treated sleepwear threatened to close some of these plants and to create unemployment and hardship in many communities.

In the face of these problems, the indemnification bill found a sympathetic ear in the United States Congress. However, opposition to the bill emerged from the Justice Department, which noted that this bill would be a bad precedent for similar actions in the future. The Senate Committee on the Judiciary, on the other hand, noted that the problem was more grave for industry and government than the Justice Department observation acknowledged. This Committee held that government regulation had turned out to be "double-edged" in this case: The industry had, in effect, been required to use Tris at great expense, and then required not to use Tris, again at great expense. This argument was successfully deployed in the Congress, and in 1978 the Senate and the House both passed the indemnification bill. This set the stage for President Carter's veto of the bill near the end of this same year.

In his veto of the indemnification bill, President Carter acknowledged that both the strict flammability standards and the subsequent ban on Tris-treated fabrics had imposed a hardship on the industry and that this was "regrettable." Nevertheless, he argued, both the imposition of the standards and the ban on Tris were fully justified in light of the available evidence. He further stated that "no basis exists to require a potential Federal expenditure of millions of dollars where the actions of the Government were fully justified."[5]

In summary, Carter maintained that:

> S. 1503 would establish an unprecedented and unwise use of taxpayers' funds to indemnify private companies for losses incurred as a result of compliance with a federal standard. The Government could be placed in the position in the future of having to pay industry each time new information arises which shows that a product used to meet regulatory stand-

[4]Earl A. Molander, "(2,3—dibromopropyl) Phosphate is a Four-Letter Word—Tris— in the Children's Sleepwear Industry," in his *Responsive Capitalism: Case Studies in Corporate Social Conduct* (New York: McGraw-Hill Book Co., 1980), p. 88.

[5]President Jimmy Carter, "The White House Memorandum of Disapproval," Office of the White House Press Secretary, November 8, 1978, quoted by Molander, "Phosphate is a Four-Letter Word," p. 88.

ards is hazardous. This would be wrong. Producers and retailers have a basic responsibility for insuring the safety of the consumer goods they market.

If this bill became law the potential would exist for compensation of firms who marketed Tris-treated material after they knew, or should have known, that such products constituted a hazard to the health of children.[6]

Members of Congress did not give up the quest for relief for the children's sleepwear manufacturers. On December 18, 1979, the Senate Committee on the Judiciary introduced Senate Bill 521, "a bill to provide for the payment of losses incurred as a result of the ban on the use of the chemical Tris in apparel, fabric, yarn, or fiber, and for other purposes."[7]

Two days later, Senator Strom Thurmond spoke on behalf of the bill:

> This is a classic case of overregulation by the Federal Government. On the one hand it required children's sleepwear manufacturers to put a flame retardant on their products, and then turned around and banned the flame retardant chemical as unsafe. All this was done at no fault to the manufacturers.
>
> This bill is not a bail out, it simply confers jurisdiction on the U.S. Court of Claims to hear claims by those who incurred losses because of the Tris ban.[8]

The bill won easy approval in the Senate, but it was never reported out of committee in the House of Representatives. As of April 1982 the status of the indemnification measure was uncertain. Once again a bill had passed the Senate, but the House Judiciary Subcommittee (on Administrative Law) had not yet considered the bill. Representative Campbell, who introduced the bill in the House, said that he had verbal assurances that, if passed, the bill would *not* be vetoed by President Reagan.[9] The Administration, however, made no public commitment and did not even send representatives to the hearing. At this point the sleepwear manufacturers' major hurdle was probably in the House of Representatives, where a new Subcommittee Chairman made prospects for considering the bill somewhat brighter.

---

[6]*Ibid.*

[7]*Congressional Record* (December 18, 1979), S 19036.

[8]*Congressional Record* (December 20, 1979), S 19343.

[9]Nikki McNamee, Spokesperson for Representative Carroll Campbell, personal communication, November 5, 1981.

The Manufacture and Regulation of Laetrile

> It has been estimated that consumers waste $500 million a year on medical quackery and another $500 million annually on some 'health foods' which have no beneficial effect. Unnecessary deaths, injuries and financial loss . . . can be expected to continue until the law requires adequate testing for safety and efficacy of products and devices before they are made available to consumers. (President John F. Kennedy in a Message to Congress.)[1]

> 'Let me choose the way I want to die.' It is not your prerogative to tell me how. (Glenn Rutherford, cancer patient and Laetrile supporter, at FDA hearing.)[2]

These two quotations express the essence of an acrimonious conflict that raged over the better part of the 1970s in the scientific and popular press, in courtrooms and hearing rooms, in prestigious research institutions, and among drug manufacturers. This conflict emerged over the regulation, manufacture, and marketing of Laetrile, a drug said to be a cure for cancer by its supporters but denounced as worthless by most of the scientific community. Some pieces of history will help us appreciate how this controversy emerged.

The Food and Drug Administration (FDA) has responsibility for determining both the safety and the efficacy of a drug before allowing it to be marketed in the United States. (However, a New Drug Application must be submitted to the FDA by a manufacturer before the agency will review the data.) This responsibility for drug licensing dates from the passage in 1906 of the Pure Food and Drug Act. This act was addressed primarily to abuses among purveyors of patent med-

---

[1]Quoted by David A. Smith, "The Laetrile Dilemma," *Pennsylvania Medicine* **80** (August 15, 1977), p. 15.

[2]Quoted by James C. Peterson and Gerald A. Markle, "The Laetrile Controversy" in *Controversy: Politics of Technical Decisions,* ed. Dorothy Nelkin (Beverly Hills, Calif.: Sage Publications, 1979), p. 175.

This case was prepared by Martha W. Elliott and revised by Tom L. Beauchamp and Linda Kern. **Not to be duplicated without permission of the authors and publisher.**

icines and required that the quantity and nature of the potent ingredients in such medicines be listed and that labels not make false claims. In 1938 the Food, Drug, and Cosmetic Act required the FDA to assess the *safety* of a drug prior to approving it for manufacture and general use. The 1962 Amendments to this act (passed partly in response to problems in the use of the drug thalidomide) strengthened the safety requirement and added the requirement that the drug must also be shown to be *effective* before it could be approved for marketing.[3] These laws state that the burden of proving both the effectiveness and the safety of a drug falls on the manufacturer.

Certain state-level decisions regarding Laetrile, especially under Oklahoma Judge Bohanon, have severely challenged the FDA's regulatory power. In the 1977 *Rutherford v. United States* case, Judge Bohanon defended Laetrile on three counts. First, he argued that Laetrile's long-time association with cancer therapy rendered it a "drug" by statutory definition. Second, he noted that Laetrile has been commercially used and sold in the U.S.A. for over 25 years while thought to be safe by qualified experts, and thus is exempt from the "new drug" requirements of the FDA. Third, he argued that by denying access to a non-toxic substance for personal health care, the FDA violated a constitutional right of privacy.[4] John F. Cannizzaro and Madelon M. Rosenfield have in turn severely challenged Judge Bohanon:

> Quite simply, Justice Bohanon avoided the "new drug" issues by arbitrarily ruling that Laetrile was not a "new drug." Based on unfounded evidence, the decision determined Laetrile to have been *generally* recognized by experts as *safe* for its intended use in cancer therapy prior to 1962, thereby avoiding the necessity of proving the drug's effectiveness. . . . There exists little doubt that the present ruling was predicated upon the earlier ruling of the court of appeals, which erroneously shifted the burden of proof to the FDA. These decisions have placed the FDA in the difficult position of having to prove by hearing that any substance which existed prior to 1962 was *not* marketed and generally recognized as safe. The necessity of having to prove a negative imposes an unbearable burden which neutralizes the FDA's function as a drug regulatory agency.[5]

---

[3]Two arguments were advanced in favor of the efficacy requirement. The economic argument had to do with consumer protection, *i.e.,* consumers were wasting money on drugs that were not benefiting them. The second argument had to do with health and safety, namely, that reliance on ineffective drugs could be dangerous when effective alternatives were available. The FDA held that although Laetrile appeared "harmless," it had not been proven effective and therefore should not be approved for manufacture and sale in the United States.

[4]*Rutherford v. United States,* 438 F. Supp. (1977).

[5]John F. Cannizzaro and Madelon M. Rosenfield, "Laetrile and the FDA: A Case of Reverse Regulation," in *The Journal of Health Politics, Policy and Law,* Vol. 3, No. 2 (Summer 1978), pp. 181–195.

The Laetrile case turns largely on the drug's efficacy and on one's right to manufacture, market, and purchase the product. During the 1970s the FDA had suffered criticisms that it was a "paternalistic" agency after it attempted to ban the manufacture and marketing of the popular artificial sweetener saccharin. Laetrile efforts came squarely on the heels of this unpopular FDA policy. By mid-1977, FDA head Donald Kennedy found himself with increasing evidence (at least to his own satisfaction) of the inefficacy of Laetrile. However, criticism of the FDA was increasing and efforts were mounting either to allow free choice of the drug or to have its efficacy demonstrated in a public trial using human subjects. A number of state legislatures and judges were also calling the FDA's determinations into question. Some states had legalized its manufacture and sale, and some courts had criticized the FDA record and policies. Even prestigious physicians and newspapers such as the *New York Times* had endorsed the right of individuals to choose the drug if it turned out to be inefficacious.

The ferocity of this debate was new in the 1970s, but Laetrile was not. Amygdalin, the chemical name for Laetrile, has been known since the first half of the eighteenth century. Modern proponents of Laetrile therapy attribute the beginning of the movement to Ernst Krebs, who began experimenting with the extract of apricot pits in the 1920s, and to his son Ernst Krebs, Jr., who refined the extract to produce the drug Laetrile in 1952. Laetrile researchers have experimented with a variety of methods and techniques for using Laetrile in the treatment of cancer, and they claim that Laetrile is in fact effective against cancer. According to Krebs, Laetrile is effective because cyanide, which is an active ingredient, attacks the cancerous cells while an enzyme called rhodanese protects the normal cells.[6]

Some supporters claim that Laetrile not only cures or controls existing cancers but can also prevent cancers from forming. Claims for the effectiveness of Laetrile are based primarily on patients' case histories (such as those published by Richardson and Griffen in *Laetrile Case Histories*) and on personal testimonials of "cured" cancer victims. However, the medical and scientific community on the whole has not been impressed with this form of "proof." The reported case histories have been viewed as too sketchy and the follow-up times too short to support claims. Moreover, few patients take Laetrile without first undergoing more traditional forms of cancer therapy. It is therefore virtually impossible to determine which treatment(s) should receive credit for improvements. Also, the natural history of cancer is not totally under-

---

[6]Thomas Donaldson, "Case Study—Laetrile: The FDA and Society," in Thomas Donaldson and Patricia Werhane, eds., *Ethical Issues in Business: A Philosophical Approach* (Englewood Cliffs, N.J.: Prentice-Hall, 1979), p. 208.

stood, and spontaneous remissions can and do occur.[7] Animal studies have also led most (but not all) researchers to conclude that Laetrile is not effective against cancer. Proponents of the drug counter that standards of proof for Laetrile research have been higher than for other cancer drugs and that pro-Laetrile results have been obtained but suppressed.[8]

The prohibition of Laetrile by the FDA has important economic implications, and both sides have accused the other of economic exploitation of cancer victims. Most Laetrile has thus far been manufactured and marketed in Mexico. It has been estimated that in 1977 alone approximately 7,000 patients were treated in two Mexican clinics at an average cost of $350 per day.[9] Proponents of Laetrile counter that traditional cancer treatments represent an enormous and profitable industry, and a cost savings for Americans would be achieved if Laetrile were marketed in the U.S. For instance, the American Cancer Society estimated that in 1972 the direct costs (hospital, nursing home care, physicians' and nurses' fees, drugs and other treatments, and research) of cancer treatment totaled over $3 billion.[10] The U. S. represents an obvious and growing market for Laetrile, and for clinics that provide it as therapeutic. Although the Food and Drug Administration does not control *intra*state commerce, it would not be profitable for any one state to manufacture Laetrile in all its stages—that is, from the farming of apricot trees all the way to the laboratory synthesis of the finished drug. Approval of the drug for *inter*state U.S. manufacture and sale would not only be a boon to U.S. business, but it would also enable customers to avoid the enormous markup now paid for black market Laetrile. Moreover, Laetrile is extremely cheap on the retail market—a tiny fraction of the cost of conventional cancer therapies.

The courts as well as the press have provided the arena for the conflict over the rights of a patient to choose a treatment and manufacturers to produce a product. While it was not the intent of Congress to impose such restrictions on choice, the patient's choice is in fact restricted as a result of the 1962 Drug Amendments. Because the market in safe drugs is restricted to industry-tested and FDA-approved products, treatment and manufacturing alternatives are inevitably constricted,[11] at least until a New Drug Application is filed. (As yet, no New Drug Application has been filed for Laetrile.)

A series of lawsuits has challenged the FDA restrictions, and a num-

---

[7]John W. Yarbro, "Laetrile 'Case Histories': A Review and Critique," *Missouri Medicine* **76** (April 1979), pp. 195–203.

[8]Peterson and Markle, "The Laetrile Controversy," p. 170.

[9]Donaldson, "Case Study—Laetrile," p. 211.

[10]Peterson and Markle, "The Laetrile Controversy," p. 172.

[11]See Don G. Rushing, "Picking your Poison: The Drug Efficacy Requirement and the Right of Privacy," *UCLA Law Review* **25** (February 1978), p. 587.

ber of states have passed laws "legalizing" its use. (The aforementioned Oklahoma Judge Bohanon has also promoted this trend in the courtroom.) The judicial and legislative challenges are not, however, without opponents. Harvard lawyer William Curran, for instance, has deplored the action of certain courts in allowing the use of Laetrile for the terminally ill. "It is understandable," he writes, "that judges have had trouble dealing objectively with the legal pleas of plaintiffs who are dying a painful death and whose only wish is to indulge in a harmless, although ineffective, gesture of hope. The courts have tried to dispense mercy. . . . Their error has been in abandoning the protection of law for these patients."[12]

As the arguments have developed, the issues of choice and fraudulent representation by business have moved to the forefront. Franz Inglefinger, the distinguished former editor of *The New England Journal of Medicine* and himself a cancer victim, was convinced that Laetrile was "useless." In 1977 he wrote, "I would not take Laetrile myself under any circumstances. If any member of my family had cancer, I would counsel them against it. If I were still in practice, I would not recommend it to my patients." On the other hand, he said, "Perhaps there are some situations in which rational medical science should yield and make some concessions. If any patient had what I thought was hopelessly advanced cancer, and if he asked for Laetrile, I should like to be able to give the substance to him to assuage his mental anguish, just as I would give him morphine to relieve his physical suffering."[13] Inglefinger did not view proper marketing of the drug as involving fraudulent misrepresentation. Dr. Inglefinger added, however, that perhaps "an evaluation [of Laetrile] should be made by a lay-professional group . . . [and] not by committees appointed by the FDA or AMA."[14]

As a result of these arguments over freedom of choice for patients and the freedom of American business, the FDA has been considerably perplexed over the exact nature of its responsibilities and how best to discharge them. This debate was fueled anew from a different perspective in October 1981. In that month, *The Washington Post* ran a series of widely discussed articles on the variety of ways in which cancer patients suffer from conventional cancer therapies.[15] The *Post* articles led many to believe that, however worthless Laetrile may be, it at least does not lead to such suffering.

---

[12]William J. Curran, "Laetrile for the Terminally Ill: Supreme Court Stops the Nonsense," *New England Journal of Medicine* 302 (March 13, 1980), p. 621.

[13]Franz Inglefinger, "Laetrilomania," (Editorial) *New England Journal of Medicine* **296** (May 19, 1977), p. 1167.

[14]*Ibid.*, p. 1168.

[15]However, the *Post* articles were widely denounced by those in cancer research as having grossly distorted the risks, safety, and efficacy of conventional cancer cures.

The OSHA-Benzene Case

In May of 1977 the Occupational Safety and Health Administration (OSHA) of the United States government issued an emergency temporary standard (ETS) ordering that worker exposure to the chemical benzene—which is widely present in industrial manufacturing—be reduced from the existing regulated level of 10 parts per million (ppm) to 1 ppm [time weighted average (TWA)]. In addition, OSHA proposed to make this a permanent standard for benzene exposure in all industries (except gasoline distribution and sales), pending a hearing (as required by section 6 of the Occupational Safety and Health Act).

OSHA's action was precipitated by a report to the National Institutes of Health in 1977 of excessive leukemia deaths related to benzene. These deaths occurred in two rubber pliofilm plants in Ohio. On this basis, and without having studies showing a relation of benzene to leukemia in humans at levels of exposure below 50–100 ppm, OSHA determined benzene to be a leukemogen (leukemia-causing agent) and ruled that worker safety demanded reduction of exposure to the lowest technologically feasible levels.

OSHA and industry both determined, subsequent to publication of the standard, that compliance costs would be in the hundreds of millions of dollars, with considerable uncertainty about the number of workers likely to be protected from cancer. OSHA's general assumption was that lowered exposure to a potential carcinogen is desirable; but little medical evidence existed of a relation between benzene and cancer at already *established* levels. Because there is some scientific evidence to indicate that there are no-effect exposure levels (harmless levels), the oil industry questioned the wisdom of OSHA's expending large public and private resources in the regulation of a chemical that most agree is a weak leukemogen.

On the other hand, benzene seems definitely to be a carcinogen, and

This case was prepared by Tom L. Beauchamp. **Not to be duplicated without permission of the author and publisher.**

workers can be seriously affected by it. OSHA therefore has a legitimate interest in the regulation of industrial manufacture involving benzene. Mainly under study throughout 1978–79 was the *level* at which the chemical would be allowed in the environment, not *whether* its use and manufacture should be regulated. Into this atmosphere of controversy stepped the United States Supreme Court, which reached a decision about certain aspects of this problem on July 2, 1980. In a case brought by the AFL-CIO (Industrial Union Department) and others against the American Petroleum Institute (the Trade Association of American Oil Companies), the Supreme Court found that the proposed OSHA standard was unjustifiably strict, but in no way rejected the legitimacy of OSHA's right to regulate such industrial manufacture on a less strict standard. Some central findings of this court, as written by Mr. Justice Stevens, are as follows:[1]

> This case concerns a standard promulgated by the Secretary of Labor to regulate occupational exposure to benzene, a substance which has been shown to cause cancer at high exposure levels. The principal question is whether such a showing is a sufficient basis for a standard that places the most stringent limitation on exposure to benzene that is technologically and economically possible.
>
> The [Occupational Safety and Health] Act delegates broad authority to the Secretary to promulgate different kinds of standards. The basic definition of an "occupational safety and health standard" is found in § 3 (8), which provides:
>
>> "The term 'occupational safety and health standard' means a standard which requires conditions, or the adoption or use of one or more practices, means, methods, operations, or processes, reasonably necessary or appropriate to provide safe or healthful employment and places of employment." 29 U. S. C. § 652 (8).
>
> Where toxic materials or harmful physical agents are concerned, a standard must also comply with § 6 (b) (5), which provides:
>
>> "The Secretary, in promulgating standards dealing with toxic materials or harmful physical agents under this subsection, shall set the standard which most adequately assures, to the extent feasible, on the basis of the best available evidence, that no employee will suffer material impairment of health or functional capacity even if such employee has regular exposure to the hazard dealt with by such standard for the period of his working life. Development of standards under this subsection shall be based upon research, demonstrations, experiments, and such other information as may be appropriate. In addition to the attainment of the highest degree of health and safety protection for the employee, other considerations shall be the latest available scientific data in the field, the feasibility

[1]The subsequent material is all quoted directly from Supreme Court of the United States, *Industrial Union Dept., AFL-CIO* v. *American Petroleum Institute et al.* (Slip Opinion of July 2, 1980), pp. 1–5, 18–23.

of the standards, and experience gained under this and other health and safety laws." 29 U. S. C. § 655 (b) (5).

Wherever the toxic material to be regulated is a carcinogen, the Secretary has taken the position that no safe exposure level can be determined and that § 6 (b) (5) requires him to set an exposure limit at the lowest technologically feasible level that will not impair the viability of the industries regulated. In this case, after having determined that there is a causal connection between benzene and leukemia (a cancer of the white blood cells), the Secretary set an exposure limit on airborne concentrations of benzene of one part benzene per million parts of air (1 ppm), regulated dermal and eye contact with solutions containing benzene, and imposed complex monitoring and medical testing requirements on employers whose workplaces contain 0.5 ppm or more of benzene.

The United States Court of Appeals for the Fifth Circuit held the regulation invalid. The court concluded that OSHA had exceeded its standard-setting authority because it had not shown that the new benzene exposure limit was "reasonably necessary or appropriate to provide safe or healthful employment" as required by § 3 (8), and because § 6 (b) (5) does "not give OSHA the unbridled discretion to adopt standards designed to create absolutely risk-free workplaces regardless of costs." Reading the two provisions together, the Fifth Circuit held that the Secretary was under a duty to determine whether the benefits expected from the new standard bore a reasonable relationship to the costs that it imposed. The court noted that OSHA had made an estimate of the costs of compliance, but that the record lacked substantial evidence of any discernible benefits.

We agree with the Fifth Circuit's holding that § 3 (8) requires the Secretary to find, as a threshold matter, that the toxic substance in question poses a significant health risk in the workplace and that a new, lower standard is therefore "reasonably necessary or appropriate to provide safe or healthful employment and places of employment." . . .

As presently formulated, the benzene standard is an expensive way of providing some additional protection for a relatively small number of employees. According to OSHA's figures, the standard will require capital investments in engineering controls of approximately $266 million, first-year operating costs (for monitoring, medical testing, employee training and respirators) of $187 million to $205 million and recurring annual costs of approximately $34 million. [43 Fed. Reg., at 5934.] The figures outlined in OSHA's explanation of the costs of compliance to various industries indicate that only 35,000 employees would gain any benefit from the regulation in terms of a reduction in their exposure to benzene. Over two-thirds of these workers (24,450) are employed in the rubber manufacturing industry. Compliance costs in that industry are estimated to be rather low with no capital costs and initial operating expenses estimated at only $34 million ($1390 per employee); recurring annual costs would also be rather low, totalling less than $1 million. By contrast, the segment of the petroleum refining industry that produces benzene would be required to incur $24 million in capital costs and $600,000 in first-year operating expenses to provide additional protection for 300 workers ($82,000 per employee), while the petrochemical industry would be required to incur $20.9 million in capital costs and

$1 million in initial operating expenses for the benefit of 552 employees ($39,675 per employee). [43 Fed. Reg., at 5936–5938.]

Although OSHA did not quantify the benefits to each category of worker in terms of decreased exposure to benzene, it appears from the economic impact study done at OSHA's direction that those benefits may be relatively small. Thus, although the current exposure limit is 10 ppm, the actual exposures outlined in that study are often considerably lower. For example, for the period 1970–1975 the petrochemical industry reported that, out of a total of 496 employees exposed to benzene, only 53 were exposed to levels between 1 and 5 ppm and only seven (all at the same plant) were exposed to between 5 and 10 ppm. . . .

Any discussion of the 1 ppm exposure limit must, of course, begin with the Agency's rationale for imposing that limit. The written explanation of the standard fills 184 pages of the printed appendix. Much of it is devoted to a discussion of the voluminous evidence of the adverse effects of exposure to benzene at levels of concentration well above 10 ppm. This discussion demonstrates that there is ample justification for regulating occupational exposure to benzene and that the prior limit of 10 ppm, with a ceiling of 25 ppm (or a peak of 50 ppm) was reasonable. It does not, however, provide direct support for the Agency's conclusion that the limit should be reduced from 10 ppm to 1 ppm.

The evidence in the administrative record of adverse effects of benzene exposure at 10 ppm is sketchy at best. OSHA noted that there was "no dispute" that certain nonmalignant blood disorders, evidenced by a reduction in the level of red or white cells or platelets in the blood, could result from exposures of 25–40 ppm. It then stated that several studies had indicated that relatively slight changes in normal blood values could result from exposures below 25 ppm and perhaps below 10 ppm. OSHA did not attempt to make any estimate based on these studies of how significant the risk of nonmalignant disease would be at exposures of 10 ppm or less. Rather, it stated that because of the lack of data concerning the linkage between low-level exposures and blood abnormalities, it was impossible to construct a dose-response curve at this time. OSHA did conclude, however, that the studies demonstrated that the current 10 ppm exposure limit was inadequate to ensure that no single worker would suffer a nonmalignant blood disorder as a result of benzene exposure. Noting that it is "customary" to set a permissible exposure limit by applying a safety factor of 10–100 to the lowest level at which adverse effects had been observed, the Agency stated that the evidence supported the conclusion that the limit should be set at a point "substantially less than 10 ppm" even if benzene's leukemic effects were not considered. . . .

Once OSHA acknowledged that the NIOSH* study it had relied upon in promulgating the emergency standard did not support its earlier view that benzene had been shown to cause leukemia at concentrations below 25 ppm, there was only one study that provided any evidence of such an increased risk. That study, conducted by the Dow Chemical Co., uncovered three leukemia deaths, versus 0.2 expected deaths, out of a population of 594 workers; it appeared that the three workers had never been

*National Institute of Occupational Safety and Health.

exposed to more than 2 to 9 ppm of benzene. The authors of the study, however, concluded that it could not be viewed as proof of a relationship between low-level benzene exposure and leukemia because all three workers had probably been occupationally exposed to a number of other potentially carcinogenic chemicals at other points in their careers and because no leukemia deaths had been uncovered among workers who had been exposed to much higher levels of benzene. In its explanation of the permanent standard, OSHA stated that the possibility that these three leukemias had been caused by benzene exposure could not be ruled out and that the study, although not evidence of an increased risk of leukemia at 10 ppm, was therefore "consistent with the findings of many studies that there is an excess leukemia risk among benzene exposed employees." 43 Fed. Reg., at 5928. The Agency made no finding that the Dow study, any other empirical evidence or any opinion testimony demonstrated that exposure to benzene at or below the 10 ppm level had ever in fact caused leukemia.

Thus, the Court refused to enforce the 1 ppm limit and OSHA had no choice but to reinstate their previous 10 ppm standard for benzene.

Air Bags and Automobile Manufacturers

In 1966 the United States Congress passed the National Traffic and Motor Vehicle Safety Act and established the National Highway Traffic Safety Administration (NHTSA) to administer the act. The purpose of the act was to develop a coordinated national safety program. One of the major thrusts of the legislation and the subsequent regulations and directives issued by the Administration was the development and enforcement of safety performance standards for motor vehicles.

One of the NHTSA's first notices, entitled "Inflatable Occupant Restraint System," was published in 1969 and clearly emphasized the controversial "air bag." It required that this "air bag" be installed in all vehicles manufactured in the United States. This notice, Motor Vehicle Safety Standard (MVSS) 208, was opposed by the automobile industry. Detailed questions were raised about safety research, engineering designs, financial burdens, and possible legal violations in order to postpone required implementation from 1972 to 1973 to 1974 to 1975, and so forth. By 1981, MVSS 208 (see Appendix I for the history of this standard) appeared doomed altogether. During the period from 1969 to 1981, millions of dollars had been spent by the automobile industry, by automobile insurance companies, by public interest groups, and by the government to promote their various views and to fight the views of the opposition.

What, then, are "air bags," and why all the controversy? Judith Reppy has described their attraction as a means of reducing the mortality and morbidity associated with automobile accidents:

> Air bags are passive restraints in that they deploy automatically in a crash without any action by the automobile's occupants. They thus represent the ultimate in a 'technological fix'—a technical solution of the social

This case was prepared by Martha W. Elliott and Tom L. Beauchamp and revised by Sarah Westrick and Linda Kern. **Not to be duplicated without permission of the authors and publisher.**

problems of traffic death and injuries. The bag, which inflates within a few milliseconds of impact, acts as a cushion to reduce the deceleration forces on the occupants and to protect them from colliding with the interior of the automobile. When worn, seat belts perform much the same function. Except for the new passive seat belts, however, they have required the active participation of the occupant to be effective, and the extent of seat belt use in the United States has been very low (approximately 20%).[1]

Reduction of deaths and injuries is clearly a major public policy problem in the United States, where approximately 50,000 persons die every year in automobile accidents. As automobiles have become more fuel-efficient, their size and weight have been reduced, and with this reduction passengers are afforded less protection in an accident. Various air bag systems have been designed that are keyed to deceleration rates and bumper contact. The bags are designed to inflate in less than 1/20 of a second and also have been designed so that a driver's vision is not unduly impaired.[2] While the basic design of the air bag is essentially the same as when first developed, the design has been improved to better accommodate the needs of small children, to decrease the weight of the system, and to prevent accidental deployment. (The air bag system was first designed in the 1960s by automobile industry researchers.)

Initial research done for NHTSA by the Cornell Aeronautical Laboratories has shown that air bags would be effective in preventing injuries and fatalities to adults in frontal crashes, but were less effective in protecting (1) smaller passengers, (2) persons involved in angled crashes, and (3) persons involved in crashes preceded by panic braking.[3] Safety research conducted by the major auto makers supports the NHTSA contention that air bags would reduce fatalities in crashes and identified the combination of passive and active restraints most effective in different types of crashes.

General Motors evaluated a series of traffic fatalities involving 706 men, women, and children and concluded that:

> If a person wears his lap belt, his potential for fatality reduction is 17%. If he wears his lap and shoulder belt, his potential for fatality reduction is 31%. If his car is equipped with air cushions his potential for fatality reduction is 18%. If his car is equipped with air cushions and he wears his lap belt, his potential for fatality reduction is 29%.[4]

[1]Judith Reppy, "The Automobile Air Bag," in Dorothy Nelkin, ed., *Controversy: Politics of Technical Decisions* (Beverly Hills, Calif.: Sage Publications, 1979), pp. 145–146.

[2]*Ibid.*, p. 147.

[3]Richard M. Hodgetts, "Air Bags and Auto Safety," in *The Business Enterprise: Social Challenge, Social Response* (Philadelphia: W. B. Saunders Co., 1977), pp. 130–131.

[4]General Motors Study, as quoted in Hodgetts, p. 131.

Further GM research showed that particular combinations of active and passive restraints were most effective in particular types of crashes. This data is summarized in the accompanying table.[5]

POTENTIAL FATALITY PROTECTION (IN PERCENTAGES)

	Restraint System			
Crash Mode	Lap Belt Only	Lap and Shoulder	Air Cushion Only	Air Cushion with Lap Belt
Frontals	14	37	38	40
Sideswipes	9	21	10	18
Sides	12	12	3	14
Rollovers	36	48	9	40
Rear	14	20	0	14

Ford Motor Company analyzed the protection that would have been offered by the various combinations of active and passive restraints in a series of several thousand accidents. Ford found that "the air bag and lap belt combination was the restraint system most likely to save the greatest number of lives, followed by the lap and shoulder belt combination,"[6] a conclusion very similar to that reached by General Motors.

Critics of this research point out, however, that air bags were never adequately "field tested," and that attempts to simulate actual crash conditions using human-like dummies and attempts to extrapolate backwards from what happens in actual crashes to what would have happened had restraints been in use are inexact and may be misleading. General Motors produced approximately 10,000 cars equipped with air bags during 1974, and these cars represent the nearest approach to a "field test." Between 1974 and 1978 these cars had been involved in only 200 crashes in which the air bag had inflated, an insufficient number of crashes to constitute a full-scale trial.[7]

Since the auto industry and NHTSA were in basic agreement about the effectiveness of air bags in reducing fatalities and injuries in at least some kinds of crashes, what was the source of disagreement that fueled the controversy? Reppy sees the controversy as follows:

> The traditional view of automobile safety has taken the 'nut behind the wheel' approach, stressing individual responsibility. This view is challenged by those who wish to focus responsibility on highway design and on the manufacturers' responsibility to make changes in the vehicle to

[5]*Ibid.*, p. 132.
[6]*Ibid.*, p. 133.
[7]Reppy, "The Automobile Air Bag," pp. 150–151.

reduce both the probability of a crash and the severity of injury if a crash occurs.[8]

Reppy points out that each side of the controversy has attracted a variety of proponents who have differing interests and differing arguments:

> The technical disagreement reached its most striking expression in the cost/benefit studies sponsored by the opposing sides which, based on conflicting assumptions, yielded opposite conclusions. On a more philosophical level, participants in the controversy have debated the proper role of government and the morality of compelling an individual to protect himself from the risk of injury.[9]

Proponents of air bags cite research on the effectiveness of passive restraints and the desirability of reducing fatalities by whatever means available as reason enough for requiring air bags; automobile manufacturers and their allies, by contrast, contend that there are many unresolved problems in the implementation of this technology. While this group agrees with the desirability of reducing traffic fatalities, they see the increased use of seat belts, through either public education or legislation, as the preferred means of achieving that goal.

Opponents of air bags have claimed that air bags could be a hazard and a potential *cause* of accidents in the case of accidental inflation. And, as noted earlier, there has not been enough actual experience with air bags to either confute or confirm such suppositions. Research on this problem under test conditions has shown, however, that while people do demonstrate a "startle" reaction to unexpected bag inflation, "drivers retained good control of the test vehicle" and "were able to see to guide their car in spite of the minimal obstruction of vision produced by the inflated air bag."[10]

Industry opposition to the air bags as revealed in Congressional hearings, court testimony, and in lobbying efforts has focused specifically on the cost of the system, the difficulties in tooling up for this addition, questions about the performance of the bag in real-life situations, and complaints about government "paternalism" and overregulation.

The auto makers consistently cite cost-of-production changes to include the air bags. This argument gained force in 1973–74 when the energy crisis shifted public and government focus from safety to fuel economy. Redesigning and retooling to make smaller and more fuel

[8]*Ibid.*, p. 146.

[9]*Ibid.*, p. 147.

[10]H. Haskell Ziperman and G. R. Smith, "Startle Reaction to Air-Bag Restraints," *Journal of the American Medical Association* **233** (August 4, 1975), p. 440.

efficient cars took precedence for auto makers over redesigning and retooling to make automobile air bags. As the decade wore on, the increasing competition from fuel efficient foreign cars, coupled with a general recession and the automobile industry's increasingly dismal economic situation, supported the auto manufacturers' contention that (1) they could not afford to absorb the cost of retooling for air bags and (2) they could not pass the additional cost on to consumers and remain competitive. Critics of this position maintained that the additional cost passed on to the consumer would be only about $100.[11]

Although automobile manufacturers remained firmly opposed to air bag regulations, air bags were supported by the automobile insurance industry because they were, and continue to be, convinced that the bags save lives and health and insurance costs. The Insurance Institute for Highway Safety provided funds and technical expertise to counter auto industry arguments. Allstate Insurance Company was particularly active in support of air bags. Allstate provided favorable advertising, support before Congressional committees, and offered discounts on insurance premiums for air bag equipped cars. A pamphlet issued by Allstate in 1976 stated:

> Allstate advocates the use of lap belts, used in conjunction with air bags. This system offers the best protection feasible now and within the foreseeable future in most types of crashes—air bags to reduce injury and lap belts to prevent ejection in rollovers.[12]

Allstate was joined by a number of consumer interest groups, who held that the technology was adequate, affordable, and would save many lives. Some estimates held that three to four times the number of lives saved by seat belts would be saved by use of air bags.

There is also some evidence that the public would support air bags. In 1976 a national telephone survey was conducted to assess the preference of individuals who planned to buy a new car within three years. The results of that survey indicated that people preferred cars with passive restraints and that they were willing to pay extra for this feature.

> . . . For improved protection in crashes, 77% of new car buyers expressed a preference for [passive restraint] protection . . .—39% exclusively and 38% in combination with protection that has to be activated by driver or passenger.[13]

[11]Hodgetts, "Air Bags and Auto Safety," p. 142.

[12]Quoted by Hodgetts, "Air Bags and Auto Safety," p. 136.

[13]As reported in Leon S. Robertson, "Study Shows Public Willing to Pay for Motor Vehicle Crash Protection," *The National Underwriter* (September 3, 1976), pp. 15–18.

Potential car buyers polled in this survey were willing to pay an additional $12 per month for 36 months ($432) on new car payments to save 6,000 lives and $17 per month to save 12,000 lives per year. This is considerably more than the $4 per month ($103 total) estimated by NHTSA as the actual cost of the air bags that would save an additional 8,800 lives per year.[14] (This $432 installation cost is apparently based on more conventional estimates between $300 and $1,100, depending on quality and production volumes.)

Strong political support for air bags has nonetheless proven difficult to arouse. With increasing financial difficulties for automobile manufacturers and the United Auto Workers, with a climate favoring government deregulation, and with increasing concern about tradeoffs in controlling traffic safety, even the *controversy* had begun to fade by the end of 1981.

In October of 1981, the NHTSA issued a final rule calling for the complete rescission of passive restraints and amended Modified Standard 208 accordingly. Within a month, on November 25, 1981, the National Association of Independent Insurers (NAII), representing 509 insurance companies, filed suit in a federal court seeking to overturn this order, which would repeal all rules requiring either air bags or automatic seat belts. The insurance companies were particularly upset by the way the matter had been handled in the Transportation Department. Raymond Peck, administrator of the NHTSA, said that the opposition of U.S. automobile companies had killed the air-bag policy. He said he made his own decision based on his firm belief that most motorists would simply disconnect the activating systems. He preferred a voluntary seat-belt campaign, but said he would try to revive interest in the development of better air bags. Mr. Peck's decision had been unanimously opposed by his senior staff, but it was praised as professionally sound by the three leading U.S. automobile manufacturers.[15]

The NAII suit challenged the claim that air bags and belts would be disconnected by owners, and argued that Mr. Peck did not understand the several different designs well enough to appreciate that it would be extremely difficult to dismantle properly engineered systems.[16] The suit also charged that the seat belt systems are highly cost effective, especially when it is considered that the insurance industry may have to increase premiums (perhaps by 30%) for motorists if cars are not

---

[14]*Ibid.*

[15]"Insurers Sue for Return of Passive Restraint Rule," *The Baltimore Sun*, November 26, 1981; and Peter Behr, "U.S. Halts Effort to Require Use of Car Air Bags," *The Washington Post*, October 24, 1981, sec. A, pp. 1, 24.

[16]*Ibid.*

equipped with such systems. The NAII was joined in this suit by State Farm Insurance and the Automobile Owners Action Council.[17]

Under the name of *State Farm Insurance* v. *Dept. of Transportation,* the case was argued in the United States Court of Appeals on March 1, 1982. The petitioners sought review of the NHTSA's final order rescinding automatic crash protection requirements ten months before the standard's effective date. They challenged the move as being "arbitrary, capricious, an abuse of discretion, and a violation of law as defined by Section 10 of the Administrative Procedure Act."[18] On June 1, 1982, the Circuit Judges agreed. They recognized the issue as highly complicated, but saw the NHTSA's role as simply defined. In this case, the NHTSA had acted outside of its legislative mandate. Circuit Judge Mikva explained:

> An administrative agency, possessing power delegated by the legislative branch of government, must comply with the legislative requirement that its decisions be reasoned and in accordance with the purposes for which power has been delegated. NHTSA's rescission of the safety standard presents a paradigm of arbitrary and capricious agency action because NHTSA drew conclusions that are unsupported by evidence in the record and then artificially narrowed the range of alternatives available to it under its legislative mandate. NHTSA thus failed to demonstrate the reasoned decisionmaking that is the essence of lawful administrative action.[19]

The court found that the NHTSA's reasons for rescinding Modified Standard 208 were insufficient. However, the agency was given 30 days to present a schedule for resolving the questions raised in the case leading either to an ultimate rescission or to implementation of the standard.

[17]*Ibid.* In early spring of 1982, the Reagan administration announced a publicity campaign in conjunction with private industry to persuade motorists to "buckle up" voluntarily. As part of this effort, Goodyear Tire & Rubber Company's blimps were used throughout the summer to display messages urging drivers to use their safety belts; Warner Communications gave the government permission to use its superhero comic book characters (e.g., Superman) in seat belt promotions; and Lorimar Productions featured safety belt use in its television series "Knots Landing." The Reagan administration's decision to pursue a vigorous but voluntary course followed on the heels of a late 1981 Department of Transportation study showing that traffic deaths could easily increase by approximately 16,000/year by 1990 if no major safety improvements or highway designs are made. The NAII argued that air bags and mandatory seat belts are essential to prevent this increase in fatalities. "Reagan Enlists Business to Cut Highway Deaths," *The Washington Post,* April 15, 1982, sec. C, pp. 1, 5; and Peter Behr, "Traffic Death Surge Feared in DOT Study," *The Washington Post,* October 14, 1981, sec. D, pp. 7, 10.

[18]United States Court of Appeals, District of Columbia Circuit, No. 81-2220, *State Farm Mutual Automobile Insurance Co.* v. *Dept. of Transportation, National Highway Traffic Safety Administration,* p. 4.

[19]*Ibid.,* pp. 4–5.

APPENDIX I

THE HISTORY OF STANDARD 208

1966: National Traffic and Motor Vehicle Safety Act passed

1967: Original Standard 208 passed
Seat belts required

1970: Standard 208 revised
Passive protection required

1972: "Final" form of Standard 208 passed
Complete passive protection required

1974: 1974 amendments passed
Entire standard of passive belts rejected by Congress
    1. Ignition interlock banned
    2. DOT's discretion to modify 208 in the future reduced

1976: Passive requirements suspended altogether (under the administration of Secretary of Transportation Coleman)

1977: Modified Standard 208 passed (under the administration of Secretary of Transportation Adams)
Passive restraint regulation mandated on a phase-in basis

1981: April: Rulemaking reopened due to automobile industry's economic difficulties (under the administration of Secretary of Transportation Lewis)
MS 208 delayed for one year
Possible rescission of entire standard proposed by NHTSA

October: Notice 25 issued, NHTSA calls for a complete rescission of passive requirements and amends MS 208 accordingly

1982: NHTSA Notice 25 ruled arbitrary and capricious by the United States Court of Appeals and remanded for further investigation

Aurora-Baxter Corporation

Mr. Jack McGowan, Chairman of the Aurora-Baxter Corporation (ABC) Audit Committee, called the meeting of his committee to order promptly at 9:30 a.m. and opened with:

> Our first item of business is one that's not on the agenda you've received. It has to do with a "questionable payments" situation that the auditors have uncovered in the Construction Materials Division. I'll ask Arnie Gates [ABC controller] to give you the background.

Aurora-Baxter Corporation, with sales in 1976 of $557 million was a diversified manufacturer of industrial products. Its Construction Materials Division sold such products as pipe (concrete, iron, and plastic), cement, sand, asphalt, tile (roofing, floor, and wall tile), and a limited line of protective coatings. Its customers included large commercial contractors as well as state and Federal government agencies.

Present at the meeting were the members of the Audit Committee, comprised of four outside directors, ABC's president, the controller, the director of the internal audit staff, and three representatives of the company's outside auditing firm, Bixby, Lyons and Bolton (BLB).

Arnie Gates, the controller spoke:

> As you know Construction Materials does a lot of business with state governments. Among our big accounts for pipe and tile is Missawba [a large midwestern state].
>
> A couple of years ago, following a scandal in the awarding of highway contracts, they enacted some very stiff legislation forbidding state purchasing officers and buyers from accepting any gifts—even free lunches. Since then our relations with Missawba buyers have gotten a little awkward in certain respects. When our marketing guys are in the middle of negotiations with them or when they've concluded a big contract, it's natural to go out with the buyers maybe for drinks and a nice meal. Every-

body knows that each person there is supposed to pay for his or her own meal. Our guys are told that they have to make that clear. So at some point one of them will say, "OK everybody, chip in. You know the rule." Maybe there are five of them and three of us and say the bill is $100. When the meal's over they've put in $2 each and we pick up the rest of the tab.

In fact, on one recent occasion our sales rep for the Missawba State Highway Department had concluded a big sale and our guys and the buyers went out to a restaurant to celebrate. The ABC rep put a big bowl in the middle of the table and made sure everybody saw him drop in 15 one-dollar bills. When we counted the money after dinner there were eight one-dollar bills! He mentioned it to a senior buyer for the state, and the response was "ABC is a big company; you ought to be able to find some way to buy me a dinner!"

On each occasion our account representative submits an expense voucher recording the amount, the place, the time and the names of those attending. Now the practice they've been following in Construction Materials is that when the voucher is approved and the claim for entertainment expenses paid, the supporting documentation is destroyed.

Ms. Rachel Stuart of the Audit Committee, a lawyer, spoke:

If you do that, you can't take it as a tax deduction and, up to certain limits, entertainment, if it is properly documented is still a deductible expense. How much money is involved anyway?

Gates responded:

It amounts to $3840 for the last fiscal year and if we do document it for tax purposes, we expose the buyers. If they're caught accepting favors, they could lose their jobs.

Jack McGowan turned to Mr. Ralph Dominick, senior BLB auditor on the ABC account:

Ralph, what do you think?

Dominick replied:

There's no reason for us to take any exception. In the first place, the expense is not being claimed as a deduction on either state or Federal tax returns. Second it's being recorded on ABC books. There's been no effort to conceal anything.

Mr. Warren Phelps, ABC's president spoke up:

Ralph, maybe BLB doesn't have a problem with it, but we surely have. I think we're "between a rock and a hard place," and we really have to do something. Our sales people do a lot of business over lunches and probably get more useful information on what competition is doing and what's going on in the customer's shops than at any other time. I don't want us to cut that off. But I also don't want our sales people being compromised.

As he spoke, Mr. Phelps had in mind the ABC Corporate Responsibility Statement, which had been promulgated less than a year before. It read in part as follows:

> The Corporation intends to comply strictly with all domestic and foreign laws which apply to its business. Employees will not be permitted to violate any law relating to the conduct of business or to engage in unethical business practices. Although customs and standards of conduct may vary from country to country, the Corporation will, at all times, conduct its business with integrity and honesty. In cases where laws or business practices are subject to interpretation, management will obtain legal advice from the General Counsel.
>
> Failure to adhere to ethical and legal standards of conduct may result in disciplinary action, including immediate suspension and eventual discharge.
>
> A complete list of illegal or unethical practices is impossible. However, areas where practices inconsistent with accepted standards commonly occur are:
>
> *Personal Gifts.* The giving or receiving of gifts, loans, favors or other services by an employee acting on behalf of the Corporation directly or indirectly to or from anyone outside the Corporation is strictly forbidden. Such gifts are not limited to tangible or cash gifts or loans but include intangibles such as promises for the future, valuable "tips," advantageous purchases or other opportunities.
>
> Excluded from this prohibition are the exchange of normal business courtesies such as luncheons or dinners, when they are proper and consistent with regular business practice. Also excluded are the advertising or promotional materials of nominal value as well as the exchange of gifts or favors because of kinship, marriage, or social relationships provided they do not violate Corporate Policy 4, *Conflict of Interest.* The criteria for deciding what is proper and reasonable is based on the judgment a disinterested third party would make under the same circumstances.

Hydrolevel Corporation
and the ASME Boiler Code

In 1971, the Hydrolevel Corporation was a small, thriving company that manufactured and marketed a small percentage of the heating boiler safety controls in the United States.

On April 12, 1971 a letter was sent to the American Society of Mechanical Engineers' (ASME) Boiler Code Committee by McDonnell & Miller, Inc., a competitor of Hydrolevel that manufactured and marketed 85% of the heating boiler safety controls in the United States. After learning about this letter, Hydrolevel maintained that both the letter and ASME's answering letter were unjustifiably intended to discredit its product and to imply falsely that it failed to meet the requirements specified in the Boiler Code—a body of rules of safety covering the design, fabrication, and inspection during construction of boiler and pressure vessels. By contrast, McDonnell & Miller executives claimed that the letter was motivated purely by their long-held concern over the safety of time-delay features in boilers.

The letters in question were as follows:

This case was prepared by Tom L. Beauchamp and Barry Smith. The following sources were consulted: Nancy Rueth, "A Case Study," *Mechanical Engineering* (June 1975), pp. 34–36, as reprinted in Robert J. Baum, ed., *Ethical Problems in Engineering,* 2nd ed. (Troy, N.Y.: Center for the Study of the Human Dimensions of Science & Technology, Rensselaer Polytechnic Institute, 1980), Vol. II: Cases, pp. 126–128; *Congressional Record* (Wednesday, March 19, 1975); *Wall Street Journal* Editorial of July 4, 1974; Associated Press report in the *Wall Street Journal* (Monday, February 5, 1979). **Not to be duplicated without permission of the authors and publisher.**

LETTER #1. TO ASME:[1]

McDonnell & Miller, Inc.,
3500 North Spaulding Avenue,
Chicago, Ill., April 12, 1971.

Subject: Par. HG–605, Section IV Heating Boilers Code.

Mr. W. B. Hoyt,
Secretary, ASME Boiler and Pressure Vessel Committee
345 East 47th Street
New York, N.Y.

Dear Mr. Hoyt:

Par. HG–605 of Section IV states that each automatically fired steam or vapor-system boiler shall have an automatic low-water fuel cut-off so located as to automatically cut off the fuel supply when the surface of the water falls to the lowest visible part of the water-gauge glass. Is it the intent of this statement that the cut-off operate immediately when the boiler water level falls to the lowest visible part of the water-gauge glass, or is it permissible to incorporate a time-delay feature in the cut-off so that it will operate after the boiler water level reaches some point below the visible range of the gauge glass?

Very truly yours,

McDonnell & Miller, Inc.,
Gene Mitchell

LETTER #2. TO MCDONNELL & MILLER:[2]

April 29, 1971.

Subject: Section IV Heating Boilers Code—Par. HG–605.

Mr. Gene Mitchell
McDonnell & Miller, Inc.
3500 North Spaulding Avenue
Chicago, Illinois 60618

Dear Mr. Mitchell:

The inquiry contained in your letter of April 12, 1971, was referred to the Chairman of the concerned Subcommittee who offers the following advice:
A low-water fuel cut-off is considered strictly as a safety device and not as some kind of an operating control. Assuming that the water gauge glass is located in accordance with the requirements of Par. HG–602(b), it is *the intent* of Par. HG–605(a) that the low-water fuel cut-off

---

[1]*Congressional Record* (Wednesday, March 19, 1975), "Exhibit B." Italics added.
[2]*Ibid.*, "Exhibit C." Italics added.

operate *immediately* and positively when the boiler water level falls to the lowest visible part of the water gauge glass.

There are many and varied designs of heating boilers. If a time delay feature were incorporated in a low-water fuel cut-off, there would be no positive assurance that the boiler water level would not fall to a dangerous point during a time delay period.

Very truly yours,

W. B. Hoyt, Secretary

At the time these letters were written, McDonnell & Miller manufactured a float or mechanically actuated fuel cut-off device, and Hydrolevel was producing a new electronically actuated sensing device that incorporated a time-delay feature, roughly as described in the letters above. Despite the possible "dangerous point" mentioned in the letter above from W. B. Hoyt, Hydrolevel was given no specific reason for thinking their mechanism might be dangerous. Hydrolevel executives, led by their aggressive president, Russell Rymer, maintained that the sudden interest in and reaction to their invention was the result purely of increased competition. Hydrolevel had just secured, for example, a sizeable account with the Brooklyn Union Gas Co. over a competitive McDonnell & Miller product. In order to impede further Hydrolevel market gains, Rymer asserted, McDonnell & Miller executives gave copies of letter #2 above to their salesmen with instructions to use it to show potential buyers that Hydrolevel's product was unsafe and did not meet code requirements. McDonnell & Miller, however, claimed that they gave the letter (at most) to three salesmen, and did not forward it to all sales personnel.

Hydrolevel then complained to ASME about the letter and the use to which it was being put. The reply from ASME to Hydrolevel, dated June 9, 1972, read as follows:

LETTER #3. TO HYDROLEVEL:

This will advise that there is no intent in Section IV to prohibit the use of low water fuel cut-offs having time delays in order to meet the requirements of Par. HG–605 (a). This paragraph relates itself to Par. HG–602 (b) which specifically delineates the location of the lowest visible part of the water gauge glass.

If a means for retarding control action is incorporated in a low-water fuel cut-off, the termination of the record function must operate to cut off the fuel supply before the boiler water level falls below the visible part of the water gauge glass.[3]

[3]Robert J. Baum, ed., *Ethical Problems in Engineering*, 2nd ed. (Troy, N.Y.: Center for the Study of the Human Dimensions of Science & Technology, Rensselaer Polytechnic Institute, 1980), Vol. II: Cases, p. 126. Italics in original.

Hydrolevel then shifted the focus of debate and discussion. Rymer and his executives vigorously and bitterly argued that throughout this entire sequence of events there had been subterfuge and collusion on the part of ASME and McDonnell & Miller. This accusation is confirmed, Hydrolevel argued, by some further features of the case reflecting a conflict of interest. The facts are that the vice-president of research and engineering of McDonnell & Miller, John James, was also vice-chairman of the ASME Subcommittee on Heating Boilers. He had worked together with the chairman of the same ASME subcommittee, T. R. Hardin, to prepare the first letter reprinted above; but they also in effect collaborated to write Hoyt's response—Letter #2.[4]

The *Wall Street Journal* investigated these charges and replies, and on July 9, 1974 published an article condemning ASME and McDonnell & Miller for actions the newspaper viewed as ethically unacceptable. The article saw as one significant issue "the close ties between the dominant company in an industry and the professional society that serves as its watchdog."[5] ASME's Professional Practice Committee then considered these questions of possible "unethical practice." This committee exonerated all accused parties (James, in particular).

On March 19, 1975, Russell Rymer presented a statement, with the appropriate letters attached, to the U.S. Senate Subcommittee on Antitrust and Monopoly of the Committee on the Judiciary. He argued that ASME Code developers used improper influence to discredit the product and thwart the market for his small but up-and-coming company.

The June 1975 issue of *Mechanical Engineering* then reviewed the case in full. This journal article, which also had an editorial purpose, concluded with the following paragraph, which was prefaced with the subtitle "The Appearance of Wrongdoing":

> No one in ASME has said that James or Hardin acted unethically by handling the situation as they did. No one is accusing them of attempting to discredit Hydrolevel. Both, all wish to believe, acted in good faith and wrote the decisions as they saw them. What is perhaps at issue is the fact that the actions may be *interpreted* as unethical. The question, it seems, is one of the *appearance* of wrongdoing as much as it is one of unethical practices.[6]

ASME officials noted that the actions taken by Hardin, James, *et al.* in every case followed standard procedures that were appropriate to

[4]James and Hardin addressed the first letter to Hoyt. Hoyt referred the inquiry back to Hardin, who then wrote the response over Hoyt's signature (letter #2).

[5]As reprinted in Baum, *Ethical Problems in Engineering*, p. 127.

[6]As reprinted in Baum, *Ethical Problems in Engineering*, p. 128. Italics added.

their positions; and ASME also maintained that drafts of letters and other suggestions were solicited from them only because of their special engineering expertise. ASME also noted that the intent of the framers of the boiler code had been to guard against dangers presented by new and inadequately tested automatic cut-off devices. Finally, ASME observed that both small and large companies are regularly involved in their affairs, and that their meetings on code revisions are open to the public, including members of consumer advocate groups.

In 1979, Hydrolevel successfully sued the American Society of Mechanical Engineers for $9.9 million (awarded by a jury), claiming that ASME had conspired against it, in violation of federal antitrust laws. Two other defendants in the case—International Telephone & Telegraph Corp., the parent company of McDonnell & Miller, and Hartford Steam Boiler Inspection and Insurance Co.—both settled out of court for a total of $800,000 between them.

chapter 6

The Multinational

INTRODUCTION   Multinational corporations often find themselves perplexed by the laws, rules, and customs of a host country in which they do business or have subsidiaries. They must reflect on whether they should do as the locals do or conform to the different, and even conflicting, moral, governmental, and cultural guidelines of their home nations. Thus, should a Canadian firm follow the rules of financial disclosure required in Canada or rather those in certain Arab countries in which it has subsidiaries? Should payments for service that are encouraged in Japan but legally prohibited in the United States be sanctioned by a U.S. firm that does business in Japan? Again, should a company sell out its stock of artificially sweetened fruit to customers in West Germany, Spain, or third-world countries, when it has been declared hazardous and outlawed in its home country? No international body has thus far answered such questions authoritatively, and there is at present no uniform agreement about the measure of control that either governments or corporations ought to introduce where standards or expectations vary. In this chapter, the cases presented cover three general areas of such multinational dilemmas: (1) The treatment of employees, (2) the marketing of products to consumers, and (3) government and cultural expectations.

(1) The employer that is manufacturing or marketing in a foreign culture cannot simply assume that workers should be governed by the same salary standards, grounds for dismissal, workplace standards, requirements of company loyalty, and promotional standards as those found back home. A well-known example of this general problem of fair and equal treatment involves the use in a foreign workplace of hazardous chemicals such as benzene (see Chapter 5) that would not be permitted in the workplaces of a home country. If a foreign nation does not require masks to be worn by workers or does not stipulate permissible dose levels of the chemical in the environment, should a multinational adopt more stringent standards than those required locally?

Although the problem of dangerous workplaces is perhaps the most established and publicized issue about the international employee, there are subtler and less explored issues, several of which are presented in this chapter by the cases of John Higgins in Japan and Polaroid in South Africa. The Higgins case raises a number of subtle issues about fairness to employees who have quite different traditions and expectations from those of a foreign owner or supervisor. Generally such employment arrangements do not involve the "informed consent" of workers to standards quite foreign to those to which they are accustomed. Rather, they arise almost unnoticed from the different presuppositions supervisors and employees bring with them to the workplace. The Higgins case explores a number of themes along these lines, while the Polaroid case raises issues about the responsibilities to employees in a country with extraordinarily different policies of racial segregation than those found in the multinational's home country. Many large companies at one time flocked to South Africa because of the friendly and stable government as well as the low wages paid to the abundant supply of black workers. This case deals with problems of alleged exploitation of workers in the region.

(2) The consumer of a company's product in a foreign culture may not be subject to the same government requirements or even have the same concerns about a product that persons in the company's home nation have. The Infant Formula and Parke, Davis Drug cases in this chapter dramatically illustrate how the highly restrictive rules on drugs and food that operate in one country may be wholly absent or starkly different in another country. Regulatory controls on the production and marketing of food and drugs in the United States are probably more stringent than those found in any other nation. These rules are framed for a culture with established views about acceptable risk and adequate testing that simply do not prevail in some nations in which multinationals market their products. Indeed a product that is banned in the United States may be welcomed by authorities in another nation; certainly nothing illegal is done by marketing the drugs in countries with no established standards. These authorities may, of course, be ignorant or too loose in formulating standards, but even so the existence of these variations presents the multinational corporation with both a ready market and a problem about whether to satisfy that market.

American companies that market internationally generally believe that the F.D.A. and other government agency requirements are too cautious, require too much testing, and are vastly too stringent when applied to other cultures. American government officials, however, tend to see standards as reasonable protections for all consumers, irrespective of their cultural affiliation. The implicit view seems to be that if there are good reasons for banning a product or restricting sales in the U.S., then it would be immoral not to conform to these standards when marketing elsewhere. Thus they tend to view American companies who violate their own government's standards as engaging in unjustifiable marketing practices. These officials have not, however, generally taken this view about foreign companies who violate rules of their own government when these rules are more stringent than those prevailing in North America.

These international marketing problems invite us to reflect on whether a food, drug, or other product should be marketed abroad if it is either known to be harmful or thought to have a significant risk. Sometimes risks are well worth taking, and risks may be more acceptable in one culture than another. The use of D.D.T. as a pesticide (when banned in the United States but not elsewhere) is one classic example. As the Infant Formula case in this chapter indicates, some countries may not see a product as harmful at all, even when they are aware of the product's alleged problems.

An alternative possibility is simply to *warn* consumers about possible harms when they purchase a product. As long as all the parties understand the terms of a transaction and it has been truly agreed to, then according to certain principles of informed consent, a company cannot be faulted for marketing a product with risks and consequences when it has informed the purchaser. However, as we shall see in the Parke, Davis case—which involves the marketing of a drug in England that has been banned in the U.S.—warnings have proved no less controversial than marketing bans. This consent approach has also been proposed in the case of marketing infant formula in the third world—a claim that has produced a protracted and unresolved controversy that affects many governments and manufacturers around the globe.

The governments in different countries also vary significantly in their rules and expectations, and these variations raise interesting questions about the responsibilities of multinationals. If moral standards, professional codes, and criteria of acceptable prudential judgments in dealing with a government vary from society to society, which system of values, if any, is binding on the multinational? Among the best known problems of this type is the facilitation of business transactions through so-called "grease payments," either to government officials or to particularly influential members of a society. These payments have commonly been defended by corporations on the ground that they are not illegal (often not illegal in either the host or home country), are in the best interests of the corporation, are harmless, provide new employment opportunities for persons at home and abroad, and provide stimulation to the economies and technological capacities of both nations. The business community has also tended to view such "sensitive payments" as extortion, or at least as demands placed on their enterprise in order to do business. The nature of these justifications and possible problems with them are explored in the case study in this chapter entitled "The Bribery Business."

Opponents have viewed grease payments and the like as simple bribery (though the U.S. Foreign Corrupt Practices Act does distinguish the two). In defense of their viewpoint, they do not simply cite laws and moral views about the unacceptability of bribery in their own culture, rather they look to a broader set of social consequences they believe will result from the practice of special payments. For example: government mismanagement is promoted; those who take the money are placed in a more favorable economic position than are other members of their society who have no source of special payments; income-tax evasion is promoted; quality products become less important to manufacturers and government officials; competing firms with quality products may be ignored; and competition is generally weakened. In general, critics say, the public interest of the foreign nation is not promoted. Critics also point out that there are many crucial, but still unanswered questions that surround sensitive payments and other clandestine practices. For example, if bribery is condoned or is a "way of life" in another nation, does this practice persist because it is approved or consented to in that culture, or only because those in power have institutionalized the practice? Even if it has become in some respect "customary," would it be regarded as scandalous if it were to come to public light in the foreign nation—as, for example, occurred some years ago in Japan when Lockheed Aircraft's payments ultimately brought down the government of Prime Minister Kakuei Tanaka. These questions and many more are raised in the final two cases in this chapter.

In the ideal, international agreements and courts would be sufficient to handle the sorts of issues encountered in the cases in this chapter. Unfortunately, there either are no international standards or they are generally inadequate—a situation likely to prevail for some time.

John Higgins: An American Goes Native in Japan

In the fall of 1962, Mr. Leonard Prescott, vice-president and general manager of the Weaver-Yamazaki Pharmaceutical Company Ltd. of Japan was considering what action, if any, to take regarding his executive assistant, Mr. John Higgins. In Mr. Prescott's opinion, Mr. Higgins had been losing his effectiveness as one who was to represent the U.S. parent company because of his extraordinary identification with the Japanese culture.

The Weaver Pharmaceutical Company was one of the outstanding concerns in the drug field in the United States. As a result of extensive research it had developed many important drugs and its product lines were constantly improved, giving the company a strong competitive advantage. It also had extensive international operations throughout many parts of the world. Operations in Japan started in the early 1930s, though they were limited to sales activities. The Yamazaki Pharmaceutical House, a major producer of drugs and chemicals in Japan, was the franchise distributor for Weaver's products in Japan.

Export sales to Japan were resumed in 1948. Due to its product superiority and the inability of major Japanese pharmaceutical houses to compete effectively because of lack of recovery from war damage, the Weaver company was able to capture a substantial share of the market for its product categories. In preparing for increasingly keen competition from Japanese producers, the company undertook local production of some of the product lines.

From its many years of international experience, the company had learned that it could not hope to establish itself firmly in a foreign country until it began manufacturing locally. Consequently, in 1953 the company began its preliminary negotiations with the Yamazaki Company Ltd., which culminated in the establishment of a jointly owned and operated manufacturing subsidiary. The company, known as the Weaver-Yamazaki Pharmaceutical Co. Ltd. of Japan, was officially organized in the summer of 1954. . . .

The subsidiary was headed by Mr. Shozo Suzuki, as president, and Mr. Leonard Prescott as executive vice-president. Since Mr. Suzuki was executive vice-president of the parent company and also was president of several other subsidiaries, his participation in the company was limited to determination of basic policies. Day-to-day operations were managed by Mr. Prescott as executive vice-president and general manager. He had an American executive assistant, Mr. Higgins, and several Japanese directors who assisted him in various phases of the operations. Though several other Americans were assigned to the Japanese ventures, they were primarily concerned with research and development and held no overall management responsibilities. . . .

Mr. Leonard Prescott arrived in Japan in 1960 to replace Mr. Richard Densely who had been in Japan since 1954. Mr. Prescott had been described as an "old hand" at international work, having spent most of his 25-year career with the company in its international work. He had served in India, the Philippines, and Mexico prior to coming to Japan. He had also spent several years in the international division of the company in New York. He was delighted with the challenge to expand further the Japanese operations. After two years of experience in Japan, he was pleased with the progress the company had made and felt a certain sense of accomplishment in developing a smooth functioning organization.

He became concerned, however, with the notable changes in Mr. Higgins' attitude and thinking. Mr. Higgins, in the opinion of Mr. Prescott, had absorbed and internalized the Japanese culture to such a point where he had lost the United States point of view and orientation. He had "gone native," so to speak, in Japan, which resulted in a substantial loss of his administrative effectiveness as a bi-cultural and -lingual executive assistant. . . .

In the summer of 1961, Mr. Higgins married a Japanese girl whom he had met shortly after he returned to Japan. His wife was an extremely attractive and intelligent woman by any standard. She had been graduated from the most prominent women's college in Japan and had studied at a well-known Eastern university in the United States for a brief period of time. Shortly after their marriage, Mr. Higgins filed a request through Mr. Prescott with the personnel director of International Division in New York, asking to extend his stay in Japan for an indefinite period of time. The personnel director approved the request upon consultation with both Mr. Densely and Mr. Prescott.

Mr. Prescott noted that marriage was a big turning point for Mr. Higgins. Until that time, he was merely interested in the Japanese culture in an intellectual sense, but since his marriage he was observed to have developed a real emotional involvement with it.

He and his wife rented an apartment in a strictly Japanese neighborhood and he was often seen relaxed in his Japanese kimono at home. He was also observed using the public bath, a well-known Japanese institution. His fluent Japanese combined with a likeable personality and interest in the Japanese culture won him many friends in the neighborhood. Everyone, including small children, greeted him with a big smile and friendly gestures addressing him as "Higgins-san" whenever they saw him.

His mode of living was almost entirely that of a typical Japanese. He seemed to have completely integrated himself with Japanese life. He was invited to weddings, neighborhood parties, and even Buddhist funerals. On these occasions, he participated actively and fulfilled whatever part was required by the customs and traditions.

The Weaver Pharmaceutical Company had a policy of granting two months home leave every two years with transportation paid for the employee and his family. When Mr. Higgins' turn came, he declined to go home even on vacation on the ground that his parents were already dead and his brothers and sisters were widely scattered throughout the United States. Consequently, he did not feel he had many home ties in the United States. Instead he and his wife took his two months leave and visited many of the remote historical sites throughout Japan.

None of these points by itself disturbed Mr. Prescott greatly. However, he was afraid that accumulations of these seemingly insignificant factors would tend to distort Higgins' cultural orientation and identification, thereby losing his effectiveness as a bi-lingual and cultural representative of the American parent company. In administrative relationships, there had been a number of incidents that tended to support Mr. Prescott's anxiety. A few of the specific examples were these.

In performing his responsibilities as executive assistant, Higgins had taken on many of the characteristics of a typical Japanese executive. For example, Mr. Higgins was reported to spend a great deal of time in listening to the personal problems of his subordinates. He maintained close social relationships with many of the men in the organization and he and his wife took an active interest in the personal lives of the employees. They even had gone as far as arranging marriages for some of the young employees.

Consequently, many of the employees sought Mr. Higgins' attention to register complaints and demands with the management. For example, a group of middle management personnel approached Mr. Higgins concerning the desirability of more liberal fringe benefits. These were particularly in the areas of company-sponsored recreational activities such as occasional out-of-town trips and the acquisition of rest houses at resort areas.

On another occasion, the middle management personnel registered their objections concerning a recent company policy of promoting personnel based upon merit rather than length of service and education, the two most important criteria in traditional Japanese approach. Shortly after Mr. Prescott took over the Japanese operations, he was appalled with Japanese promotion practices and decided to change these to a merit system. In the process, he consulted with Mr. Higgins as to its applicability in Japan.

The latter objected to the idea, saying that the Japanese were not quite ready to accept what he considered a radical approach. Since Mr. Prescott did not see it as a radical concept, he went ahead and announced the policy. At the same time, he installed an annual review system, whereby every one of the management personnel would be evaluated by his immediate superior and this would constitute an important basis for promotion.

The Japanese objections were primarily based upon the ground that their traditional personnel practices were so different from those of the United States, that a mechanical imposition of the U.S. method would not work in Japan. The system had, as Higgins expected, created many undesirable problems. The Japanese group contended that Mr. Prescott, who did not understand the language, was not aware of the magnitude of the anxiety and insecurity the policy had caused. Because of the traditional superior-subordinate relationship characterized by distance, fear, and obedience, they were not willing to take these problems directly to Mr. Prescott. Therefore they asked Mr. Higgins to intercede on their behalf by reporting their feelings to Mr. Prescott.

Mr. Prescott felt that though it was helpful to have Mr. Higgins report back to him the feelings and opinions of the middle management personnel, which otherwise might never come to his attention, he did not appreciate the latter's attitude in so doing. In these cases, Mr. Higgins' sympathy was with the Japanese group, and he usually insisted that these demands were reasonable and well justified according to the Japanese standard and traditions. Mr. Prescott found it necessary to deal with Mr. Higgins on these demands instead of being able to work with him as it had been in the past. His perception had been so colored that Mr. Prescott became hesitant to ask Mr. Higgins' opinions on these matters. Lately, whenever Mr. Prescott proposed a change in administrative procedures that might be contrary to Japanese traditions or culture, Mr. Higgins invariably raised objections. In Mr. Prescott's thinking, there were dynamic changes taking place in traditional Japanese customs and culture, and he was confident that many of the points Mr. Higgins objected to were not tied to the cultural patterns as rigidly as he thought they might be. Besides, Mr. Prescott thought that there was no point for a progressive American company to copy the local customs and felt that its real contribution to the Japanese society was in bringing in new ideas and innovations.

To substantiate this point, he learned that some of his Japanese subordinates were much more susceptible to new ideas and more willing to try them out than Mr. Higgins. This fact had convinced Mr. Prescott that Mr. Higgins was too closely identified with the traditional pattern of the Japanese culture, not sensing the new and radically different development taking place in Japan.

Moreover, two recent incidents raised some doubts in Mr. Prescott's mind as to the soundness of Mr. Higgins' judgment, which he, heretofore, had never questioned. The first incident was in connection with the dismissal of Mr. Nonogaki, chief of subsection in the Purchasing Department. In the opinion of Mr. Prescott, Mr. Nonogaki lacked initiative, leadership, and general competency. After two years of continued prodding by his superiors, including Mr. Prescott himself, he had shown little interest in self-improvement. As a result, Prescott had decided to dismiss him from the organization. Both Higgins and Takahinshi, personnel manager of the subsidiary, objected vigorously on the ground that this had never been done in the company. Besides, in Japan the management was required to live with a certain amount of incompetent executives as long as their honesty and loyalty were not questioned. They further claimed that the company was partially responsible for recruiting him initially and had kept him on for the last ten years without spotting his incompetency, thus it was not completely fair to require Mr. Nonogaki alone to take the full burden. Mr. Prescott, unimpressed by their arguments, dismissed him after serving proper notice.

A few weeks later, Mr. Prescott learned quite accidentally that Mr. Nonogaki was re-employed by one of the other subsidiaries of the Japanese parent company, the Yamazaki Pharmaceutical Co., Ltd. Upon investigating, he found, to his surprise, that Messrs. Higgins and Takahinshi had interceded and arranged for him to be taken back without informing Mr. Prescott. For understandable reasons, Mr. Prescott did not appreciate their action and confronted Mr. Higgins with this, who in turn told Mr. Prescott that he had only done what was expected of a superior in any Japanese company.

Another incident was in connection with his relationship with the government. In Japan, the government plays a substantially greater part in business and economic activities than it does in the United States. It is important for companies to maintain a good working relationship with government officials of those agencies that have control over their activities. This is particularly true of foreign subsidiaries. Because of many complicated intricacies, government relations had been entrusted to Mr. Higgins and his two Japanese assistants.

Mr. Prescott had observed a basic difference in the view with which he and Higgins looked upon practices of this sort. Prescott, knowing the differences in business ethics in various countries, accepted some of these activities as a necessary evil but felt that they had to be kept to a minimum in order to preserve the overall integrity of the company; whereas, Mr. Prescott felt Mr. Higgins had become a willing participant in the system without much reservation or restraint.

Mr. Prescott believed these problems to be quite serious. Mr. Higgins had been an effective as well as efficient executive assistant and his knowledge of the language and the people had proved invaluable. On numerous occasions, his American friends envied Prescott for having a man of his qualifications as an assistant. He also knew that Mr. Higgins had received several outstanding offers to go with other American companies in Japan.

Prescott felt that Higgins would be far more effective could he take a more emotionally detached attitude toward the Japanese people and culture. In Mr. Prescott's view, the best international executive was the one who retained a belief in the fundamentals of the U.S. point of view while also understanding foreign attitudes. This understanding, of course, should be thorough or even instinctive, but it also should be objective, characterized by neither disdain nor strong emotional attachment.

He was wondering how he could best assist Mr. Higgins to see his point of view, so that they could collaborate more effectively in fulfilling their administrative responsibilities.

Polaroid In and Out of South Africa

American companies operating in South Africa have become increasingly sensitive to charges that their activities bolster a regime that practices apartheid—a legal system of racial segregation and oppression widely agreed to be immoral.

Apartheid is an ancient Afrikaan term, meaning "apartness," in this case racial apartness. This policy of white domination has been the cornerstone of social policy in South Africa since the beginning of the Union of South Africa in 1910. According to the classification scheme implementing this policy, South Africa's population is composed of 17 percent white, 70 percent African, 10 percent Coloured (mixed descent), and 3 percent Asian. Whites alone may be members of Parliament and the cabinet, and only whites may possess firearms or be arms-carrying members of the police and military forces. Organizations doctrinally opposed to apartheid are banned. There has also been a history of political involvement by indigenous industry aimed at promoting apartheid because industrialists have worked to keep labor both cheap and unorganized.

Despite these modes of enforced segregation, most nonwhites reside in white-owned urban territory or on white-owned farms whose economies depend upon their labor. Under this system, blacks are allowed to own only 13 percent of the land surface. These lands are designated "native reserves." Though whites constitute 17 percent of the population, they control 87 percent of the land. Whites also control all major business activities, and the system is constructed so that black workers are paid less than white workers for comparable work.

About 320 American companies currently have operations in South Africa. These include such major and respectable companies as General Motors, Exxon, Eli Lilly, Kodak, IBM, etc. South Africa is an attractive place for American investment, and a part of the attraction de-

This case was prepared by Tom L. Beauchamp, with assistance from R. Jay Wallace and Barbara Humes. **Not to be duplicated without permission of the authors and publisher.**

rives from the economic benefits of apartheid: Profits are very substantial, labor is remarkably cheap, capital is not threatened by the political insecurity created by unstable governments, the market is thriving and currency is hard and convertible, and South Africa is rich in natural resources, especially minerals. The United States is the second largest direct foreign investor in South Africa, a nation of 30 million people, 5 million of whom are whites. U.S. investments in South Africa were approximately $1.7 billion in 1976. American companies control 43% of South Africa's petroleum market, 23% of auto sales, 70% of its computer business, and are easily the main suppliers of most major consumer products. Thus the American presence in South Africa is not an insignificant factor in the country's economic health.[1]

American corporations began to trade in South Africa around 1880, when the white South African community alone was involved in commerce and employment. That is, whites at that time held all the available jobs, even in factories. There were no "black employees." Gradually, however, the South African economy was so spectacularly successful that there were not enough whites to fill available positions, and blacks began to move into factories and other low-paying jobs. Though salaries have always been extremely low, blacks have made enough money to purchase goods and become a factor in the South African economy. The more they interacted in the economy, the more repressive apartheid laws became, and this in turn bluntly presented dilemmas for American corporations about participation in the immoral activities of the South African government.

While American corporations have become increasingly sensitive to charges of immoral exploitation and opportunism in South Africa, very few have taken the initiative of complete withdrawal. Polaroid, however, has had a long history of sharply criticizing the South African government and—as we shall see in detail—has now withdrawn completely from all entanglement in South Africa. Not surprisingly, Polaroid was one of the first American firms to publicly condemn apartheid and to assume responsibility for the uses that government made of Polaroid technology. Polaroid views itself as a "corporation with a conscience" and has been a pacesetter in both race-relations policies and community-relations programs in the United States.[2]

Nonetheless, in 1970 Polaroid too found itself embroiled in a controversy over its involvement in South Africa. The events in this contro-

[1]See Richard DeGeorge, "U.S. Firms in South Africa," in his *Business Ethics*, pp. 253–55; and Dharmendra T. Verma, "Polaroid in South Africa" (Bentley College, 1978), distributed by Harvard Business School, HBS Case Services, p. 6.

[2]C. L. Suzman, "Polaroid Experiment in South Africa" (Johannesburg, South Africa: Graduate School of Business Administration, University of Witwatersrand, 1974, revised 1977), distributed by Harvard Business School, HBS Case Services, p. 2.

versy began in 1970 when a few of Polaroid's black American employees formed a group called Polaroid Revolutionary Workers Movement (PRWM). They were outraged in particular because they believed Polaroid products were being used in South Africa's repressive Pass Book system. The hated Pass laws were designed by the South African government to control the movement of blacks in urban areas. This practice has been described by Bishop Desmond Tutu, head of the South African Council of Churches, as ". . . among the most humiliating of the dehumanizing laws and regulations applied to this country."[3] In brief summary form, these laws require: (1) that all African citizens over 16 carry a Pass Book that enters details of where the person is permitted to be and other personal details such as the person's place of work and payment of taxes; (2) that Africans may not remain in an urban area longer than 72 hours without a permit unless special permission has been granted or the person has a long history of approved residence and work in the area.[4]

PRWM employees at Polaroid in the United States distributed leaflets that charged in its title, "Polaroid Imprisons Black People in 60 Seconds." These leaflets were also placed on company bulletin boards. This campaign intensified and came to a point of confrontation in October 1970. The general charge by the employees was that Polaroid was (like other American companies) exploiting cheap black labor in South Africa, and (unlike other American corporations) was actually having its technology used to support the more repressive aspects of the apartheid system.[5] The above-mentioned pamphlet and this last charge refer to the use of film and cameras involved in implementing the South African government's Pass Book system. At least one Polaroid executive (Tom Wyman, Vice-President of SALES) admitted an awareness that Polaroid products were being used at that time in the Pass Book identification program. The supply source was Frank and Hirsch Ltd., Polaroid's (independent) South African distributor.[6]

On October 27, 1970 some large demonstrations organized by PRWM were held in Boston, and the more activist-minded members of PRWM called for a worldwide boycott of Polaroid products. In this same month Polaroid officials denied that the company's equipment

[3]Marjorie Chan and John Steiner, "Corporate America Confronts the Apartheid System," in George A. Steiner and John F. Steiner, *Casebook for Business, Government, and Society,* 2nd ed. (New York: Random House, Business Division, 1980), pp. 86f.

[4]See Muriel Horrel, *South Africa: Basic Facts and Figures* (South African Institute of Race Relations, 1973).

[5]David Vogel, *Lobbying the Corporation: Citizen Challenges to Business Authority* (New York: Basic Books, Inc., 1978), p. 173; Chan and Steiner, "Corporate America Confronts," pp. 86f; and Suzman, "Polaroid Experiment," p. 6.

[6]See accounts in the *Boston Globe,* October 18, 1964, p. 64, and Suzman, "Polaroid Experiment," p. 7.

was being used in the Pass law program. Polaroid's director of community relations was authorized to make the following statement in response to PRWM charges: "We have a responsibility for the ultimate use of our product. . . . In response to the charge we articulated a very strict policy of refusing to do business directly with the South African government. . . . We as a corporation will not sell our products in instances where its use constitutes a potential abridgement of human freedom."[7] Mr. Edwin Land, owner and manager of the corporation, also reiterated his "personal ban" on the sale of Polaroid products to the South African government, a ban originally instituted in 1948, but less than diligently enforced in some years.[8]

Instead of yielding to PRWM demands to have Polaroid put an end to all activities in South Africa, Polaroid management determined that it would rather investigate less radical alternatives. Management at Polaroid then formed a committee of fourteen employees, representing a cross section of the company's work force. This group was mandated to make a final withdraw-or-stay decision. This committee first recommended:

1. That a four member fact finding group be sent to South Africa to review the feeling of blacks in South Africa first hand. The four-man team was to report on the use of Polaroid products in South Africa, conditions of Frank and Hirsch, the use of Polaroid film in the Pass Book Program, and was to give recommendations on the engagement-disengagement decision.

2. That the committee would consult outside experts in economics, African history, politics, and other fields in order to assist them in making recommendations about Polaroid's future in South Africa and Polaroid's future business in "free Black Africa".[9]

This travel group had a reasonably free hand to assemble data and conduct interviews while in South Africa. Their final recommendation was that Polaroid should not pull out of South African operations, but instead should initiate a program that would come to be known as "The Polaroid Experiment." The program had four main points:

1. Sales to the South African government were to be discontinued, but the company would not disengage from the Republic and would set up an experimental program for one year.

2. Polaroid's local distributor and its suppliers were going to improve salaries and other benefits for black employees.

[7]As quoted in Vogel, p. 173.

[8]H. Landis Gabel, "Polaroid Experiment in South Africa" (Charlottesville, Va.: The Colgate Darden School of Business Administration, University of Virginia, 1981), distributed by Harvard Business School, HBS Case Services, p. 1; Suzman, "Polaroid Experiment," p. 7. See also *Business Week* (November 14, 1970), p. 32.

[9]Suzman, "Polaroid Experiment," p. 10.

3. The company's South African associates were to be obliged to start a training program for blacks so as to enable them to take up important posts.

4. A proportion of Polaroid's South African profits was to be devoted to encouraging black education.[10]

The South African government agreed to permit these employment practices by an American company, so long as no law was violated. The government specified, however, that any promotion of nonwhites into positions of authority over whites would not be permitted.

One year later Polaroid evaluated the effects of this experiment and found that great improvements had been made in the salaries, advancement, and benefits of its nonwhite employees. The average monthly salary for blacks had increased 22% (including a "bonus" for black employees). The principle of the same pay for the same job had been accepted. Eight black employees were promoted to supervisory positions. Three programs were designed to improve the education of black employees' children, to establish a foundation to support black students and teachers, and to promote black leadership. Polaroid also contributed $75,000 in grants to black educational groups in South Africa.[11]

This program continued successfully for six years. However, the actual measure of "success" can easily be disputed. Frank and Hirsch noted at the time, and Polaroid knew, that it would be extremely difficult to enforce a complete ban on the sale of all products to the South African government. It was easy to stop *direct* sales, but indirect sales through private photographers and retailers in other countries would be difficult to stop. Thus the effectiveness of the ban on the sale of Polaroid products during these years was questionable. Nonetheless, during these six years both Polaroid and Frank and Hirsch expressed virtually complete satisfaction with the program. The Managing Director of Frank and Hirsch noted that it was also a period when racial discrimination was attacked and virtually eliminated at Frank and Hirsch. Blacks and whites came to share the same offices and have the same working hours. Frank and Hirsch employees grew to be almost 50% black, and the company donated money to upgrade the education of black African children.[12]

However, in November 1977 a dramatic new development occurred in Polaroid's "Experiment." On November 21 the *Boston Globe* ran a first-page story claiming that Frank and Hirsch had been clandestinely selling Polaroid products to the South African government in complete violation of its 1971 standing agreement not to permit such sales. This

[10]*Ibid.*, p. 12; see also Gabel, "Polaroid Experiment," p. 2.
[11]Chan and Steiner, "Corporate America Confronts," p. 89.
[12]Suzman, "Polaroid Experiment," p. 14.

story emerged through the whistleblowing efforts of a former employee in the shipping department of Frank and Hirsch—a South African Indian named Indrus Naidoo. Mr. Naidoo had made photostatic copies of invoices documenting the delivery of Polaroid products to the Bantu Reference Bureau on September 22, 1975. This is an agency that issues Pass Books for nonwhites. Mr. Naidoo passed on this photostatic copy and other information to Mr. Paul Irish, a staff member of the American Committee on Africa in New York. Irish then released the copy to the *Boston Globe* after a time when Naidoo was able to leave South Africa (as an exile, after discharge from his job). Naidoo's documentation showed that Frank and Hirsch had for years billed all its shipments to the South African government through a drugstore in Johannesburg. These shipments were packed in unmarked cartons containing both film and cameras. Deliveries had also been made to the military, including a large shipment of Polaroid sunglasses. Since all billing was done through the pharmacy, there was no record of direct sales.[13]

Polaroid had been informed by the *Boston Globe* of these charges five days prior to the appearance of the story in their newspaper. The company immediately sent their Export Sales Manager to South Africa to investigate the charges. The Sales Manager was able to document several deliveries to the South African government, and to interview Mr. Hirsch (the owner of Frank and Hirsch), who expressed shock and complete ignorance of these sales. (Polaroid officials indicated at the time that they had long had suspicions about Frank and Hirsch, and had periodically attempted investigations.) Polaroid then immediately announced—on the same day the story appeared in the *Boston Globe*—that it was terminating its distributorship and all involvement in South Africa. Polaroid issued an official statement saying it "abhorred" the policy of apartheid, that it was largely the recommendations of black Africans that had led to continued sales in 1971, that Polaroid's contributions to black African scholarships during this period amounted to approximately one-half million dollars, that there was considerable evidence that Polaroid had had a positive effect on black employees and on foreign investors, and that they would not establish a new distributorship in South Africa.[14] At this time Polaroid's South African annual sales were between three and four million dollars; the company's universal 1977 sales were over one billion dollars.[15]

[13]George M. Houser, "Polaroid's Dramatic Withdrawal from South Africa," *The Christian Century* (April 12, 1978), pp. 392–93. Mr. Houser was then Executive Director of the American Committee on Africa, located in New York. See also Verma, p. 3; Vogel, p. 173; and Gabel, p. 1.

[14]Letter from the Polaroid Corporation, Monday, November 21, 1977.

[15]Verma, "Polaroid in South Africa," pp. 1–4, and Houser, "Polaroid's Dramatic Withdrawal," p. 392.

Marketing Infant Formula

On May 21, 1981 the Thirty-fourth World Health Assembly of the World Health Organization (WHO) passed a resolution adopting the International Code of Marketing of Breastmilk Substitutes, urging all member states "to give full and unanimous support to the implementation of the recommendations made by the joint WHO/UNICEF Meeting on Infant and Young Child Feeding and of the provisions of the International Code in its entirety as an expression of the collective will of the membership of the World Health Organization."[1] The code is designed to regulate marketing practices related to prepared infant formula and other products designed as partial or total substitutes for breastmilk, but the code specifies that it is a recommendation and not a requirement for member nations. Article 5 of this code states that:

> There should be no advertising or other form of promotion to the general public of products within the scope of this Code.
>
> Manufacturers and distributors should not provide, directly or indirectly to pregnant women, mothers or members of their families, samples of products within the scope of this Code. . . .
>
> There should be no point-of-sale advertising, giving of samples, or any other promotion device to induce sales directly to the consumer at the retail level, such as special displays, discount coupons, premiums, special sales, loss-leaders and tie-in sales, for products within the scope of this Code. . . .
>
> Manufacturers and distributors should not distribute to pregnant women or mothers of infants and young children any gifts of articles or utensils which may promote the use of breastmilk substitutes or bottle-feeding.
>
> Marketing personnel, in their business capacity, should not seek direct

---

[1] Thirty-fourth World Health Assembly, "International Code of Marketing of Breastmilk Substitutes," World Health Assembly 34.22 (May 21, 1981), p. 1. Passed under Article 23 of the WHO Constitution.

or indirect contact of any kind with pregnant women or with mothers of infants and young children.[2]

While these limitations on the marketing of breastmilk substitutes are designed to apply in all WHO-member countries, they are in fact directed specifically to a controversy that has raged over the past decade regarding the marketing of prepared infant formulas in Third-World countries.

Annual sales of infant formula by approximately 20 multinational corporations amount to roughly $2 billion. Figures in the Third World were estimated in 1981 to be no less than $690 million.[3] Abbott Laboratories, through its Ross Laboratories nutritional division, is the largest domestic manufacturer of infant formula in the United States, with 65% of the market. In the Third World the market is dominated by the Swiss conglomerate, Nestle, S.A., with 60% of total sales. Chicago-based Abbott/Ross has approximately 6% of the remaining Third World market, along with Mead Johnson (Bristol-Myers), Wyeth Laboratories (American Home Products), and numerous foreign competitors.[4]

Since 1970 Abbott/Ross and Nestle, along with all the other companies who market infant formula in the Third World, have been involved in a controversy over (1) the morality of *any* infant formula marketing in the Third World and (2) the morality of specific promotional and marketing techniques. This controversy has been played out in various health organizations (e.g., UNICEF, the World Health Organization, and the Pan American Health Organization), in the popular press, in consumer boycotts organized primarily by religious groups, in the annual meetings of the corporations involved, in the SEC, in the courts, and in Federal and international hearing rooms.

The basic charges against these corporations are that in the Third World countries: (1) prepared infant formula is likely to be improperly used and so to lead to malnutrition, diarrhea, and death; and (2) the "aggressive" marketing tactics used by certain companies encourage women to choose bottlefeeding and thereby cause a decline in breastfeeding. While prepared infant formulas do provide adequate nourishment if properly used, it is almost universally agreed that from a medical, nutritional, and psychological standpoint breastfeeding is the

[2]*Ibid.*, p. 7.

[3]David O. Cox, "The Infant Formula Issue: A Story in Escalation and Complication," a paper delivered at the Conference on Business Environment/Public Policy and the Business School of the 1980s (College Park, Md., July 12–17, 1981), p. 5.

[4]Earl A. Molander, "Abbott Laboratories Puts Restraints on Marketing Infant Formulas in the Third World," in his *Responsive Capitalism: Case Studies in Corporate Social Conduct* (New York: McGraw-Hill Book Co., 1980), p. 265.

superior way to feed infants (assuming a healthy mother). In Third World countries the use of prepared infant formulas often is complicated by ignorance and consequent failures to understand the instructions, by poverty, and by poor sanitation and lack of adequate water supplies, which lead to improperly cleansed bottles and to mixing the formula with impure water. Because infant formula can cost 25–40% of a family's income, mothers sometimes over-dilute the preparation in order to make it "go further." Over-dilution, coupled with poor sanitation, leads to malnutrition, diarrhea, and increased susceptibility to infectious disease. Unfortunately, there is no room for a "trial" at bottlefeeding, as breastfeeding must be instituted shortly after birth if it is to be used.

Marketing strategies to sell infant formula in Third World countries include direct mass media advertising by radio, television, newspapers, and billboards. Free samples are also distributed through health professionals in hospitals and clinics. "Milk nurses," who are company employees dressed like nurses, have in some regions called on prospective and new mothers at home and in hospitals to promote the product and leave samples. These promotional strategies are viewed by critics as a major cause of the decline of breastfeeding in some Third World countries. The use of company "milk nurses" has been denounced as a deceptive practice because they are easily confused with *bona fide* nurses. The provision of free samples of formula is detrimental to breastfeeding because using the samples may irreversibly suppress lactation, thus leaving the mother with no choice but to continue with the formula.

It is important, however, not to overgeneralize complex situations by use of the term "Third World countries." Many of these countries have substantially different situations, and within each the mothers using the formula vary dramatically in socioeconomic background. Perhaps three-fourths of the women in the Third World are not in the cash economy in their country, and could not purchase formula even if they wanted to. For example, socialist Algeria permits no advertising whatever, but the Algerian government purchases in excess of 20 million pounds of infant formula, which it then distributes. Breast feeding rates remain high in this country.[5]

The controversy over infant formula has a long history, but there is still considerable lack of clarity and disagreement about all the relevant cause-and-effect relationships and about the importance of related cultural practices. Health and nutritional experts disagree as to the exact

[5]Based on data supplied by Tom McCollough of Ross Laboratories (on February 24, 1982).

relationship of bottlefeeding to infant mortality and morbidity and to the continuing decline of breastfeeding. It is, however, agreed that the relationships are complex and multifactorial.

In 1970 the problem of "bottle illness" was brought to the attention of Abbott/Ross, Nestle, and other infant-formula manufacturers by Dr. Derrick B. Jelliffe, then head of the Caribbean Food and Nutrition Institute in Jamaica, who charged that "infant morbidity and mortality in general were linked in a significant way to the promotion and use of commercial formulas." Jelliffe recommended that prepared formulas be entirely withdrawn from the developing countries.[6] Many medical and nutritional experts agreed with Dr. Jelliffe, and in 1971 an *ad hoc* committee of the United Nation's Protein Advisory Group observed that "The extensive introduction and indiscriminate promotion of expensive processed milk-based infant foods in some situations may constitute a grave threat to the nutritional status of the infants for whom they are intended." In 1974 the governing body of the World Health Organization (WHO) passed a resolution that stressed the problems caused by advertisements promoting the superiority of bottlefeeding over breastfeeding. The resolution urged member countries to "review sales promotion activities on baby foods and to introduce appropriate remedial measures, including advertisement codes and legislation where necessary."[7]

However, other medical and nutritional experts disagreed with these views. A group led by Dr. Fernando Monkeberg of the Institute of Nutrition and Food Technology at the University of Chile maintained that even more serious health and nutrition problems would exist if prepared infant formulas were *not* available. This group argued that the decline in breastfeeding ". . . was largely independent of prepared infant formula promotion." This group insisted "that data on morbidity and mortality had to be examined as part of a much larger picture that included maternal nutrition, sanitation, access to health care, purchasing power, education, lactation failure due to family disruption, urbanization with subsequent life-style changes, etc." The Protein Advisory Group also modified its earlier position on the basis of a series of international meetings on infant nutrition. While still critical of industry *promotional* practices, their report included the recommendation that "infant formulas be developed and introduced to satisfy the special needs of infants who are *not* breast fed."[8]

A recent study done by Jose Villar of the Johns Hopkins School of Hygiene and Public Health and Jose M. Belizan of the Institute of Nu-

---

[6]Molander, "Abbott Laboratories," p. 266.

[7]David Vogel, "Infant Formulas" in his *Lobbying the Corporation: Citizen Challengers to Business Authority* (New York: Basic Books, Inc., 1978), p. 189.

[8]Molander, "Abbott Laboratories," p. 267.

trition of Central America and Panama can be viewed as supportive of the availability of prepared infant formula (when used properly) in the poorer countries:

> UNSUPPLEMENTED human milk from a well-nourished, well-motivated mother is all that a baby in optimal nutritional condition may require to sustain growth and good nutrition during the first 4 to 6 months of life. To have a healthy, well-nourished, and well-developed infant, the mother must have laid down adequate nutritional reserves during pregnancy, including subcutaneous fat, and must remain well-fed throughout lactation. Unfortunately, in developing countries poorly nourished women give birth to infants of low birthweight (LBW) in bad environmental and sanitary conditions. The frequency of low birthweight (<2500 g) is, on the average, three times greater in underdeveloped (17%) than in developed countries (6%). In some areas 30–40% of birthweights may be below 2500 g with 75% of the infants intrauterine-growth-retarded (IUGR). IUGR infants are the ones most at risk of perinatal death, illness, and subsequent handicap. . . .
>
> A healthy, well-nourished woman must be prepared for successful lactation in two ways:
>
> a) By the physiological changes of pregnancy, especially the accumulation of fat reserves (an average of 4 kg during a normal gestation period). This represents an additional 36,000 kcal.
>
> b) By an increased dietary intake during lactation (600–800 additional kcal/day) to give a total daily intake of 2800–3000 kcal. Greater consumption of all essential nutrients, including an additional 20 g of protein/day, is also necessary for adequate lactation. . . .
>
> Neither of the two physiological processes required for successful lactation is found in poorly nourished mothers from developing countries and these women are, from their first pregnancy, in a state of general "maternal depletion," characterized by progressive weight loss and/or specific nutritional deficiencies.[9]

Villar and Belizan conclude that in the case of malnourished children born to already malnourished mothers, breastfeeding alone neither corrects

> malnutrition nor modifies its basic courses. When the infant is already malnourished at birth, as are about 40% in developing countries, breastfeeding alone during the first four months of life is unlikely to provide adequate nutrition.[10]

Drs. Villar and Belizan do not go so far as to take a general position on the controversy surrounding economic and sanitation factors or

---

[9]Jose Villar and Jose M. Belizan, "Breastfeeding in Developing Countries," *The Lancet* (September 19, 1981), pp. 621–22.

[10]*Ibid.*, p. 623.

about marketing practices in the Third World. While this recent study supports the contention that *some* forms of supplemental feeding are needed for some Third World infants, questions remain unanswered about what kind of maternal and child supplements should be used (prepared formula or selected foods), who should pay for the supplement (government or family), and what kinds of marketing tactics are permissible.

The accumulating evidence of the need for foods to supplement breastmilk in Third World countries has not answered important questions about the advertising tactics and marketing strategies used by the infant formula manufacturers. The United Nations, in a widely circulated but undocumented statistic, estimated that one million infant deaths per year are directly related to the use of breastmilk substitutes; and in developing the Code of Marketing of Breastmilk Substitutes the joint WHO/UNICEF group accepted the existence of a cause-and-effect relationship between the marketing of prepared infant formulas and the decline of breastfeeding in the Third World. They link both infant mortality and morbidity to the use of these products. It has been generally agreed by critics of infant formula marketing practices that the greatest offenders are members of an association named the International Council of Infant Formula Industries (ICIFI), which is led by Nestle. The only company in the United States that joined this group is Wyeth Laboratories. Abbott/Ross refused to join the association when its proposals for voluntary restrictions on marketing practices were consistently voted down at the first association meeting in November 1975.[11]

THE ABBOTT/ROSS RESPONSE

David Cox, Chairman of Ross Laboratories, agrees with many of the criticisms leveled at some of the companies that market infant formula in the Third World. He strongly disagrees, however, both with the notion that infant formula sales are *responsible* for the decline in breastfeeding, and the across-the-board condemnation of infant formula producers (by the press, the public, and specific action groups). Cox points out that infant mortality is closely related to the general level of a country's economic and technological development, to the general health status of the population, to child spacing, to the nutritional and educational status of the mother, and to the availability of adequate supplies of pure water. Cox also notes that "infant mortality is often highest in areas where lactation is universal and extended, for example

[11]Molander, "Abbott Laboratories," p. 268.

in the rural areas of the Third World."[12] Cox agrees, however, that (while not a panacea for Third World ills) breastfeeding is the "desirable" means of infant feeding and should not be *unnecessarily* replaced by substitutes. "Breast milk is a relatively inexpensive, nutritionally ideal first food for infants. As a natural fertility regulator, exclusive breastfeeding tends to increase the spacing between births; additionally, its immunological properties can be passively transmitted to the newborn, offering some protection from environmental insult."[13]

Tom McCollough, Director of Business Practices Research for Ross Laboratories, takes issue with the tendency of the critics of infant formula sales to lump all "Third World mothers" together "implying that infant formula is widely used by the poor and that all Third World women and their situations are alike."[14]

Cox holds that, despite accusations to the contrary, Abbott/Ross has consistently demonstrated responsible "stewardship" in this matter:

> In 1972, we published our first Marketing Code of Ethics in Developing Countries; it was later strengthened in 1977.
> We were the first member of industry to develop such an ethical regulation and believe it remains the most stringent one in the industry. For the most part, our code development was but a clarification of policies already in place and based on the following three marketing philosophies:
>
> (1) Breast feeding is superior and the preferred method of feeding;
> (2) Our marketing practices should in no way discourage the adoption of breast feeding; and
> (3) Promotion of our product is limited to the health professional community.
>
> It is our belief that health professionals are best qualified to evaluate and recommend the appropriate use of our products for babies in their care. It is our policy, that where no health care counseling is available, the use of our product is inappropriate.
> New labels stress the importance of breastfeeding as the most desirable feeding for infants. The labels also include written and graphic instructions for use, emphasize that the product should only be used under the supervision of a qualified health professional, and warn against the dangers of improper preparation.[15]

[In (3) above Cox is referring to a policy and organizational difference between Abbott/Ross and some competitors. Abbott/Ross deals with pharmaceuticals and health care products, not with food products, as

[12]Cox, "The Infant Formula Issue," p. 2.

[13]*Ibid.*

[14]McCollough correspondence.

[15]Villar and Belizan, "Breastfeeding in Developing Countries."

do some competitors. Abbott/Ross therefore has marketed by calls on professionals rather than through mass marketing practices.]

Other Abbott/Ross measures initiated by the company to control infant formula abuses included: (1) placing an insert in each carton of formula asking Third World distributors to limit the product to consumers who can afford and properly prepare the product; (2) a similar request to Third World health professionals; (3) the limitation of samples to health professionals; (4) the reduction of sample size from 250 grams to 125 grams to preclude the chances of interference with the establishment of lactation; (5) the elimination of bonuses to employees based on sales; and (6) the banning of nurses' uniforms for nurses and midwives hired as company representatives.

Abbott/Ross has also undertaken an extensive program to promote maternal and child health in the Third World, and in 1976 formed a permanent team that includes a nutritionist, an anthropologist, a medical education specialist, and a pediatric consultant to study infant nutrition, formula, and breastfeeding in the Third World. Projects undertaken by the company as a result of this effort include the preparation of posters, sample radio announcements, and films advocating the merits of breastfeeding for distribution to Third World Health Ministries and the development of instructional material for training traditional birth attendants in the Arab world.[16]

THE NESTLE RESPONSE

The campaign against Nestle began in 1974 when a Swiss political organization published a translated version of an earlier United Kingdom report on infant formula marketing in developing countries under the title, "Nestle Kills Babies." In response Nestle filed a libel suit in a Swiss court. Nestle won the suit on the point of the libelous title, but the court, in rendering its judgment, called on the company to adjust its marketing practices in Third World countries. Specific mention was made of Nestle's mass advertising and sales promotion techniques.[17]

While Abbott/Ross relied on health professionals for distribution and promotion of its products, Nestle, which is basically a producer and distributor of foods rather than pharmaceuticals, advertised its infant formula on billboards, posters, through radio and television messages, and in newspapers and booklets, as well as providing free samples to hospitals and health professionals. Critics of Nestle cite the following radio message as an example of Nestle's "aggressive advertising":

[16]Cox, "The Infant Formula Issue."

[17]"Infant Formula: An Activist Campaign," reprinted from *Europe's Consumer Movement: Key Issues and Corporate Responses* (Geneva: Business International, S.A., undated), p. 9.

Bring up your baby with love and Lactogen.

Important news for mothers/ Now Lactogen is even better, because it contains more proteins plus vitamins and iron, all essential for making your baby strong and healthy.

Lactogen Full Protein now has an even creamier taste and is guaranteed by Nestle.

Lactogen and love.[18]

Nestle has also been criticized for using free gift schemes and premiums to promote its milk products and for the establishment of baby clubs.[19] And like the other infant formula manufacturers, Nestle has been attacked for the use of milk nurses, or as the company prefers to call them, "mothercraft" nurses. In response to these criticisms Nestle has made changes in its advertising and marketing tactics, suspending "all consumer advertising of infant formula products in developing countries in order to reevaluate the role of advertising in educating Third World peoples about the use of infant formula."[20] The company also changed the outfits worn by the "mothercraft" nurses from white nurses' uniforms to colored company uniforms.

Nestle agreed early to endorse "the principle" behind the marketing code recommended by the World Health Assembly. On March 16, 1982 Nestle agreed to abide strictly by the Code in the 120 countries in which its product is marketed.[21] However, Nestle executives have voiced concerns over the prohibition of contact between company representatives and consumers. The company holds that improvements in labeling are not adequate to fulfill (often illiterate) consumers' need for accurate information and that a "show and tell" approach is necessary.

> What we're talking about is not necessarily the *right* but the *responsibility* of industry to communicate with its consumers. . . . If consumers—mothers in this case—are not given adequate instructions which can help them to use a product correctly, there are certain circumstances under which a manufacturer could be held responsible. So if you say, 'Treat it like lettuce and just put it on the shelves' you are neglecting what is seen as a manufacturer's basic responsibility to do everything in his power to ensure that the product he sells is used correctly and appropriately.[22]

---

[18]Marjorie Chan, "Nestle under Fire for Hyping Infant Formula," in George A. Steiner and John F. Steiner, *Casebook for Business, Government, and Society,* 2nd ed. (New York: Random House, Business Division, 1980), p. 197.

[19]*Ibid.*

[20]John A. Sparks, "The Nestle Controversy—Anatomy of a Boycott," Public Policy Education Fund, Inc. (Grove City, Pa., undated).

[21]Philip J. Hilts, "Nestle to Comply with Tougher Code on Infant Formula," *The Washington Post,* March 17, 1982, sec. A, p. 8.

[22]"Infant Formula: An Activist Campaign," p. 13.

In June 1981 Dr. Thad M. Jackson, Vice-President for Nutrition and Development, Nestle Coordination Center for Nutrition, testified before Subcommittees of the Foreign Affairs Committee, U.S. House of Representatives on the WHO Infant Formula Code. In his testimony Dr. Jackson reviewed the company's past practices and stated their position on a number of elements in the ongoing controversy:

> The Nestle Company's involvement in infant nutrition began in 1867 when Henri Nestle, a Swiss chemist, developed and marketed a milk food that he used to nourish a premature infant who could not take any food and was in immediate danger of dying.
>
> Nestle's concern for the quality of its products, especially infant and child nutrition products, has not diminished from its earliest history. And just as Henri Nestle's first use of his milk food saved a baby's life in Switzerland more than a century ago, our products save thousands of lives today. For example, Nestle infant food products have been used to fight famine and feed starving refugees in Thailand, Somalia, Nicaragua, Bangladesh and elsewhere. Our products have been used by the International Red Cross, the Save the Children Fund and the Baptists Missions of Thailand to fight starvation and to save the lives of babies. . . .
>
> The need for breastmilk supplements and substitutes is clearly supported by the World Health Organization and eminent pediatric authorities. We fully recognize our responsibility to market infant formula in ways that do not discourage breastfeeding. We have been conscious of the need to modify our policies to meet changing conditions and to maintain our commitment to breastfeeding.
>
> In 1974, Nestle's president, Dr. Arthur Furer, aware of changing social patterns in the developing world and the increased access to radio and television there, reviewed the company's marketing practices on a region-by-region basis. As a result, mass media advertising of infant formula began to be phased out immediately in certain markets and, by 1978, was banned worldwide by the company.
>
> Nestle then undertook to carry out more comprehensive health education programs so as to ensure that an understanding of the proper use of our products reached mothers, particularly in rural areas. . . .
>
> Nestle fully supports the aim of the Code of Marketing of Breastmilk Substitutes recently adopted by the World Health Assembly: the provison of safe and adequate nutrition for infants by the protection and promotion of breastfeeding and by ensuring the proper use of breastmilk substitutes, when they are necessary, on the basis of adequate information and through appropriate marketing and distribution.
>
> Moreover, Nestle welcomes the World Health Assembly's decision to adopt the WHO Code as a recommendation, rather than as a regulation, so as to encourage individual countries to introduce, where needed, specific national codes most appropriate to their socio-economic, educational and cultural backgrounds, and best suited to protect the health of infants in each sovereign nation.
>
> Many countries have already adopted individual national codes, and several more are in the process of doing so. Nestle currently markets infant formula in ten nations that have their own codes, and it abides by

all ten of the codes, as it will abide by new codes as they are developed and enacted if needed by individual nations. . . .

Nestle continually refines its policies to meet the needs of individual nations, and it will continue to do so. We reviewed our infant formula marketing practices seven years ago and made significant changes. We have made many more changes since then. We will continue to review current marketing practices to ensure that they are in agreement with national codes.[23]

The International Council of Infant Food Industries, of which Nestle is a founding member, has also issued a statement regarding the World Health Assembly Code of Marketing, which holds that national rather than international codes would be preferable:

ICIFI members firmly support this WHO/UNICEF principle that marketing should not discourage breastfeeding. At the same time, ICIFI members believe 'it is essential to make formulas, foods, and instructions for good nutrition for their infants available to those mothers who do not breast-feed for various reasons.'

ICIFI members have criticized the proposed single, detailed, international code which does not take into consideration varied socio-economic and cultural differences and, therefore, does not help infant nutrition in specific countries.

Instead, ICIFI members are convinced that national codes or marketing—adaptable as they are to the very diverse conditions of developed countries as well as the Third World—are a much better way to guide business practices.[24]

CONTINUING CRITICISMS

In spite of the above responses, Abbott/Ross and Nestle have been sharply criticized by certain church, medical, and public health groups. One ecumenical agency of the National Council of Churches has argued that corporate "development" often means *creating* a market for a product (i.e., creating a need that previously did not exist). They hold Abbott/Ross and Nestle responsible for increasing the incidence of infant malnutrition and mortality. They are willing to agree that an infant-formula product can be "benign" in developed countries, but they hold that the same product seriously endangers health and welfare levels in underdeveloped countries. This group has occasionally met and had serious discussions with representatives of Abbott/Ross. The company believes it has done all it can to satisfy their proposed changes in marketing, but the church group cites two remaining prob-

[23]Thad M. Jackson, "Nestle Discusses the Recommended WHO Infant Formula Code."

[24]International Council of Infant Food Industries, "Infant Formula Marketing in the Third World," *National Journal* (May 9, 1981), p. 854.

lems: (1) the company continues to offer "large quantities of free formula" that flow through health professionals to mothers; and (2) the company continues to pay its representatives to *sell* its products. However, the church group has specifically cited Abbott's code of marketing ethics as making important strides in proper marketing, and further holds that whether the code is or is not adequate will depend more on how progressively the company monitors its implementation, including the reporting of abuses, than on the literal wording of the code.

Numerous medical and public-health groups are also still critical of industry marketing practices, and some have joined in an arranged boycott of Nestle products. The following official "Statement" on the WHO "Code of Marketing of Breastmilk Substitutes" by the Board of Directors of the Ambulatory Pediatric Association is representative of these ongoing concerns:

> Despite claims to the contrary, marketing of infant formula influences maternal feeding practices. In recent testimony before the House Subcommittee on International Economic Policy and Trade, Carl Taylor, Professor and Head of the Department of International Health at the Johns Hopkins School of Hygiene and Public Health, presented some evidence: Massive advertising and availability of formula have been associated with a decline in breastfeeding in oil-rich Arab countries so that only 15% of mothers are nursing their babies at 3 months of age. In 1977 in Papua, New Guinea, promotion of infant formula was banned and feeding bottles could only be obtained with prescriptions from health workers; breastfeeding increased from 65% to 88%, and by 1980 there was a statistically significant association with decreased incidence of gastroenteritis and malnutrition. With the institution of practices to encourage breastfeeding in an area in rural Costa Rica, neonatal mortality from diarrheal infections decreased from 3.9/1,000 in 1976 to near zero in 1980. . . .
>
> Recent hearings by the House Subcommittee on Domestic Marketing, Consumer Relations, and Nutrition, and an administrative petition by Public Advocates, Inc. to 'alleviate domestic infant formula misuse' indicate growing public concern about the policies of infant formula manufacturers in the United States. The free distribution of formula within health facilities makes health professionals conduits for free advertising. . . .[25]

Abbott/Ross vigorously denies that these claims have been adequately validated in New Guinea, the Arab countries, or elsewhere. Both Nestle and Abbott/Ross continue to believe they are providing a product vitally needed by *some* Third World infants and that they are providing this product in a way that is not detrimental to the ideal of breastfeeding. Furthermore, they believe that no solid evidence linking

[25]"Statement," *Pediatrics* **68** (3) (September 1981), pp. 432–33.

infant formula sales to the decline of breastfeeding has yet been produced.[26] Abbott/Ross argues that it has developed a good marketing code and is attempting to enforce it, and that it is providing a valuable service in the Third World. Tom McCollough, of Ross Laboratories, argues in addition that this controversy is a "cover" for a number of other agendas that are less openly discussed. In particular he mentions the conflicts between North and South, between private enterprise and centralized ownership, and between conservative and liberal philosophy.[27]

Anthropologist Luther P. Gerlach of the University of Minnesota has argued for an even greater complexity to the issues:

> The issue is, of course, not simple. Nutritional status is embedded in a sociocultural and biophysical system. Changes in food use and diet are related to changes in social, political, economic, technological, religious, and environmental factors. Third World societies are open systems which are changed by forces from within and without. It is very difficult to control these forces for change. . . .
>
> It seems likely that industry, protest groups, and church organizations will continue to interact along with international health and development agencies and governments to deal with this infant formula issue and that such interaction will lead not to simple marketing changes but rather to complex system interventions.[28]

[26]Cox, "The Infant Formula Issue," p. 7.

[27]McCollough correspondence.

[28]Luther P. Gerlach, "The Flea and the Elephant: Infant Formula Controversy," *Society* **17** (September/October 1980), p. 56.

Parke, Davis, and Drug Warnings

Government regulation of the drug industry has a long history, with some peaks in that history being more pronounced and influential than others. Persistent members of the press and Congress have played a major role in this regulation by placing issues before the public about the fairness and responsibility of various business practices. Thus, accusations of monopoly control, huge profits, misleading advertising, inadequate research and development, nondisclosure of risks, and the like have filled congressional hearing rooms and newspaper columns.

Such a setting was present in some 1967–68 U.S. Senate subcommittee hearings about the responsibilities of drug companies, chaired by Senator Gaylord Nelson. In the transcript below, the Senator is interrogating Dr. Leslie M. Lueck, an official spokesperson for Parke, Davis Co., where he was the director of quality control. These hearings focused on advertising, product testing and safety, and information disclosure. Dr. Lueck had been asked to testify specifically on his own area of expertise—quality control and the generic counterparts of his company's drug Chloromycetin. However, Senator Nelson was chiefly concerned about advertising and information disclosure, and his interrogation of the witness—together with questions by a staff economist to his subcommittee, Mr. Gordon—quickly moved to these subjects.

THE 1967–68 HEARINGS

SENATOR NELSON: Now, Doctor, I understand that your product, Chloromycetin, has been responsible for deaths resulting from bone marrow disorders, is that correct?

This case was prepared by Tom L. Beauchamp and consists in part of excerpts from the *Hearings Before the Subcommittee on Monopoly of the Select Committee on Small Business,* on "Present Status of Competition in the Pharmaceutical Industry," Part 6 (Nov. 29, 1967– February 29, 1968). Washington, D.C.: U.S. Government Printing Office, 1968, pp. 2167–68, 2170–71, 2178–79, 2222–25. **Not to be duplicated without permission of the author and publisher.**

DR. LUECK: I do not know in what frame of reference you are phrasing the question. If you mean Chloromycetin and all chloramphenicol products have official labeling approved by the Food and Drug Administration, required statements on the labeling, that include indications for use, how to use the product, with warnings, actions, and side effects, that information is explicitly—

SENATOR NELSON: Maybe you did not understand the question. I said I understand that your product, Chloromycetin, has been responsible for deaths from bone marrow disorders. Is that correct or incorrect?

DR. LUECK: I do not know in what reference you are phrasing that question. I know that Chloromycetin, the Parke, Davis brand of chloramphenicol—

SENATOR NELSON: Has never resulted in any deaths?

DR. LUECK: No, I did not say that.

SENATOR NELSON: Maybe I did not put the question correctly.

Some people have died from the administration of Chloromycetin, I understand. Will you tell me what you know about that?

DR. LUECK: I understand that Chloromycetin has been alleged to be related to or associated with some serious side effects, some serious reactions. Those things are related and detailed in considerable length in the package information, in the labeling, Mr. Chairman.

SENATOR NELSON: You say you understand. You really are not sure that any deaths have resulted from this drug?

DR. LUECK: I think that there have been instances where some reactions can be related to the use of Chloromycetin.

SENATOR NELSON: Have you ever read the warning that your company now belatedly puts in its advertising for this drug? Here is an ad from the Journal of the American Medical Association, February 20, 1967:

Warning: Serious and even fatal blood dyscrasias-aplastic anemia, hypoplastic anemia—

And so forth—

are known to occur after the administration of chloramphenicol.

Were you aware of that?

DR. LUECK: Yes, sir.

SENATOR NELSON: That was my question, Doctor: Do you know of any cases of fatal side effects occurring after the administration of Chloromycetin?

DR. LUECK: I was attempting to respond to your question by referring to this warning statement in the labeling, which is precisely

	identical to that in the advertising. I am sorry if I misled you.
SENATOR NELSON:	You did not mislead me. You are aware, then, that deaths have occurred in this case?
DR. LUECK:	Absolutely
SENATOR NELSON:	What has Parke, Davis done about quality control to overcome that problem?
DR. LUECK:	I would like to state, Mr. Chairman, tha Chloromycetin, like many other drugs, is very potent drug. . . .

The National Research Council has responded, as I said, on two occasions to inquiries from the Food and Drug Administration as to the place of Chloromycetin in the therapeutic armamentarium of physicians.

I might quote, on January 11, 1961, the Chairman of the Division of Medical Sciences of the National Research Council replied by letter and among other things, he commented as follows:

Chloramphenicol is considered to be a valuable drug that should remain on the market. In fact in certain infections, it is a drug of choice. The newer antibiotics that have appeared on the market since chloramphenicol was last evaluated by the National Academy of Science's National Research Council in 1952 can't replace satisfactorily in all cases.

Point 2, and I quote further:

A restriction of the usage of chloramphenicol to hospitalized patients is not deemed to be indicated. . . .

3. A knowledge of the untoward side effects that may occur with this drug should be adequately known to all prescribers. The information should be disseminated as a warning on the drug label and elaborated in an enclosure in the drug package. Beyond this, there is need for the continuing education of the physician through the media of medical meetings and the medical literature. This, of course, is a responsibility of the leaders of medicine and not of the FDA.

Point 6. Almost, if not all, potent therapeutic agents cause some undesirable side effects. Therefore, it should be pointed out that chloramphenicol is not the only antibiotic that may cause unfavorable reactions of a serious and sometimes fatal nature.

In addition to the National Research Council review, the Food and Drug Administration in 1957 published comparative data of side effects comparing various antibiotics.

Now, Mr. Chairman, let us look at this article in this publication, and let us look at the potential dangers of chloramphenicol in true perspective; in other words, comparing it to other anti-infective agents or other antibiotics. Let us take a look at disabling and death-dealing reactions that may occur with the other antibiotics. The last significant and overall review of severe reactions to antibiotics was communicated to the medical literature by personnel of the FDA in 1957. Now, it consisted of a nationwide study, including more than 800 hospitals and interviews with 1,600 physicians, and uncovered 1,070 severe antibiotic reactions that were life-threatening.

SENATOR NELSON: Any deaths in that list?

DR. LUECK: Yes. In a paper published in Antibiotic Medicine and Clinical Therapeutics, 1957, these authors brought out the fact that penicillin was found to produce the greatest number and the most severe reactions of all antibiotics presently available.

MR. GORDON: This was when?

DR. LUECK: 1957.

MR. GORDON: And when did Chloromycetin appear on the market?

DR. LUECK: 1949.

Further, in order of their frequency, the life-threatening reactions to antibiotics are anaphylactoid shock, super-infections, severe skin reactions, blood dyscrasias and anguineurotic edema, with respiratory-tract involvement. Please note, Mr. Chairman, that blood dyscrasias—which can be related to chloramphenicol therapy—are next to the last on the list of life-threatening reactions.

These authors further noted that the tetracyclines account for most of the cases of super-infections.

MR. GORDON: Excuse me, sir. What was the date of that particular report?

DR. LUECK: The specific date I don't know. It was 1957.

MR. GORDON: Are you aware of the fact, however, that the risk at that time was considered to be considerably less than it is today? For example, I think the risk at that time was considered to be one in 800,000. A recent report to the California State Assembly and Senate by the California Medical Association and the State Department of Public Health, has revealed that the risk, on the basis of an average dose of 7.5 grams, is 1 in 24,000.

DR. LUECK: Mr. Gordon, with your permission, I would like to comment on the California report and I will finish my brief review of the 1957 FDA publication in just a moment. Then I would go on to the California report.

MR. GORDON: But isn't it correct that considerably more is known today about the effects of chloramphenicol than was known, say, 12 or 13 years ago? Is that not correct?

DR. LUECK: I do not know that we have a higher incidence of side effects now than we had in 1957. I will treat that subject in a moment, Mr. Gordon.

But at any rate, the 1957—

MR. GORDON: Could you answer my question, Doctor?

DR. LUECK: I am sorry.

MR. GORDON: I asked the question: Is it not correct that we know considerably more today about the side effects and dangers of chloramphenicol than we did say 12 or 13 years ago when that particular report was written?

DR. LUECK: No, sir; I do not believe we do.

MR. GORDON: You do not believe we know any more today than we did at that time?

DR. LUECK: I do not believe we know any more. The California report is largely the same as the National Research Council report. The recommendations are largely the same. . . .

SENATOR NELSON: How do you explain that you knew how serious these effects could be 10 years ago and yet in 1960, you were running an ad that did not call this sharply to the attention of the doctor, but then suddenly, 7 years later, you are running this ad?

DR. LUECK: Mr. Chairman, I would like to comment on the fact that since 1952, every ad, every advertisement that has appeared on Chloromycetin, has first been reviewed with the Food and Drug Administration before that ad was ever submitted for publication in any journal.

SENATOR NELSON: I am prepared to indict the FDA along with your company for that.

DR. LUECK: This was the opinion, the combined opinion, apparently, of the experts in Parke, Davis, the experts in the Food and Drug Administration, that adequate warning was included in those ads and in the labeling at any given time. We have diligently worked with the Food and Drug Administration and disseminated the information to the best of our ability on any changes or improvements in that labeling through the years. And to carry the message to the physician, Mr. Chairman, each and every time.

SENATOR NELSON: Do you really mean to tell me, Doctor, that you think this first ad [1960] says the same thing as the second ad [1967]? Do you really mean to say that?

DR. LUECK: I am not saying that they say the same thing.

SENATOR NELSON: Do they give the same warning?

DR. LUECK: Yes; I think they give the essential warning.

SENATOR NELSON: Let's read it again. I think that this is preposterous.

MR. CUTLER: Mr. Chairman, I hope I will not sound impertinent, but may I ask what this has to do with the evidence Dr. Lueck has submitted with regard to the evidences of differences of therapeutic brands?

SENATOR NELSON: I can give you several answers, but I will give you one that ought to satisfy you. If quality control is important, and I think it is as important as you say it is in the production of drugs for the marketplace, quality control of advertising is just as important.

It does not do any good to have good quality control so the drug will do exactly what you expect it to do and then be outright dishonest about what it will do. I think quality control in advertising is as important as quality control in the production of a drug. That is exactly what I am getting at.

Now, I will read the two ads again. I will let the public judge this one. You tell me if they both tell the doctor the same thing, and I am going to ask the doctors who testify what their opinion is. We will put into this record the opinion of distinguished doctors on this question. And, if you want me to, you can select a number of doctors to appear on this question.

The testimony has been that you knew as much about the dangers of this drug 10 years ago as you know now, and your ad stated in April 1960:

Chloromycetin is a potent therapeutic agent and, because certain blood dyscrasias have been associated with its administration, it should not be used indiscriminately or for minor infections. Furthermore, as with certain other drugs, adequate blood studies should be made if the patient requires prolonged or intermittent therapy.

If the doctor reads that, is there anything in there to alert him that there have been deaths indirectly attributed to this drug?

If you knew 10 years ago what you know today, why, in 1967, do you have a severe warning boxed in heavy print:

Warning: Serious and even fatal blood dyscrasias (aplastic anemia, hypoplastic anemia, thrombocytopenia—

And so forth—

are known to occur after the administration of chloramphenicol. Blood dyscrasias have occurred after both short-term and prolonged therapy with this drug. Bearing in mind the possibility that such reactions may occur, chloramphenicol should be used only for serious infections caused by organisms which are susceptible to its antibacterial effects.

Do you consider these to be equivalent warnings?

DR. LUECK: The second warning is an exact duplicate of the package insert and, in my opinion, would be considered a stronger warning, Mr. Chairman.

SENATOR NELSON: I bless you for that.

DR. LUECK: I would like to repeat that all of the ads on Chloromycetin were reviewed by Parke, Davis & Co., with the Food and Drug Administration since 1952 before they were published or submitted to a journal or any advertising media. Also, I would like to—

SENATOR NELSON: Let me say at this point, if I may, that I do not have any higher opinion of the FDA's judgment in permitting this kind of advertising then than I do of the company's running this ad. I do not think it protects you any to come up and say the FDA approved of a lousy ad. Most of the industry is attacking the FDA most of the time, anyway.

DR. LUECK: Well, I think if Parke, Davis & Co. had improper ads, we would have been cited by the Food and Drug Administration, as some people have, and we have not. . . .

So, Mr. Chairman, I think our advertising of all our products has been much in order with the keeping of the day and regulatory requirements appropriate to advertising the product and to inform the advertising.

SENATOR NELSON: Well, my questions have been directed at the proposition that the evidence was available several years ago that there were some major serious side effects, and that the ads did not indicate it. For example, there had already been known deaths—I think that is indisputable—by 1954. . . .

Now, let me ask you another question: This [second] ad was published February 20, 1967?

DR. LUECK: Yes, sir.

SENATOR NELSON: I have here an ad from the British Medical Journal of February 11, 1967, just 9 days away from this very detailed ad. That British ad does not have any warning in it at all. It says:

Clinically Unexcelled.
Clinical use throughout the world has established Chloromycetin (chloramphenicol B. P. Parke, Davis) as an antibiotic of outstanding efficacy in a wide variety of bacterial, viral and rickettsial infections. Chloromycetin possesses extremely high anti-microbial activity, crosses tissue barriers readily, diffuses widely and rapidly through nearly all body tissues and fluids, and is well tolerated. It is rapidly absorbed and bacterial resistance is minimal. And because of these notable properties, therapy with Chloromycetin generally results in prompt response and rapid recovery.

No warning at all in that ad. How do you explain that? . . .

DR. LUECK: I would like to comment that the medical feeling and impressions on the warning requirements on Chloromycetin are different in practically every country of the world. Parke, Davis & Co., has always met all the requirements, the legal requirements of whatever country we distributed our products in and we have met the necessity of the medical profession in that country. These ads, so far as I know, met all of those requirements.

SENATOR NELSON: Well, the effect of the drug is the same on people in other countries as it is here; is it not?

DR. LUECK:	Largely.
SENATOR NELSON:	Do you know of some differentiation?
DR. LUECK:	Yes; there are some minor differentiations, but for the sake of this discussion, let us say they are the same.
MR. CUTLER:	Mr. Chairman, I think you will find that the point you are developing is true of every single ad in this magazine, which is a distinguished magazine of the British Medical Society and I assume it meets all of what they consider to be appropriate requirements.
SENATOR NELSON:	I have not questioned whether or not it met their requirements. I have assumed that. There is a very serious moral question involved that ought to be brought up. It sure shocks me. What the witness says is we will meet the standards of the country where the drug is sold. That means, of course, there is not a single underdeveloped country in the world that has any defense against the exploitation of their people for profit by an American corporation who does not warn them of the serious, mighty serious, possibly fatal consequences here. So you mean to testify that your company will stand on the proposition that we will send drugs to Tanganyika, we will send drugs to Latin American countries, we will send drugs to all the underdeveloped countries in the world and since they do not have any standards, we will fool them all we can and make a great big profit and never tell the doctors that there is a risk of serious blood dyscrasias. Is that what you are telling the committee?
MR. CUTLER:	No, sir. I think you know that, sir. This is a British Medical Society. The British doctors are sophisticated doctors, just as sophisticated as the doctors in this country. This meets all their requirements. This is, of course, only a small part of the information that goes to a British doctor.
SENATOR NELSON:	That is not the testimony.
MR. CUTLER:	You are indicting every drug company in Great Britain and the United States.
SENATOR NELSON:	Any company, drug company or any other kind of company, that would do that, I would be pleased to indict on moral grounds. I think they ought to be indicted on moral grounds. Your testimony is that you will meet the standards of the country in which you are advertising, not the standards of safety which the witness has testified is a proper standard, the proper ad which gives this warning that is put in ads in this country. But in countries where the people do not know any better, where the country is not protected by laws, you will tell us that you have no compunction about running an ad that will fool a doctor, as you did in California in 1961.
	I will read this to you. I would think you would not sleep

at night, frankly, you or any drug company that would do that.

On page 11 of "By Prescription Only," by Morton Mintz, it says that Dr. L. A. M. Watkins, La Canada, Calif., physician, prescribed Chloromycetin to his own son. In 1952, the boy died. In November 1961, the physician went before a California Senate committee and testified: "I do not know of one single victim who would not be alive today had he only been permitted to get well by himself; by nature without the use of antibiotics." Here is an American doctor. I do not know what he read about chloramphenicol. But if he read these ads without any warning, he might very well prescribe it and lose his own son. I do not understand what standard of ethics would govern a great industry of this country that would find it satisfactory to finally, under compulsion in this country, warn the public and warn the doctors about serious blood dyscrasias and then cavalierly advertise in another country without telling those people about the risks. I should think you people would not be able to sleep.

MR. CUTLER: Mr. Chairman, I think you are reaching awfully far to criticize a witness and a company that brought you some evidence that you have been asking for, for months, about therapeutic equivalency of various drugs. It so happens that the pharmaceutical industry, as you know, has believed that advertisements of drugs are not the primary source of information on which the doctor relies. In 1962, this issue was fought out in this Congress and it was decided by the Congress that all advertisements should contain brief summaries, warnings, of complications and side effects, and the FDA was given power to regulate in that area. These companies have done their very best to live up to that law, the need for which they did not agree with at the time. They have observed that law, and you are digging back to 1952, some 15 years ago, to whip this company which brought you some evidence.

I must object to that, Mr. Chairman, most respectfully.

This witness did not come to testify about advertising. Neither you nor Mr. Gordon said anything to him in advance to indicate you intended to question him about advertising. If you want to query Parke, Davis about its advertising, give them notice and they will produce a witness to reply to you.

SENATOR NELSON: I am perfectly happy to have any statement you want to make in the record. I did not tell you what witnesses to bring. You are familiar with the questions that have been raised. . . .

But it shocks me that you do not even blush when you defend a company advertising drugs in another country without the warning required here when the reason it is required in this country is because the ad without the warning does mislead doctors, it does cause people to prescribe a dangerous drug for illnesses that are not serious. That is why the ad is run with the warning. And you know it and everybody else knew it, too.

I would like an answer to that. If this is the standard of ethics by which the industry operates, I tell you, you fellows are in for some sad trouble. I do not think this country will stand for it.

I do not have any more questions of this witness.

Thank you, Dr. Lueck.

CHANGES IN 1971

Three years after these hearings, Parke, Davis Company was acquired by the Warner-Lambert Company of Morris Plains, New Jersey. For a period of eight years following this acquisition, Warner-Lambert had to keep their new division at arm's length due to anti-trust legislation. Within five months, however, the Senior Management of Warner-Lambert undertook, by their own account, a major study of the labeling "for all ethical pharmaceuticals marketed . . . throughout the world."* The objective of the policy was declared to be "the standardization of labeling." The policy, which Warner-Lambert claims to be the most demanding in the industry, contains the following key proposals and explanations:

I. Labeling of a pharmaceutical product must give to the practicing physician that information which he must have to prescribe the drug for the diseases and pathological conditions for which it is intended. This necessarily must include all warnings, precautions, contraindications and adverse reactions as these data allow the physician to make a decision as to the benefit for the patient and the risk involved. . . .

II. Warner-Lambert will make available to governments in the process of approving a drug for sale or marketing a drug, all information, favorable or adverse, that will allow the government regulatory agency to make decisions as to the safety and efficacy of the drug involved.

Management is aware that some regulatory agencies outside the United States do not require that pharmaceutical companies report serious, unexpected or fatal adverse reactions occurring in other countries.

*This quotation, and all subsequent citations, are from "Public Affairs Report No. 77-1: Warner-Lambert Policy Statements," published by Warner-Lambert.

This policy decision establishes the responsibility of the Corporation to inform governments of the existence of unusual or serious problems so that the regulatory agency can study the situation and make the decision as to the benefit/risk ratio. It is believed that regulatory agencies of developed countries can make decisions based on the facts presented and the health needs of their country. In countries where regulatory agencies appear under-staffed or lacking in the latest medical and scientific expertise, Warner-Lambert recognizes that its medical/scientific group must submit changes in labeling which, when adopted, will provide the basis for correct decisions.

III. A centralized control system is established and must operate in such a way that the objectives defined in I and II above will be met in all countries where Warner-Lambert pharmaceuticals are sold. . . .

Example

Chloromycetin In the standardization of labeling for this widely used antibiotic, "labeling" was defined as all information given to the health profession and included package inserts, labels on bottles and cartons, advertising in medical journals, descriptions published in drug compendia and courses of instruction given to salesmen. The reference document selected was the package insert approved by the U. S. FDA.

Official labeling such as package inserts, data sheets (used in the United Kingdom) or monographs (used in Canada) cannot be changed in most countries without a formal request. Submissions for requests to change were submitted to all regulatory agencies of countries in which Chloromycetin was marketed. Because this antibiotic was given in capsules, liquid suspensions and by injection, a total of 88 official package inserts or their equivalents had to be standardized.

In most countries, approval for change was granted in three to four months; in others, delays occurred because of bureaucratic structure. In countries such as Malaysia, Singapore and the Hong Kong Crown Colony, labeling changes would not be acceptable until the regulatory agency of the United Kingdom had indicated acceptance.

Recognizing that due to unavoidable delays the standardization in official package inserts or their equivalent would not necessarily be available to the practicing physician for some time, Warner-Lambert management made the decision to inform the medical profession directly—a program without precedent because of its magnitude and complexity.

The Chloromycetin Monograph This was a document known in the United States as an expanded package insert that contained in considerable detail the medical position on where this antibiotic fits into modern therapeutics. The document was translated from English into the language of the country where it was distributed so that there would be no problems as to the precise meaning of the various medical terms. When this portion of the program was completed, translations were available in the following languages:

Afrikaans   Greek
Chinese   Italian
Danish   Norwegian
Dutch   Portuguese
English   Spanish
Farsi   Swedish
French   Turkish
German

The majority of countries readily gave permission to distribute the monograph to physicians; a small number of governments were reluctant initially then subsequently agreed. In countries where mailing lists of physicians were available, the monograph was distributed through the postal system; in the remainder, by sales representatives. Centralized monitoring made certain that distribution was as complete as possible. This program began in 1972 and was virtually complete by the end of 1973.

Countries—Package Inserts Not Permitted In some Latin American countries, inserts inside bottles and cartons giving indications for use, dosage and other information are not permitted. This prohibition was put into law to discourage over-the-counter buying of ethical pharmaceuticals by the non-medically trained consumer and to force the layman to seek medical attention. In these countries, warnings were placed on the bottle and carton as follows:

Precautions & Warnings

To be taken according to the directions of a medical practitioner.
Not to be used for trivial infections.
Blood dyscrasias including aplastic anemia may be associated with the administration of chloramphenicol. Blood studies should be performed at appropriate intervals where possible in the event of prolonged or repeated administration. . . .

Chloromycetin Advertising Chloromycetin is not heavily promoted by advertising. However, all advertising for pharmaceuticals sold outside the United States must be approved by the Medical Affairs Department, International Group, based at the Corporate Headquarters in New Jersey.

The Chloromycetin program is similar to that undertaken for all company drugs and represents Corporate responsibility in action.

Other Drugs Labeling for other potent drugs such as Dilantin (an anticonvulsant), Norlestrin (an oral contraceptive) and Ketalar (general anesthetic) as well as others marketed by Warner-Lambert are modified any time that new significant data are available. The same procedure used for Chloromycetin has been followed with the exception of the preparation and distribution of a monograph.

New Drugs Before any new drug is marketed in any country, approval must be obtained from the senior medical officer of the Medical Affairs

Department, International Group. The approval, if given, states the basis on which safety and efficacy have been established and specifies the indications for use, warnings, precautions, contraindications and adverse reactions that must be included in the labeling. This approval must be obtained for all new drug entities whether a major drug to be sold in many countries or a simple reformulation of an existing drug that is to be sold in a single country. This procedure ensures that the Corporate standards for safety and efficacy as well as content of labeling are met in countries without sophisticated regulatory agencies.

THE CURRENT IFPMA CODE

The International Federation of Pharmaceutical Manufacturers Associations (IFPMA) is a pharmaceutical industry association spanning 47 countries. It was started in 1968, the same year the above congressional hearings were completed. The association was admitted into an official relationship with the World Health Organization in 1971, the same year of the Warner-Lambert policy statement issued above. Warner-Lambert is an active member of this association. In IFPMA's current professional "Code of Pharmaceutical Marketing Practices," General Principle #2 is worded as follows:

Information on pharmaceutical products should be accurate, fair and objective, and presented in such a way as to conform not only to legal requirements but also to ethical standards and to standards of good taste.

General Principle #6 reads as follows:

Particular care should be taken that essential information as to pharmaceutical products' safety, contraindications, and side effects or toxic hazards is appropriately and consistently communicated subject to the legal, regulatory, and medical practices of each nation. The word "safe" must not be used without qualification.

Warner-Lambert implemented sweeping reforms in their Parke, Davis division, but not until 8 years after the initial acquisition. They were forced to take a "hands-off" stand during this period due to antitrust legislation. In 1978, however, they took steps toward reform with such additions as the IFPMA Code, the distribution of detailed information to foreign health authorities, and the inclusion of a package insert.

Italian Tax Mores

The Italian federal corporate tax system has an official, legal tax structure and tax rates just as the U.S. system does. However, all similarity between the two systems ends there.

The Italian tax authorities assume that no Italian corporation would ever submit a tax return which shows its true profits but rather would submit a return which understates actual profits by anywhere between 30 percent and 70 percent; their assumption is essentially correct. Therefore, about six months after the annual deadline for filing corporate tax returns, the tax authorities issue to each corporation an "invitation to discuss" its tax return. The purpose of this notice is to arrange a personal meeting between them and representatives of the corporation. At this meeting, the Italian revenue service states the amount of corporate income tax which it believes is due. Its position is developed from both prior years' taxes actually paid and the current year's return; the amount which the tax authorities claim is due is generally several times that shown on the corporation's return for the current year. In short, the corporation's tax return and the revenue service's stated position are the opening offers for the several rounds of bargaining which will follow.

The Italian corporation is typically represented in such negotiations by its *commercialista*, a function which exists in Italian society for the primary purpose of negotiating corporate (and individual) tax payments with the Italian tax authorities; thus, the management of an Italian corporation seldom, if ever, has to meet directly with the Italian revenue service and probably has a minimum awareness of the details of the negotiation other than the final settlement.

Both the final settlement and the negotiation are extremely important to the corporation, the tax authorities, and the *commercialista*. Since

This case was prepared by Arthur L. Kelly, and is published here with the permission of the author. **Not to be duplicated without permission of the author and publisher.**

the tax authorities assume that a corporation *always* earned more money this year than last year and *never* has a loss, the amount of the final settlement, i.e., corporate taxes which will actually be paid, becomes, for all practical purposes, the floor for the start of next year's negotiations. The final settlement also represents the amount of revenue the Italian government will collect in taxes to help finance the cost of running the country. However, since large amounts of money are involved and two individuals having vested personal interests are conducting the negotiations, the amount of *bustarella*—typically a substantial cash payment "requested" by the Italian revenue agent from the *commercialista*—usually determines whether the final settlement is closer to the corporation's original tax return or to the fiscal authority's original negotiating position.

Whatever *bustarella* is paid during the negotiation is usually included by the *commercialista* in his lump-sum fee "for services rendered" to his corporate client. If the final settlement is favorable to the corporation, and it is the *commercialista*'s job to see that it is, then the corporation is not likely to complain about the amount of its *commercialista*'s fee, nor will it ever know how much of that fee was represented by *bustarella* and how much remained for the *commercialista* as payment for his negotiating services. In any case, the tax authorities will recognize the full amount of the fee as a tax deductible expense on the corporation's tax return for the following year.

About ten years ago, a leading American bank opened a banking subsidiary in a major Italian city. At the end of its first year of operation, the bank was advised by its local lawyers and tax accountants, both from branches of U.S. companies, to file its tax return "Italian-style," i.e., to understate its actual profits by a significant amount. The American general manager of the bank, who was on his first overseas assignment, refused to do so both because he considered it dishonest and because it was inconsistent with the practices of his parent company in the United States.

About six months after filing its "American-style" tax return, the bank received an "invitation to discuss" notice from the Italian tax authorities. The bank's general manager consulted with his lawyers and tax accountants who suggested he hire a *commercialista*. He rejected this advice and instead wrote a letter to the Italian revenue service not only stating that his firm's corporate return was correct as filed but also requesting that they inform him of any specific items about which they had questions. His letter was never answered.

About sixty days after receiving the initial "invitation to discuss" notice, the bank received a formal tax assessment notice calling for a tax of approximately three times that shown on the bank's corporate tax return; the tax authorities simply assumed the bank's original return had been based on generally accepted Italian practices, and they re-acted accordingly. The bank's general manager again consulted with his lawyers and tax accountants who again suggested he hire a *commercialista* who knew how to handle these matters. Upon learning that the *commercialista* would probably have to pay *bustarella* to his revenue service counterpart in order to reach a settlement, the general manager again chose to ignore his advisors. Instead, he responded by sending the Italian revenue service a check for the full amount of taxes due according to the bank's American-style tax return even though the due date for the payment was almost six months hence; he made no reference to the amount of corporate taxes shown on the formal tax assessment notice.

Ninety days after paying its taxes, the bank received a third notice from the fiscal authorities. This one contained the statement, "We have reviewed your corporate tax return for 19____ and have determined that [the lira equivalent of] $6,000,000 of interest paid on deposits is not an allowable expense for federal tax purposes. Accordingly, the total tax due for 19____ is lira____." Since interest paid on deposits is any bank's largest single expense item, the new tax assessment was for an amount many times larger than that shown in the initial tax assessment notice and almost fifteen times larger than the taxes which the bank had actually paid.

The bank's general manager was understandably very upset. He immediately arranged an appointment to meet personally with the manager of the Italian revenue service's local office. Shortly after the start of their meeting, the conversation went something like this:

GENERAL MANAGER: "You can't really be serious about disallowing interest paid on deposits as a tax deductible expense."

ITALIAN REVENUE SERVICE: "Perhaps. However, we thought it would get your attention. Now that you're here, shall we begin our negotiations?"[1]

[1]For readers interested in what happened subsequently, the bank was forced to pay the taxes shown on the initial tax assessment, and the American manager was recalled to the United States and replaced.

The Bribery Business

On February 3, 1975, Mr. Eli Black, Chairman of the United Brands, Inc., smashed the window of his 44th floor Manhattan office with his briefcase and jumped to his death on the street below. Mr. Black, who had been ordained as a rabbi in his youth, was widely respected as a business leader who had done much to try to make business corporations more responsive to the needs of American society. Since no explanation of his decision to commit suicide was found, there was a great deal of speculation about why this man of seemingly exemplary character had done so.

It is the practice of the Securities and Exchange Commission to make an immediate investigation of the financial affairs of any important corporation whenever one of its senior officers takes his own life. The S.E.C. began such an investigation of United Brands shortly after Mr. Black's death and quickly discovered that the company had recently paid some $1.25 million into the Swiss bank accounts of government officials of Honduras. The major business of United Brands is the cultivation and sale of bananas, and the company owns 28,000 acres of banana plantations in Honduras. The Honduran government had announced its intention to double the export tax on bananas, but shortly after the payment by United Brands, the proposed tax increase was cancelled. Actual ownership of the Swiss bank account was never publicly identified, but shortly after the S.E.C. announced its finding, General Oswaldo Lopez, the president of Honduras, was ousted. The record of payment had been falsified in United Brands' accounts.

This case was prepared from published sources by Professor Dwight R. Ladd, Dean of the Whittemore School of Business and Economics, University of New Hampshire, with the collaboration of Professor Blair Little of the University of Western Ontario. It is intended as a basis for classroom discussion and not to illustrate either effective or ineffective handling of an administrative situation. Copyright © 1975 by the University of New Hampshire, and reprinted with the permission of the authors. The Postscript was prepared by Tom L. Beauchamp, with the permission of Professor Ladd. **Not to be duplicated without permission of the authors and publisher.**

FURTHER DEVELOPMENTS

This disclosure, coming more or less on the heels of the resignation of Richard Nixon from the U.S. presidency amid, among other things, evidence of widespread illegal corporate payments to the Nixon campaign fund, caused a good deal of public clamor. Further investigations by the S.E.C. and the opening of hearings by a Senate committee quickly followed. As a result, it has become clear that corporate payments to government officials, political parties, "influential persons," and so on, in many parts of the world were well-established practice. Gulf, Northrop, Carnation, Johnson and Johnson, Goodyear, Phillips, and Lockheed are among the major corporations whose officials have admitted such activities.

The sums involved have not been trivial. Gulf, for example, admitted to the payment of $4.2 million to the party of President Park of South Korea. Lockheed has acknowledged payments of $22 million to various officials, mostly in the Middle East. In general these payments have not been recorded on the companies' books but were "laundered" in one way or another through overseas subsidiaries. Gulf, for example, created a Bahamian subsidiary which was used as a conduit for making political contributions that were unlawful in the United States. Perhaps the most notorious case was that of Lockheed. The notoriety was undoubtedly related to Lockheed's having been kept from bankruptcy by a loan guarantee from the government, to governmental crises in Japan and the Netherlands as a result of testimony that Prince Bernhard of The Netherlands and senior government figures in Japan had received Lockheed money, and to the continuing and rigorous arguments of Lockheed's Chairman Haughton that payoffs were just good business.

These events, and continuing disclosures of additional companies involved, have raised a number of rather troublesome issues and questions about the international business system. The balance of this case attempts to define and discuss these issues.

THE LEGAL SITUATION
BEFORE THE FEDERAL
CORRUPT PRACTICES ACT

In the United States, bribery of public officials is a criminal offense. the U.S. government and many state governments have strict rules against the taking of gifts of any value by purchasing agents, contract officers, and so on. Corporate contributions to political parties or candidates are also forbidden by law. Many business corporations have regulations against giving or receiving of gifts which could be construed as bribes or payoffs. While it is known that these rules and regulations are violated from time to time, it is clear that the practices described are considered to be improper in the United States and this is reflected in the laws and regulations which prohibit them. However, these laws did not apply to actions by Americans—individuals or corporations—outside the United States until the Foreign Corrupt Practices Act was passed in 1977. When an American company did business in country X it was (until this Act was passed) exclusively governed by the laws of X, just as a company from X would be governed by U.S. law when it does business here. Thus, at least in those countries where payments to public officials or political contributions by corporations are (or were) not illegal, the described actions of the companies were not illegal until 1977.

Before 1977 there were two possible exceptions to the foregoing: The S.E.C. has long assumed the power to require that American-based companies disclose any such material payments to investors and to penalize companies that fail to do so. A second possible exception involves the Internal Revenue Code which requires that expense deductions for tax purposes be "necessary and proper" business expenses. The courts could obviously hold that bribes and payoffs are neither "necessary" nor "proper," in which case companies making such deductions would be in violation of the tax code or perhaps would be misstating profits to investors. That is, bribing and paying-off foreign officials were not until the Foreign Corrupt Practices Act *illegal*. The *ethical* issues were the truly troublesome and contentious ones, but this is probably no less true *after* passage of this Act.

OTHER CUSTOMS

It is a fact that in many parts of the world some forms of what we call bribery or payoffs are not only legal, but are widely accepted ways of conducting affairs. "Baksheesh" as it is known in Arabian countries, or "La Mordida" as Latin Americans style it, is commonplace. Not only for sales of military hardware, but for such routine transactions as purchasing a railway ticket, getting a telephone installed, or customs clearances, one is expected to make some sort of payment to those empowered to further or complete the transaction. Simply getting an appointment in order to further one's business may be virtually impossible without "La Mordida."

In many countries, such things as beginning and operating a business or getting import or export licenses, are not more or less simple matters of meeting a few uniformly applied regulations as is the case in the U.S. and most industrial countries. Some payoff to those officials who have virtually complete latitude to grant or withhold necessary approvals is both expected and accepted practice. The following paragraphs provide a recent (1975) description of such a situation.

For 18 months Del Monte Corp. tried to buy a 55,000 acre banana plantation in Guatemala, but the government said no.

Then the company hired an influence-wielding "business consultant" and agreed to pay him nearly $500,000. Suddenly, the Guatemalan government reversed itself. Now, Del Monte owns the profitable banana-growing properties, for which it paid $20.5 million.

The California food packer declines to identify the Guatemalan consultant, citing his fear that disclosure of his relationship with the large U.S. company could diminish his influence in Guatemala and perhaps provoke left-wing threats against his life. For these reasons, he demanded and received company assurances on anonymity.

To protect him, Del Monte paid him outside the country. It charged his fee to general and administrative expenses on the books of several Panamanian shipping subsidiaries. His fee was entirely contingent on his ability to influence the balky Guatemalan government. Del Monte hasn't publicly disclosed these facts, but it confirms them.

The company says that the fat fee secretly paid to its agent was entirely proper. It concedes that the consultant, a wealthy businessman, frequently contributes to political parties in Guatemala. But the consultant has assured Del Monte that no corporate cash went to any government officials there, a company spokesman says. Thus, Del Monte says its payments to the consultant shouldn't be compared to foreign bribes paid by United Brands Co. and Northrop Corp. or to illegal political contributions made abroad by Gulf Oil Corporation.

Still, Del Monte's experience suggests why many U.S. companies find it necessary to hire well-connected fixers—a practice that would seem irregular in the U.S.—to help swing foreign transactions. Sometimes a fat fee paid to the right intermediary can quickly produce a few crucial phone calls and a favorable decision. Whether or not things went that way in the Del Monte case, a company spokesman does recall: "For a year we pounded on doors and waited for meetings. Then we hired this guy and things started occurring."[1]

General political "contributions" are in a somewhat different category for they are usually not related to specific transactions, but rather are intended to foster a generally favorable climate for the companies' activities. In the most general case, they may simply be intended to preserve a favorable "climate," as in the case of Exxon's openly accounted for gifts to Canadian political parties. "Obviously, Imperial (Exxon's Canadian subsidiary) doesn't contribute to such parties as the New Democratic Party (a Socialist party) whose ideologies would nationalize us or put us out of business."[2] In a time when governments are more and more involved in activities relating to business, there is a tendency to forestall retaliation of a general sort. This was the motivation expressed by some of the companies "contributing" to the Nixon reelection fund. Then there is the rather specific payoff of protection money. In South Korea, for example, Chairman Bob Dorsey of Gulf

[1]*Wall Street Journal,* July 14, 1975.
[2]*Wall Street Journal,* May 19, 1975.

Oil reported that the threats made by the financial chairman of President Park's party—threats against Gulf's $300 million investment—"left little to the imagination."[3] Mr. Dorsey claimed not to have learned until after having made contributions of some $4 million, that doing so might have been illegal under South Korean law, but since President Park was a dictator, this presumably made little difference.

Finally, it must be observed that forms of corruption such as bribery have long been neither legal nor tolerated in some countries in the world. In March, 1975 Yuri Sosnovsky, head of a furniture-making organization in the Ministry of Timber and Wood Processing of the Soviet Union was shot by a firing squad after being convicted of accepting a $150,000 bribe from Walter Haeflin, representative of an unidentified Swiss company. Mr. Haeflin was sentenced to ten years in prison.[4]

THE ISSUES

Most of the discussions resulting from these revelations of corporate practices have centered around the ethical issue, and around the question of what, if anything, should be done at the governmental level in the United States or elsewhere. The ethical discussions center on two closely related issues: First, are ethical considerations in any way involved, and, second, is it appropriate to attempt to transfer the ethical standards of one culture to another?

WHAT SHOULD BE DONE?

If one argues that whatever local customs may be, the practice of bribery and payoffs should not be continued, one is faced with what to do to insure control. While there are obvious barriers to attempting to impose U.S. law outside the United States, some argue that if American-based corporations face strong sanctions for engaging in bribery overseas, and if everyone knows that to be the case, an individual company can refuse to go along with the practice without much fear of reprisal or economic loss. No one has suggested that Mr. Dorsey of Gulf or Mr. Haughton of Lockheed should have been shot like Mr. Sosnovsky of the Ministry of Timber and Wood Processing, but one may assume that with such a precedent, Russian businessmen can put up a pretty strong defense against demands for bribes or payoffs if they choose to do so. As Mr. Dorsey said in urging Congress to pass legislation outlawing bribes overseas, it would "make it easier to resist the very intense pressures which are placed on us from time to time."[5]

[3]*Newsweek* (International Division), May 26, 1975.
[4]*International Herald Tribune*, May 19, 1975.
[5]*International Herald Tribune*, May 23, 1975.

On the other hand, it is feared by some that American legislative initiatives inevitably put American-based corporations at a disadvantage vis-a-vis German, Japanese, French and other competitors not facing similar sanctions. There is ample evidence that businessmen from other countries are not reluctant to make payoffs in order to obtain sales. Viewed in this way the specific issue of bribery merges into the broader question of overall control of multinational corporations. Some feel that if the United States were to act first it would be easier to push other governments—German, Japanese, Swiss, Dutch, British, French—to follow. Others argue that the issue is best tackled through existing mechanisms for regulation such as the Common Market, the OECD, the International Monetary Fund, and so on.

Others, notably the business press, have tended to argue against legislative solutions. *Business Week* argued editorially in 1975:

> It is time for top management of U.S. companies to establish a single standard of ethical behavior for their executives at home and abroad. Competition should be in terms of product quality, price and financing— not in the purchase of local politicians. Each company must look past short-term profit to the long-term results of corruption.[6]

The *Wall Street Journal* argued:

> It is easy for moralists on the side-lines to say that business executives should not buckle to pressures from politicians. No doubt it is a great deal harder to make such decisions when the price of a bribe must be weighed against a perceived threat to a large business and all the jobs and shareholder investments tied up in the enterprise.
>
> Nevertheless, we can't help feeling that executives who bend to illicit political pressures either in the U.S. or abroad are buying only short-term success. The whole history of extortion at any level suggests that a strong resistance to the first approaches is the most effective response. There is a great deal of bargaining strength to be gained from taking a position that is morally and ethically strong.[7]

WHAT HAS BEEN DONE?

By mid-1976, the Securities and Exchange Commission had drawn up much more specific and sweeping regulations for the control and disclosures of foreign payments, though it had been reported[8] that the S.E.C. had considerable difficulty in doing so. One issue was whether or not the names of recipients of bribes and payoffs should be disclosed. Some argued that such disclosures could result in nationaliza-

[6]*Business Week,* June 23, 1975.
[7]*Wall Street Journal,* June 1975.
[8]*Wall Street Journal,* September 9, 1975.

tion of companies, or cancellation of valuable business concessions. Another issue was how to distinguish, in regulations, between bribes and $5 tips. Some of the same issues were involved in legislation being considered by the Senate Banking Committee. This legislation was more directed towards elimination rather than disclosure and control and was opposed by the Ford Administration, ostensibly because of enforcement problems. The OECD nations were also in the process of developing an international code to limit these practices, but the group as such had no enforcement power, depending, rather, on individual governments.

In February of 1976, the Conference Board published the results of a survey of 73 senior international executives. About three-quarters of the respondents did not think foreign payoffs or bribes were an important problem in their industries—though many of these felt they were a problem for other industries. Only one-quarter of the companies had any formal, written policy covering the matter. On the other hand, the Directors of Gulf Oil, acting on the report of an investigating committee which they had created, rather pointedly discharged Chairman Dorsey and two other senior officials. As Exhibit I, a summary of the status of a number of corporate officials who had admitted to or been convicted of illegal payoffs by mid-1975, suggests, Gulf's example was not widely followed, and the practice of bribery and payoffs was not regarded as a very serious matter in the boardrooms of the United States. (See p. 258 for Exhibit I.)

POSTSCRIPT—1982

On December 20, 1977, President Jimmy Carter signed into law the Foreign Corrupt Practices Act. This Act received its impetus from the aforementioned disclosures during the Watergate hearings of large slush funds maintained by a number of American corporations (at least 117 of the Fortune 500, by one S.E.C. account). The Act makes it a criminal offense for a representative of an American corporation to offer or transmit payments to the officials of other governments for the purpose of facilitating business. A number of reporting measures and fines are specified in the Act, including up to five years in prison. The Act does not, however, prohibit so-called "grease" payments to lower officials in foreign governments, because these officials often will not perform their normal specified functions without such payments.

The Foreign Corrupt Practices Act has been the focus of intense and ongoing debate, especially in the business community, since its initial voyage through Congress. Even some U.S. government officials have spoken publicly in opposition to the Act, on grounds of its potentially serious implications for the frustration of American business. The most common argument is that in many countries payments are a *necessary condition* of doing business, and are far more akin to an approved system of extortion than to bribery. Questions have also been raised about whether there is anything *unethical* or *corrupt* in making such payments.[9]

Such questions have been raised about many recent cases. For example, on June 30, 1982, the Boeing Aircraft Co. pleaded guilty to making over $7 million in secret payments from 1973 to 1977 to middlepersons in foreign countries (Spain, Lebanon, Honduras, and the Dominican Republic) for facilitating the sale of $343 million of passenger planes. These payments were not at that time illegal, although they would be now. Boeing pleaded guilty for illegally *concealing* the payments from the Export-Import Bank, which financed up to 45% of the purchases. Boeing and Judge John H. Pratt concurred, in a plea agreement, that Boeing would pay $450,000.[10]

---

[9]For information on this Act and the ethical issues that surround it, see Mark Pastin and Michael Hooker, "Ethics and the Foreign Corrupt Practices Act," *Business Horizons* (December 1980).

[10]Al Kamen, "Boeing Draws Fine for Secret Payments in Overseas Plan Sales," *The Washington Post,* July 1, 1982, sec. A, p. 7.

What Happened to Convicted Watergate Donors?[11]

American Ship Building	George M. Steinbrenner 3d	$15,000	Still chairman at $50,000/yr.
	John H. Melcher, Jr.	$2,500	Discharged. Practicing law in Cleveland.
Ashland Oil	Orin E. Atkins*	$1,000	Still chairman at $314,000/yr.
Associated Milk Producers	Harold S. Nelson	4 mos. prison $10,000	Resigned. Now in commodities exports.
	David L. Parr	4 mos. prison $10,000	Resigned.
	Stuart H. Russell	2 yrs. prison**	Resigned. Now in private law practice.
Braniff International	Harding L. Lawrence	$1,000	Still chairman at $335,000/yr.
Carnation	H. Everett Olson	$1,000	Still chairman at $212,500/yr.
Diamond International	Ray Dubrowin	$1,000	Still V.P. for public affairs.
Goodyear Tire & Rubber	Russell DeYoung	$1,000	Still chairman of 2 committees at $305,000/yr. Also collecting pension of $144,000/yr.
Gulf Oil	Claude C. Wild, Jr.	$1,000	Consultant in Washington, D.C.
HMS Electric	Charles N. Huserman	$1,000	Still president.
IBC&W Inc.	William G. Lyles, Sr.	$2,000	Still chairman.
Lehigh Valley Cooperative Farmers	Richard L. Albson	Suspended fine of $1,000	Discharged.
3M	Harry Heltzer	$500	Retired as chairman, but does special projects at $100,000/yr.
Northrop	Thomas V. Jones	$5,000	Still chief executive at $286,000/yr.
	James Allen	$1,000	Retired as V.P. with pension est. at $36,000/yr.
Phillips Petroleum	William W. Keeler	$1,000	Retired with pension at $201,742/yr.
Ratrie, Robbins & Schweizer	Harry Ratrie	1 mo. probation	Still president.
	Augustus Robbins 3d	1 mo. probation	Still Exec. V.P.
Time Oil	Raymond Abendroth	$2,000	Still president.

*Pleaded no contest
**Under appeal

[11]Data taken from *New York Times*, August 24, 1975. Not updated after 1975.